Serjeant Musgr[...]
Armstrong's Last Goodnight

As well as *Serjeant Musgrave's Dance*, first performed at the Royal Court Theatre in 1959 and now acknowledged as one of the best plays of the last two decades, this volume contains two further well-known Arden plays from the early sixties. *The Workhouse Donkey*, first staged at the 1963 Chichester Festival, is 'Arden's masterpiece' according to Michael Billington of *The Guardian*: 'it hit me amidships and left me feeling it was after all possible to unite passion, politics, poetry, sex and song in a living theatrical form'. The third play is *Armstrong's Last Goodnight*, staged first by the Glasgow Citizens' Theatre, then by the National Theatre at the Old Vic, which Ronald Bryden in the *New Statesman* found to be 'Arden's strongest play. Each of his thirty speakers is beautifully alive, a realized private existence integrated into a huge social canvas ... Arden has steeped himself in the marvellous language of Dunbar and the real Lindsay, lovingly recreating it into a theatrical speech thorny with images, knotted with strength, rough and springy as an uncombed fleece.' Introducing the three plays is a short Preface by the author specially written for this volume.

JOHN ARDEN was born in Barnsley, Yorkshire, in 1930. While studying architecture at Cambridge and Edinburgh Universities, he began writing plays, three of which have been produced at the Royal Court Theatre: The Waters of Babylon *(1957),* Live Like Pigs *(1958) and* Serjeant Musgrave's Dance *(1959), while a fourth,* The Workhouse Donkey, *was staged at the Chichester Festival in 1963. For a year he held an Annual Fellowship in Playwriting at Bristol University, and Bristol Old Vic staged* Ironhand, *his free adaptation of Goethe's* Goetz von Berlichingen. Armstrong's Last Goodnight *was first seen at the Glasgow Citizens' Theatre in 1964 and subsequently at the National Theatre.* Left-Handed Liberty *was commissioned to commemorate the 750th Anniversary of Magna Carta and was performed at the Mermaid Theatre in 1965. John Arden has collaborated with Margaretta D'Arcy on several plays. These include* The Happy Haven *(1960),* The Business of Good Government *(1960),* The Royal Pardon *(1966),* The Hero Rises Up *(1968),* The Island of the Mighty *(1972),* The Ballygombeen Bequest *(1972) and* The Non-Stop Connolly Show *(1975). John Arden has just published his own selection of essays by him and D'Arcy on the theatre and its public entitled* To Present the Pretence.

*The front cover shows a detail from an untitled painting by Clem Beer,
which was created in July 1967 from a scenario provided by John Arden.
It is reproduced by courtesy of Clem Beer. The photograph of John Arden
on the back cover is by Roger Mayne and is reproduced with his permission.*

JOHN ARDEN

Plays : One

Serjeant Musgrave's Dance
The Workhouse Donkey
Armstrong's Last Goodnight

With a Preface by the Author

The Master Playwrights
EYRE METHUEN
London

Contents

This volume first published in the Master Playwrights series in 1977 by Eyre Methuen Ltd, 11 New Fetter Lane, London EC4P 4EE

Serjeant Musgrave's Dance first published by Methuen & Co. in 1960.
Copyright © 1960 by John Arden
The Workhouse Donkey first published by Methuen & Co. in 1964.
Copyright © 1964 by John Arden
Armstrong's Last Goodnight first published by Methuen & Co. in 1965.
Copyright © 1965, 1966 by John Arden
This collection and Author's Preface © 1977 by John Arden.

Printed in Great Britain by Cox & Wyman Ltd,
London, Reading and Fakenham

ISBN 0 413 38460 8

Author's Preface

The late George Devine of the Royal Court Theatre used to make a noble affirmation of his belief in the playwright's 'right to fail': and as an illustration of this doctrine in action he would frequently quote the case of *Serjeant Musgrave's Dance* – a play which lost the theatre (I think) ten thousand pounds, but which he nevertheless had insisted upon presenting in the teeth of hostile critics and indifferent audiences until acceptance of its qualities was finally secured. Grateful though I was to George Devine, and also to Lindsay Anderson, for their strong championship of my play, I always found this particular invocation of it embarrassing. Not because of the amount of money dropped – for there is no doubt that Anderson's beautiful production had not been a box-office success – but rather for the implication that the play was now a 'modern classic', and that in consequence I had achieved the status of an 'established writer'.

I did not know exactly at that time (the early 1960s) what kind of life an established writer might be expected to lead, but I was quite sure that I was not leading it. I earned a reasonable income from royalties, translation-rights and the like; I was invited to give the occasional lecture to a university or literary society; I did not have my next few plays rejected by the managements to whom I offered them: and I was courteously consulted by directors as to how I would wish them staged. But somehow I was never able to feel that I belonged in the modern theatre. I had some of the best actors and actresses in the country on my cast-lists, and I never got to know any of them very much better than if I had been merely a member of their audiences. The audiences themselves came and went and applauded politely enough, but the distance between them in their seats and the play on the stage seemed irreducible.

I was not quite certain what could be done about this – I was not looking for the sort of 'participatory' exercises that involve actors crawling about the auditorium demanding direct person-to-person responses from individuals among the public – it was rather that I was troubled by a general lack of warmth, a withdrawn coldness, a too-precisely-defined correctitude of artistic technique which seemed to tell the audience: 'thus far and no further – we are the professionals – actors, director, designer, author – and you are to contemplate the work we choose to show you – if you take it in the right spirit you will probably be the better for it.' (To which the audiences naturally responded with a mute defiance and an obvious reluctance to be impressed.) When I was actually writing my scripts I had no such attitude of mind. I regarded myself as preparing a story which would be told to the audience on my behalf by the actors, which would in fact be *me* saying something of interest to a whole crowd of people whom I would have liked to believe my friends. If I personally told

5

such a story to a group of real friends round a supper-table I would
have expected them to react, to interrupt, to comment in a manner
provocative of some more prolonged discourse. If this did not happen
in the theatre, was I to blame for my style of writing, were the public
to blame for their false expectations, or should one blame the entire
theatre and its inherited manner of presentation, publicity, and
technical device?

It did happen, once, and that was at the Glasgow première of
Armstrong's Last Goodnight: where the production – in comparison
with the Royal Court or Chichester – was under-budgeted, unevenly
cast, hastily-prepared, and yet there was a vigorous sharing of a lively
experience with the audience – it was of course the experience of
Scotland – of a discontented 'region' of the United Kingdom aware
of its historical claim to its own unique identity and language, and
aware of a theatrical reflection of that claim in the play upon the stage,
a reflection consciously projected by the actors in response to a
realized demand for it. After *The Workhouse Donkey* had been so
skilfully presented at the Chichester Festival I wrote the preface to it
that appears in this volume: it will readily be understood that the type
of experience alluded to there would not have been possible under any
circumstances in that theatre at that time. Yet when I wrote the play
I had vainly hoped that it might.

In 1967 I found myself working with Margaretta D'Arcy on a vast
'war-carnival' political show in the University of New York – there
was little or no 'literary' or 'classical' content in the work (which was
both improvised and collectively-assembled), and my 'established'
status was very much at a discount in that environment – the Viet-
namese subject-matter had put us both under suspicion from all sorts
of respectable quarters – and the result was a remarkable fulfilment of
exactly the kind of aspiration I had given voice to in the *Donkey*'s
preface. Particularly in regard to the number of writers, actors and
other artists with whom we were able to develop warm and reciprocal
relationships in New York.

An 'established writer', I came to understand, if he is anything at all,
is a writer of whom some are jealous, many are wary, and who is above
all not expected to desire an intense and integrated part in the presentation of his work. He stands outside the working theatre to which
he gives over his scripts complete for others to breathe life into* : he
stands outside the general stream of non-theatrical society, except

* I should mention that unlike some other dramatists I never had a
permanent working relationship with any one director. The diversity
of the plots and moods of my plays may have had something to do with
this. But I don't know whether it would anyway have made much
difference. Also one hears of these professional partnerships that
suddenly break up after years of fruitful work, leaving the playwright
cast adrift and feeling bitterly betrayed – directors can always find
another script elsewhere . . .

insofar as he may be occasionally made use of to sign appeals and protests for the furtherance of some good cause.

I remember, when *Armstrong's Last Goodnight* had been running for a few weeks in the repertory at Chichester, I revisited the show to see how it was getting along. (I had been at the rehearsals and at the first night, and then I had gone back home to Yorkshire.) I looked forward so much to that revisit, as I thought highly of the production and performances, and I longed to discover how the audiences were continuing to respond to them. It was a terrible disappointment. The actors whom I met before the show and after it were pleasant, chatted amiably, and quite obviously had no idea what on earth I was doing there. Afterwards I asked myself the same question and could find no sensible answer. The play was no longer mine, it was not me but the National Theatre Company who was telling the story of the Scottish bandit to the public each evening. I had already fulfilled my function, and I ought to have stayed away.

A few years later (1972) Margaretta D'Arcy and myself had a dispute with the Royal Shakespeare Company about their production of a play of ours: we felt, as we made our case public, that we were speaking not only for ourselves but for playwrights in general, and, by extension, for actors in general whom we knew to be only too often as unhappy as we were with the bureaucracy of big subsidised managements. Some actors supported us, so did several writers, but there was a surprising degree of complete incomprehension, and an alarming attitude on the part of many younger 'fringe-theatre' people that the whole thing served me right for having become an 'established writer' all those years ago with *Serjeant Musgrave* – that notorious box-office calamity . . .

I am still paying back George Devine's ten thousand pounds – not in cash, but in reputation. I am presently waiting to be sued for libel ('exemplary damages'): I am continually informed in all manner of print by all manner of critics that my later work (post-1967, which is to say since I started regularly working as the older half of the Arden/ D'Arcy writing-production partnership) shows a distinct falling-off in dramatic tension and inspiration: I am accused of having turned my back upon the professional theatre – whereas the professional theatre, at least in certain large and influential areas, has let it be known that Arden's work is only acceptable if D'Arcy is not impertinently attached to it: I am regarded by the 'established' English theatre as having abdicated my responsibilities by living and working in the Republic of Ireland, while in Ireland I am held by many to be a foreign interloper only over for the tax-benefits (largely illusory, I might add, unless one is not only 'established' but also a millionaire) who is doing honest Irishmen out of their inalienable place in the sun: and yet I have been working consistently at plays and projects which have aroused audience-enthusiasm and involvement to a degree I could not have conceived fifteen years ago – except as it were in a dream, like my preface to *The Workhouse Donkey*.

Meanwhile in England there is now an organization of playwrights, the Theatre Writers' Union, which, if it succeeds in its currently-expressed intentions, should once and for all put back the writer where he or she historically belongs – in the active interior of the chaotic working theatre. Within such a union there need be no isolation for the established playwright, nor sense of exclusion for the beginner. I think that if this organization had existed when I wrote the three plays in this book, the plays themselves would not necessarily have been very different, but the conditions under which they would have been produced, and the experience of those productions upon the development of their author would have been utterly at variance from what happened to me . . .

As it is, they are here offered in one volume to the reader as examples of the kind of script by which some of us once vainly believed that the whole nature of the theatre could be changed, regardless of its financial and political position within society, and regardless of the then universal isolation of the playwright. This book is perhaps a little like Vitruvius' famous handbook of the ancient architecture, which he wrote, during the days of Imperial Rome, as though the god-like proportions of the Doric, Ionic and Corinthian Orders (devised for the simple small-scale rectangular temples of obsolete Greek city-states) were still the basic principles of structure. In fact they had long been degraded to applied decoration upon the huge hulks of brick-encased concrete by which the Caesars confirmed their military power, while outside the bounds of Empire the barbarians were already developing those frames of wood and wattle that eventually grew into the cathedrals of the Gothic middle-age. *Progress* in the arts is an indeterminate, very relative concept. It does not and cannot invariably mean 'going forward and doing better'. More frequently it denotes mere movement, in what direction no-one can say until after we have got there. I wonder will I ever have reason to write any stage-plays quite like these again . . . ?

J.A.

1977

Serjeant
Musgrave's Dance

AN UN-HISTORICAL PARABLE

To Margaret

INTRODUCTION

This is a realistic, but not a naturalistic, play. Therefore the design of the scenes and costumes must be in some sense stylised. The paintings of L. S. Lowry might suggest a suitable mood. Scenery must be sparing – only those pieces of architecture, furniture, and properties actually used in the action need be present: and they should be thoroughly realistic, so that the audience sees a selection from the details of everyday life rather than a generalised impression of the whole of it. A similar rule should also govern the direction and the acting. If this is done, the obvious difficulties, caused by the mixture of verse, prose, and song in the play, will be considerably lessened.

The exact date of the play is deliberately not given. In the London production, the details of costume covered approximately the years between 1860 and 1880. For instance, the soldiers wore the scarlet tunics and spiked helmets characteristic of the later (or 'Kipling') epoch, while the Constable was dressed in tall hat and tail coat as an early Peeler – his role in the play suggesting a rather primitive type of police organisation.

The songs should be sung to folk-song airs. There are many available tunes which equally well suit the various songs – perhaps these are as good as any:

Sparky's song (Act One, Scene 1): 'Six Jolly Wee Miners' – Scottish.

Sparky's song and chorus (Act Two, Scene 2): 'Blow away the Morning Dew' – English.

Sparky's song (Act Two, Scene 3): 'The Black Horse' – Irish.

Attercliffe's song (Act Three, Scene 2): First three stanzas – 'John Barleycorn' – English Air. Final stanza – 'John Barleycorn' – Irish Air.

Musgrave's song (Act Three, Scene 1) proved in production to be more satisfactory if the words were spoken against a background of drum rolls and recorded music.

The characters perhaps need a few notes of description:

The Soldiers: these are regulars and seasoned men. They should all have moustaches and an ingrained sense of discipline. Musgrave is aged between thirty and forty, tall, swart, commanding, sardonic but never humorous; he could well have served under Cromwell. Attercliffe is aged about fifty, grey-haired, melancholy, a little embittered. He is the senior O.R. of the party and conscious of his responsibility. Hurst, in his twenties, is bloody-minded, quick-tempered, handsome, cynical, tough, but not quite as intelligent as he thinks he is. Sparky, also in his twenties, is easily led, easily driven, inclined to hide from himself behind a screen of silly stories and irritating clownishness. The Dragoon Officer is little more than the deus-ex-machina at the end of the play. All he needs to be is tall, calm, cold, and commanding. His Trooper is a tough, reliable soldier.

The Townsmen: The Mayor is a bustling, shrewd, superficially jovial man with a coarse accent and an underlying inclination to bully. The Parson is very much a gentleman: he is conscious of the ungentlemanly nature of the community in which he lives. He must have the accent and manners of a balked aristocrat rather than a stage-clergyman. He too has some inclination to bully. The Constable has a continual inclination to bully, except when in the presence of his superiors. He is as inefficient as he is noisy. The Colliers are all embittered but not so as to make them unpleasant. Walsh is a strong man, physically and morally. He knows what he wants and is entirely impatient with those who are not so single-minded. The Slow Collier is not particularly intelligent but has a vacuous good humour. The Pugnacious Collier is pugnacious, and very quick to show it. The Bargee is something of a grotesque, a hunchback (though this should not be over-emphasised), very rapid in his movements, with a natural urge towards intrigue and mischief.

The Women: The Landlady is a large, immobile widow of about fifty. She sits behind her bar and watches everything that happens. She is clearly a woman of deep sympathies and intelligence, which she disguises with the normal north-country sombre pessimism. Annie is a big-boned girl, not particularly attractive, but in an aggressive sort of way she provokes the men. Her emotional confusion expresses itself in a deliberately enigmatic style of speech and behaviour. Her voice is harsh.

As for the 'Meaning of the Play': I do not think that an introductory note is a suitable place for a lengthy analysis of the work, but in view of the obvious puzzlement with which it was greeted by the critics, perhaps a few points may be made. This is not a nihilistic play. This is not (except perhaps unconsciously) a symbolist play. Nor does it advocate bloody revolution. I have endeavoured to write about the violence that is so evident in the world, and to do so through a story that is partly one of wish-fulfilment. I think that many of us must at some time have felt an overpowering urge to match some particularly outrageous piece of violence with an even greater and more outrageous retaliation. Musgrave tries to do this: and the fact that the sympathies of the play are clearly with him in his original horror, and then turn against him and his intended remedy, seems to have bewildered many people. I would suggest, however, that a study of the roles of the women, and of Private Attercliffe, should be sufficient to remove any doubts as to where the 'moral' of the play lies. Accusations of nihilism seem to derive from the scene where the Colliers turn away from Musgrave and join in the general dance around the beer barrel. Again, I would suggest, that an unwillingness to dwell upon unpleasant situations that do not immediately concern us is a general human trait, and recognition of it need imply neither cynicism nor despair. Complete pacifism is a very hard doctrine: and if this play appears to advocate it with perhaps some timidity, it is probably because I am naturally a timid man – and also because I know that if I am hit I very easily hit back: and I do not care to preach too confidently what I am not sure I can practise.

J.A.

Serjeant Musgrave's Dance was first performed at the Royal Court Theatre on 22 October 1959, with the following cast:

PRIVATE SPARKY	Donal Donnelly
PRIVATE HURST	Alan Dobie
PRIVATE ATTERCLIFFE	Frank Finlay
BLUDGEON, *a bargee*	James Bree
SERJEANT MUSGRAVE	Ian Bannen
THE PARSON	Richard Caldicot
MRS. HITCHCOCK	Freda Jackson
ANNIE	Patsy Byrne
THE CONSTABLE	Michael Hunt
THE MAYOR	Stratford Johns
A SLOW COLLIER	Jack Smethurst
A PUGNACIOUS COLLIER	Colin Blakely
WALSH, *an earnest collier*	Harry Gwynn Davies
A TROOPER OF DRAGOONS	Barry Wilsher
AN OFFICER OF DRAGOONS	Clinton Greyn

Produced by LINDSAY ANDERSON
Music by DUDLEY MOORE
Decor by JOCELYN HERBERT

The play is set in a mining town in the north of England eighty years ago. It is winter.

Act One

A canal wharf. Evening.

HURST *and* ATTERCLIFFE *are playing cards on the top of a side-drum. A few yards away* SPARKY *stands, as though on guard, clapping himself to keep warm. There is a pile of three or four heavy wooden boxes with the WD broad arrow stencilled on them, and a lantern set on top.*

SPARKY. Brr, oh a cold winter, snow, dark. We wait too long, that's the trouble. Once you've started, keep on travelling. No good sitting to wait in the middle of it. Only makes the cold night colder. (*He sings*):

> One day I was drunk, boys, on the Queen's Highway
> When a recruiting party come beating that way.
> I was enlisted and attested before I did know
> And to the Royal Barracks they forced me to go.

Brr! And they talk of the Crimea! Did I ever tell you that one about the field kitchens at Sebastopol? Well, there was this red-haired provost-sarnt, y'see . . . and then the corporal-cook – now *he'd* got no hair at all . . . now the Commissary in that Regiment was – oh . . . (*He finds no one paying attention.*) Who's winning?

HURST. I'm winning.

ATTERCLIFFE. Oho, no you're not. The black spades carry the day. Jack, King and Ace. *We* throw the red Queen over. That's another shilling, you know. Let's have it.

HURST. All right. Deal agen, boy. Or no, no, *my* deal, this game. Now let's see if I can't turn some good cards on to my side for a difference. Here: one, two, three, four . . . (*He deals the cards.*)

SPARKY. How much longer we got to wait, I'd like to know. I want to be off aboard that damned barge and away. What's happened to our Black Jack Musgrave, eh? Why don't he come and give us the word to get going?

ATTERCLIFFE. He'll come on the stroke, as he said. He works his life to bugle and drum, this serjeant. You ever seen him late?

SPARKY. No. (*He sings*):

> When first I deserted I thought myself free
> Till my cruel sweetheart informed upon me –

ATTERCLIFFE (*sharply*). I don't think you ought to sing *that* one.

SPARKY. Why not? It's true, isn't it? (*He sings*):

> Court martial, court martial, they held upon me
> And the sentence they passed was the high gallows tree.

HURST (*dropping cards and springing up in a rage*). Now shut it, will you! God-damned devil of a song to sing on this sort of a journey! He said you didn't ought to, so don't! (*He glances nervously around.*)

SPARKY. Ha, there's nobody to hear us. You're safe as a bloody blockhouse out here – I'm on the sentry, boy, *I'm* your protection.

ATTERCLIFFE (*irritably*). You make sure you are then. Go on: keep watching.

SPARKY (*returns to his guard*). Ah. Ha-ha . . . Or did you think *he* could hear you? (*He gestures towards the boxes.*) Maybe, maybe . . . *I* thought I heard him laugh.

ATTERCLIFFE. Steady, boy.

SPARKY (*a little wildly*). Steady yourself, you crumbling old cuckold. He might laugh, who knows? Well, make a rattling any road. Mightn't he, soldier boy?

HURST. Are you coming funny wi' me –

SPARKY. Funny? About *him*? You don't tell me he don't know what we're at. Why shouldn't he have a laugh at it, if that's how he feels?

HURST. Arrh, you're talking daft.

SPARKY. Now don't you be nervous, boy: not for *you* to be nervous. You're a man and a soldier! Or an old red rag stretched over four pair o' bones – well, what's the odds? Eh?

HURST (*after glaring angrily, sits down again*). *All right . . . All right, play.*

They play in silence. SPARKY *hums and blows his knuckles. Then he starts.*

SPARKY. Who goes there!

The BARGEE *enters with a lantern, whistling 'Michael Finnegan'.*

BARGEE. Hooroar, my jolly buckos! It's only old Joe Bludgeon, the Captain of the Lugger. Crooked old Joe. Heh heh. And what's the news with you? Are we ready yet, are we?

SPARKY. Ready for what?

BARGEE. Ready for off, of course, what do you think? Are we?

ATTERCLIFFE. No.

BARGEE. Why not, then?

ATTERCLIFFE. 'Cos it's not time, that's why not. Half-past seven, you was told.

BARGEE. Oh, it's as near as –

ATTERCLIFFE. No begod it's not, and he won't be here till it is.

BARGEE. Ah, the serjeant, eh?

ATTERCLIFFE. Aye, the serjeant. Is your barge up yet?

BARGEE. It's up. And the old horse waiting.

ATTERCLIFFE. Then we'll start to load.

HURST. Hey, we've not finished the game.

ATTERCLIFFE. Save it, mucker. You heard what Black Jack said.

HURST. All right. All right.

BARGEE. You can load these smaller cases 'side of the cabin. What you got in 'em, for Godsake? Ten ton and a half here.

SPARKY (*kicking one of them*). There's a Gatling gun in that one. You know what a Gatling gun is, friend?

BARGEE. I don't, and I don't care neither, tell you truth of it. By Lordy, what a life, the bloody Army. Do they still tie you fellers up and stripe you across with the cat-o'-nine-tails, eh?

HURST. No they don't.

ATTERCLIFFE *and* HURST *start carrying the cases out.*

BARGEE (*gloating*). Heheh, when I wor a young lad they told me, they did. Whack, whack, whack. Ooh, cruel it was. You know what they used to call 'em in them days – soldiers, I mean? Eh?

SPARKY. I know a lot o' names for calling soldiers.

BARGEE. I'll bet you don't know this one, though. Heh. Bloodred roses, that was it. What d'you think o' that, eh? Whack, whack, whack. Bloodred roses, eh? (*He calls off-stage.*) Not there, don't put it there, give me some room to swing me tiller, can't you! Soldiers. Get 'em aboard a barge, you'd be as well off wi' a row of deaf niggers from Peru. That's right, now leave it where you've dropped it, and come ashore before you capsize her—you bloodred bloody roses, you!

HURST *re-enters.*

HURST. That's enough of that, matey. Watch it.

MUSGRAVE *enters.*

MUSGRAVE (*to the* BARGEE). Aye, you watch it. Now I'll tell you just once, old man, and that's all. We travel on your

barge, passengers: we pay our fare. So don't you talk to my
men like they're deck-hands. Clear?

BARGEE. Oh it's clear, serjeant, I only wanted a little joke.

MUSGRAVE. Aye. And now you've had one. So be thankful.

ATTERCLIFFE *re-enters.*

ATTERCLIFFE (*as he and* HURST *pick up the remaining smaller
boxes*). We got the Gatling loaded on serjeant, and we're
fetching the rest of it. Then there's just the drum and the
other box left. Any news?

MUSGRAVE (*quietly to him*). We're all all right. Don't worry.

ATTERCLIFFE *and* HURST *go out with their load.* MUS-
GRAVE *taps the drum meditatively and turns to the* BARGEE.

I say, you, bargee. Is it going to snow again before tomorrow?

BARGEE. Likely. There's ice coming on the water too. Give
her another day and this canal'll be closed. They say the
road over the moors is fast already with the drifts. You've
chose a merry time o' year beating up for recruities, haven't
you? What you got in here? Another Gatling gun? (*He
smacks the last box.*)

MUSGRAVE. Why not? Show 'em all the best equipment,
glamourise 'em, man, fetch 'em in like conies . . . Now get
this last box loaded, and be careful. And then we're all
ready. You can start.

ATTERCLIFFE *and* HURST, *having returned, pick up the box
and carry it out,* SPARKY *going with them, the drum slung
on his shoulder.* MUSGRAVE *takes the soldiers' lantern and
makes a rapid circuit of the stage to see if anything is left. He
stands for a moment looking out in the direction from which
he has come in.*

BARGEE (*waiting for him*). This your first trip to the coal-mining
towns, serjeant?

MUSGRAVE. It is.

BARGEE. Ooh, brr, bitter and bleak: hungry men for the Queen. If you're used to a full belly, you'll want it when you get there.

MUSGRAVE (*curtly*). It's not material. We have our duty. A soldier's duty is a soldier's life.

BARGEE. Ah, duty.

> The Empire wars are far away
> For duty's sake we sail away
> Me arms and legs is shot away
> And all for the wink of a shilling and a drink . . .

Come on, me cheery serjeant, you've not left nowt behind.

They go out after the soldiers.

SCENE TWO

The bar of a public house.

MRS. HITCHCOCK *is sitting in the body of the room, talking to the* PARSON, *who is very much at his ease, with a glass of brandy in his hand.* ANNIE *is polishing glasses etc. behind the bar.*

PARSON. No. No, madam, no. I cannot be seen to countenance idleness, pauperism, beggary. If no one comes to buy your drink, I am sorry for you. But the fact is, madam, a little less drunkenness and disorder will do this town no harm. The Church is not a speculative bank, you know, to subsidise pot-houses.

MRS. HITCHCOCK (*sulkily*). Always a respectable house.

PARSON. What?

MRS. HITCHCOCK. Always a respectable house, reverend. Aye. If not, why renew the licence? You're a magistrate,

you know. You could have spoke agen me on me application.
But you didn't.

PARSON. That is not to the purpose, Mrs. Hitchcock. The
Bench allows that there have to be public houses to permit
an outlet for the poorer sort of people, but in times of
regrettable industrial conflict it is better that as many of
them as possible remain empty. If the colliers cannot afford
drink because of the strike – because of their own stupidity –
then there is the less likelihood of their being inflamed to acts
of violence. I am not at all certain that the Bench ought not
to withdraw all licences altogether until the pits are working.

MRS. HITCHCOCK. That'd be grand. See half a dozen publi-
cans going on the parish – beer-dregs from the workhouse
served to the Trade – ooh, talk of arsy-versy! (*She laughs
throatily.*)

PARSON. I'm quite sure that would not be necessary.

MRS. HITCHCOCK (*reasonably*). Now, look, reverend, you've
been taking me crossroads since the minute I began. All I
asked you in to say is this: this strike is bad for the town.
Well, I mean, of course, that means me. But it means you
too. *And* it means His Worship the Mayor: oh aye, aye:

> I am a proud coalowner
> And in scarlet here I stand.
> Who shall come or who shall go
> Through all my coal-black land?

(*She laughs again.*) Eh, if we can't have a laugh, we'll
starve!

PARSON. You are impertinent. I have nothing more to say.

MRS. HITCHCOCK. Ah, but I come to you because you're
Church, you're charity. Go on, reverend, you tell the Mayor
to agree with his men and give them a good price, then
they'll buy and sell in the town and they'll drink in this
taproom, and – ho-hoo – who knows, they might even
come to church! That'll be the day.

The PARSON *turns irritably from her and goes to the door.*
The BARGEE *enters and confronts him.*

BARGEE (*touching his cap mockingly*). Parson.

PARSON (*coldly*). Good afternoon.

BARGEE. Cold enough for you, eh?

PARSON (*trying to pass*). It is cold, yes.

BARGEE. How's the strike?

PARSON. It is not yet settled.

BARGEE. No, I bet it's not, and all. Hey missus!

MRS. HITCHCOCK. Hello.

BARGEE. A quart o' taddy. Best!

MRS. HITCHCOCK (*impassive*). Can you pay for it?

BARGEE. 'Course I can pay – wait a minute, Parson, just a
minute, all under control – I'm not one of your colliery
agitators, you know. *I'm* still in work. I've news for you.

MRS. HITCHCOCK (*to* ANNIE). He says he can pay. Draw him
his quart.

BARGEE (*to the* PARSON). I didn't think, like, to find you here,
but, eh, well, seeing as how here you are – canal's froze up,
you know.

PARSON. Well?

BARGEE. Well. Last barge come in this morning. *My* barge.
There was passengers.

PARSON. I am not really interested.

BARGEE (*significantly*). Four on 'em, Parson. Soldiers.

ANNIE *hands the* BARGEE *his tankard.*

PARSON (*in some alarm*). Soldiers! Already? Who sent for
them? Why was I not told? This could be very dangerous –

BARGEE. They're not here for what you think, you know. Not
yet, any road. You see, they've come recruiting.

PARSON (*relieved, but vexed*). Oh . . . Well, what if they have?
Why bother me with it? You're just wasting time, man.
Come on, get out of my way . . .

BARGEE (*still detaining him*). Eh, but, Parson, you're a magistrate.

PARSON. Of course I'm a magistrate.

BARGEE. You're a power, you are: in a town of trouble, in a place of danger. Yes. You're the word and the book, aren't you? Well then: soldiers. Recruiting. Useful?

PARSON (*beginning to follow his drift*). H'm. I do not think the Bench is in any real need of *your* suggestions. But I am obliged to you for the news. Thank you.

He gives the BARGEE *a coin and leaves.*

BARGEE (*flipping the coin*). Heh, heh, I said I could pay.

He gives it to ANNIE *and starts whistling 'Michael Finnegan'.* ANNIE *goes back to the bar.* MRS. HITCHCOCK *takes the coin from her and tests it between her teeth.*

MRS. HITCHCOCK. Soldiers. Annie, love, you could tell us what soldiers is good for.

ANNIE (*sullen*). Why should I tell you?

BARGEE (*gleefully*). Go on, go on, lassie, tell us about the soldiers. She knows the good redcoat button-to-back, I'll bet. Go on, it's a cold day, warm it up for us. Heh, heh, our strong Annie's the champion, eh?

He smacks her on the bottom. She swerves angrily.

ANNIE. *When* I've given you leave: and not afore. You bloody dog, sit down.

BARGEE (*subsiding in mock terror*). Ooh, sharp, sharp.

MRS. HITCHCOCK. Aye, so sit down . . . Go on, Annie, tell us.

ANNIE. I'll tell you for what a soldier's good:

> To march behind his roaring drum,
> Shout to us all: 'Here I come
> I've killed as many as I could –
> I'm stamping into your fat town

From the war and to the war
And every girl can be my whore
Just watch me lay them squealing down.
And that's what he does and so do we.
Because we know he'll soon be dead
We strap our arms round the scarlet red
Then send him weeping over the sea.
Oh he will go and a long long way.
Before he goes we'll make him pay
Between the night and the next cold day –
By God there's a whole lot more I could say –

What good's a bloody soldier 'cept to be dropped into a
slit in the ground like a letter in a box. How many did you
bring with you – is it four?

BARGEE. Aye. Four.

ANNIE. That's four beds in this house?

MRS. HITCHCOCK. I should hope it's in this house. It's the
best house in town.

ANNIE (*in a sudden outburst*). Then you'd do well to see they
stay four nights because I'll not go with more nor one in
one night, no, not for you nor for all of Egypt!

*She lets out a howl and rushes out of the door behind the bar,
clattering a tin tray full of tankards on to the floor.*

BARGEE. Ooh, Lordy! Champion, strong, and sharp. Annie!
Tell us some more!

MRS. HITCHCOCK (*crossly*). Let her alone. She's said enough
for you, hasn't she? It's not right to set her off . . . I
suppose they *are* coming to this house?

BARGEE. Oh surely, aye, surely. *I* told 'em: *I* took care.

A rat-tat-tat on the drum heard, off.

There, you see, they're coming.

SPARKY *enters magnificently, beating the drum.*

SPARKY. Ho-ho, atten-tion! Stand by your beds! Name of the Queen, missus – has he told you – there's four on us: we three, we'll settle for palliasses in the loft, but the serjeant he wants a big brass bed with knobs on, that's his fancy! Can you do it?

MRS. HITCHCOCK. So here they are, the gay recruiters. Aye, I can do it, young man. I've only one room in the house. The serjeant can have that. The three of you'll have to doss down in me old stable, out back, but there's a good stove, you'll be warm. Now, who's going to pay? You or the Queen?

SPARKY. Oh, Queen at end of it all, I suppose.

MRS. HITCHCOCK. But you at beginning, eh?

SPARKY. Oh-oh, chalk it up, you know . . . we've brought some gear with us too.

BARGEE. Ten and a half ton. Nigh foundered the old barge, it did, I can tell you.

SPARKY. But we got here, friend, didn't we? Like we get ourselves to everywhere we go, we do. No question o' that, y'see.

BARGEE. Heh, heh, none.

SPARKY (*calls to offstage*). Serjeant! We're fixed!

MUSGRAVE (*off*). And the equipment?

SPARKY. And the equipment, missus?

MRS. HITCHCOCK. There's a coach-house across the yard.

SPARKY (*calls to offstage*). Coach-house across the yard, serjeant! . . . While they're taking it round there, missus, let's have a pint apiece drawn ready. Like what *he* drinks, eh? Recommend it, friend?

BARGEE. You could stand your bayonet up in this, you could.

SPARKY. Right, then. And we'll give you another while we're at it. That's five on 'em, pints, unless *you're* drinking with us, too, are you?

MRS. HITCHCOCK. Why not, soldier? Queen as pays . . . Annie! Hey Annie!

As there is no reply, she goes herself behind the bar and starts filling the tankards. MUSGRAVE *enters.*

MUSGRAVE. Is the padlock on your coach-house door a strong one, ma'am?

MRS. HITCHCOCK. Likely so.

MUSGRAVE. Valuable equipment, y'see. Your window in there's barred, I notice.

MRS. HITCHCOCK. That's right.

MUSGRAVE (*picking up a tankard*). Good . . . This for me?

MRS. HITCHCOCK. If you want it.

The other two soldiers enter.

ATTERCLIFFE. The cases are all locked up and safe, serjeant.

MUSGRAVE (*indicates drinks*). Very good. Here you are.

HURST and ATTERCLIFFE. Thank you, serjeant.

BARGEE (*raising his drink*). Good health to Her Majesty; to Her Majesty's wars; to the girls we leave behind us. Drink!

They all drink.

MRS. HITCHCOCK (*raising her drink*) :

>   Into the river, out of the river
>   Once I was dry, now I am wet
>   But hunger and cold they hold me yet.

They drink again, with a certain puzzlement at the toast.

MRS. HITCHCOCK. They hold this town today, any road, serjeant; or had you been told?

MUSGRAVE. What's the matter?

MRS. HITCHCOCK. No work in the colliery. The owner calls it a strike, the men call it a lock-out, we call it starvation.

The CONSTABLE *enters violently.*

CONSTABLE. His Worship the Mayor.

MRS. HITCHCOCK. Eh?

CONSTABLE. I said, His Worship the Mayor!

BARGEE. Oho, *now*, me jolly buckos, give attention, stand-to, to the present!

CONSTABLE (*to the* BARGEE]. Sssssh – ssh –

BARGEE. Heh, heh, heh –

The MAYOR *enters at speed, wearing his gold chain. After him comes the* PARSON. MUSGRAVE *calls his men to attention.*

MAYOR. Mrs. Hitchcock, I'm seeking the soldiers. Ah, here they are! Well, I'm the Mayor of this town, I own the colliery, I'm a worried man. So I come seeking you when I could send for you, what do you think to that? Let's have a look at you . . . Ah. Haha . . . Clear the snug a minute, missus. I want a private word with the Parson. Serjeant, be ready outside when I send for you.

MUSGRAVE. At your service, sir . . . Come on.

Beckoned by MRS. HITCHCOCK, *he leads his party out behind the bar.*

CONSTABLE (*propelling the* BARGEE *to the street door*). Go on, you, out this road.

BARGEE (*dodging him*). Oo-er –

> Constable Constable alive or dead
> His head is of leather and his belly's of lead.

Go – whoops . . . How are you, Parson?

He ducks out, whistling 'Michael Finnegan'.

MRS. HITCHCOCK (*sourly, to the* MAYOR). Do you want a drink?

MAYOR. No.

MRS. HITCHCOCK. *At* your service, when you do.

She curtsies and goes out behind the bar.

MAYOR. What do you think to 'em, Parson?

PARSON. Fine strong men. They make me proud of my country. Mr. Mayor, Britain depends upon these spirits. It is a great pity that their courage is betrayed at home by skulkers and shirkers. What do *you* think?

MAYOR (*looking at him sideways*). *I* think we'll use 'em, Parson. Temporary expedient, but it'll do. The price of coal has fell, I've had to cut me wages, I've had to turn men off. They say they'll strike, so I close me gates. We can't live like that for ever. There's two ways to solve this colliery – one is build the railway here and cut me costs of haulage, *that* takes two years and an Act of Parliament, though God knows I want to do it. The other is clear out half the population, stir up a diversion, turn their minds to summat else. The Queen's got wars, she's got rebellions. Over the sea. All right. Beat these fellers' drums high around the town, I'll put one pound down for every Royal Shilling the serjeant pays. Red coats and flags. Get rid o' the trouble-makers. Drums and fifes and glory.

PARSON (*severely*). The soldier's calling is one of honour.

MAYOR. It's more than that. It's bloody convenient. Town Constable, fetch that serjeant in!

CONSTABLE (*nervously*). Er, excuse me, Your Worship. A point. Soldiers, you see. Now, I've got a very small force in this town. Only one other regular officer, you know: the rest is them deputy-specials – I can't trust *that* lot to stand fast and fear nowt when the time comes.

PARSON. What time?

CONSTABLE. There's been stone-throwing this morning. Two of my office windows is broke. And I'm nervous—that's frank, you know – I *am*.

MAYOR. Well?

CONSTABLE. Your Worship. I want these soldiers added to my force. It's all right recruiting. But what we need's patrols.

MAYOR. Not yet.

CONSTABLE. Your Worship. I'm asking you formal. You've got agitators here, and they won't stop at throwing stones: that's frank.

MAYOR (*angrily*). I said not yet. We'll try it my road first. Godsake, man, what's four soldiers agen the lot of 'em? This town's wintered up, you'll get no more help till there's a thaw. So work on that. Call in the serjeant.

CONSTABLE. Right, Your Worship. Serjeant! Come in here!

MUSGRAVE *re-enters.*

MUSGRAVE. Sir?

MAYOR. Serjeant, we're very glad to have you. I speak for the Council, I speak for the magistrates. Now listen: there's loyal hearts and true here, and we're every man-jack of us keen to see our best lads flock to the colours. Isn't that so, Parson?

PARSON (*taken a little by surprise*). Ha-h'm – with great pride, yes.

MAYOR. Right. For every Queen's Shilling you give out, I give out a golden sovereign – no, two. One for the recruit, and one to be divided among you and your three good lads. What do you say to that?

MUSGRAVE. That's most handsome, sir.

MAYOR. I should damn well think it is. How do you propose to work?

MUSGRAVE. Sir?

MAYOR. Aye, I mean, d'you tramp around the streets drumming, or set on your fannies in a pub—or what?

MUSGRAVE. Depends what's most appropriate, sir, according to the type of town. I've not had time for a look at yours yet. But the pubs seem pretty empty, if this one's owt to go by.

PARSON. They *are* empty.

MUSGRAVE. Aye. Well, in that case, I'll have to make a reconnaissance, won't I? When I'm decided, I'll let you know.

CONSTABLE. And let me know, serjeant. I'll see you get facilities.

MUSGRAVE. Thank you, mister.

MAYOR. And while you're on about them facilities, constable, perhaps you might let in the serjeant on a few likely names for his list, eh? Could you pick him some passable strong-set men, could you?

CONSTABLE (*significantly*). I could have a try, Your Worship.

MAYOR. Right. Then if that's settled, I'll be off back to town hall. I've not got time to waste wi' nattering, snug and all though it is in here. Come along, Constable. I want a little word wi' you about them stones.

MAYOR *and* CONSTABLE *go out.*

PARSON (*severely*). I think I ought to make one thing clear, serjeant. I know that it is customary for recruiting-parties to impress themselves upon the young men of the district as dashingly as possible, and no doubt upon the young women also. Now I am not having any of that. There's enough trouble in the place as it is. So remember.

MUSGRAVE. Yes, sir. I'll remember.

PARSON. I want no drunkenness, and no fornication, from your soldiers. Need I speak plainer?

MUSGRAVE. No, sir. There will be none. I am a religious man.

PARSON. Very well. Good day to you.

MUSGRAVE. Good day, sir.

The PARSON *goes.* MUSGRAVE *sits down, takes out a small pocket bible and reads.* MRS. HITCHCOCK *enters.*

MRS. HITCHCOCK. What, they've not all gone, already?

MUSGRAVE. They have, ma'am.

MRS. HITCHCOCK. Just like, isn't it? Use my bar for a council-parlour, leave nowt behind 'em but bad breath and a shiny bench – *they* take care. I'm giving your three their dinners in back. You eating with 'em?

MUSGRAVE (*of-handed*). No. I'll have a hand of bread and cheese and eat it here.

MRS. HITCHCOCK. Drink with it?

MUSGRAVE (*still at his book*). No . . . Thanks, no. Just the cheese.

MRS. HITCHCOCK (*sourly*). H'm, another on 'em . . . Hey, Annie! Slice o' bread and a piece o' cheese in here for this one! Pickles?

MUSGRAVE. Eh?

MRS. HITCHCOCK (*annoyed*). Pickles!

MUSGRAVE. No . . . (*He looks up suddenly.*) Tell me, ma'am, is there many from this town lately have gone for a soldier?

MRS. HITCHCOCK. Some. It's not a common pleasure here – not as long as the coal wor right to sell, any road. But there was some. You'll know the sort o' reasons, I daresay?

> The yellow-haired boy lay in my bed
> A-kissing me up from me toes to me head.
> But when my apron it did grow too short
> He thought it good time to leave his sport.

Enter ANNIE *with the bread and cheese. She gives it to* MUS-GRAVE.

MUSGRAVE. Thank you.

ANNIE (*confronting him*). Serjeant you are.

MUSGRAVE. That's right.

ANNIE. You seem a piece stronger than the rest of 'em.

He nods.

And they call you Black Jack Musgrave?

He looks at her.

Well, I'm looking at your face, mister serjeant. Now do you know what I'd say?

MUSGRAVE. What?

ANNIE. The North Wind in a pair of millstones
    Was your father and your mother
    They got you in a cold grinding.
    God help us all if they get you a brother.

She looks at him another minute, then nods her head and goes out.

MUSGRAVE (*wryly*). She talks a kind of truth, that lassie. Is she daft?

MRS. HITCHCOCK. No, no, no, I wouldn't say daft. But there's not many would let her bide in their house.

MUSGRAVE. Tell me, ma'am. It sticks on my mind that I once had a sort of a comrade came from this town. . . Long, yellow-haired lad, like in your little verse. Name of, oh, Hickson, was it, Hickman?

MRS. HITCHCOCK (*astonished and disturbed*). Ey, ey –

MUSGRAVE. What was it now, his name – Billy – Billy –

MRS. HITCHCOCK (*very upset*). Billy Hicks. Hicks. Aye, oh, strange, serjeant, strange roads bringing you along, I'd not wonder.

MUSGRAVE. What do you mean? . . . It *was* Hicks – I remember.

MRS. HITCHCOCK (*reminiscently*). Not what you'd call a bad young feller, you know – but he weren't no good neither. He'd come in here pissed of a Sat'dy night – I'd tell him straight out, 'You needn't reckon on to get any more here.' But he'd lean on this bar and he'd look at me, and he'd sing. You know – *hymns* – 'Uplift your heads, you gates of brass' – church hymns, he'd sing. Like he'd say to me, 'I'll sing for me drinking, missus' . . . hymns . . .

She hums the tune of 'Uplift your heads' and breaks off sharply.

He gave her a baby, and he went straight off to the war. Or the rebellions, they called it. They told us he was killed.

MUSGRAVE (*without emotion*). Aye, he was killed. He was shot
dead last year . . . Gave a baby to who?

MRS. HITCHCOCK (*jerks her thumb to door behind bar*). Her.

MUSGRAVE (*truly surprised*). Go on?

MRS. HITCHCOCK. True. But when it wor born, it came a
kind of bad shape, pale, sick: it wor dead and in the ground
in no more nor two month. About the time they called
him dead, y'see. What d'you reckon to that?

MUSGRAVE (*carelessly*). It's not material. He was no great
friend to me. But maybe, as you said, strange. He did use
to sing. And yellow hair he had, didn't he? (*He goes to the
door behind the bar and calls.*) Have ye finished your dinners?
Because we'll take a look at the town before it gets dark.
(*Confidently to* MRS. HITCHCOCK) What you've just
been telling me, don't tell it to these. Dead men and dead
children should bide where they're put and not be rose up
to the thoughts of the living. It's bad for discipline . . . (*He
calls again.*) Come on, let's be having you!

The SOLDIERS *come in.* MUSGRAVE *points to each one as they
enter.*

East; south; west; I'll go north; I'm told it suits my nature.
Then meet at the churchyard rail and tell me what you've
seen. Let's make it sharp.

They go out.

SCENE THREE

The churchyard.

Sunset. HURST *enters and walks about, whistling nervously. The*
SLOW COLLIER *enters and looks at him. They pass each other,
giving each other good hard stares. The* SLOW COLLIER *is about
to leave the stage when he turns round and calls.*

SLOW COLLIER. Hey! Soldier!

HURST. Aye?

SLOW COLLIER. How many on you is there?

HURST. Four.

SLOW COLLIER. Four . . . Four dead red rooks and be damned.

HURST. What? What's that?

SLOW COLLIER (*contemptuously*). Arrh . . .

He slouches out.

HURST *makes to follow, but decides not to, and continues walking about.*

MUSGRAVE *enters.*

MUSGRAVE. Coldest town I ever was in. What did you see?

HURST. Hardly a thing. Street empty, windows shut, two old wives on a doorstep go indoors the minute I come. Three men on one corner, two men on another, dirty looks and no words from any on 'em. There's one man swears a curse at me just now. That's all.

MUSGRAVE. H'm . . .

He calls to offstage.

Hello! We're over here!

ATTERCLIFFE *enters.*

What did you see?

ATTERCLIFFE. Hardly a thing. Street empty, doors locked, windows blind, shops cold and empty. A young lass calls her kids in from playing in the dirt—she sees me coming, so she calls 'em. There's someone throws a stone –

MUSGRAVE. A stone?

ATTERCLIFFE. Aye. I don't know who did it and it didn't hit me, but it was thrown.

HURST. It's a cold poor town, I'm telling you, serjeant.

MUSGRAVE. Coldest town I ever was in. And here's the fourth of us.

Enter SPARKY.

What did you see?

SPARKY. Hardly a thing. Street empty, no chimneys smoking, no horses, yesterday's horsedung frozen on the road. Three men at a corner-post, four men leaning on a wall. No words: but some chalked up on a closed door – they said: 'Soldiers go home'.

HURST. Go home?

SPARKY. That's it, boy: home. It's a place they think we have somewhere. And what did *you* see, serjeant?

MUSGRAVE. Nothing different from you . . . So, here is our town and here are we. All fit and appropriate.

HURST (*breaking out suddenly*). Appropriate? Serjeant, now we've come with you so far. And every day we're in great danger. We're on the run, in red uniforms, in a black-and-white coalfield; and it's cold; and the money's running out that you stole from the Company office; and we don't know who's heard of us or how much they've heard. Isn't it time you brought out clear just what you've got in mind?

MUSGRAVE (*ominously*). Aye? Is it? And any man else care to tell me what the time is?

ATTERCLIFFE (*reasonably*). Now serjeant, please, easy—we're all your men, and we agreed –

HURST. All right: if we *are* your men, we've rights.

MUSGRAVE (*savagely*). The only right *you* have is a rope around your throat and six foot six to drop from. On the run? Stolen money? I'm talking of a murdered officer, shot down in a street fight, shot down in one night's work. They put that to the rebels, but *I* know *you* were the man. We deserted, but you killed.

HURST. I'd a good reason . . .

MUSGRAVE. I know you had reason, else I'd not have left you alive to come with us. All I'm concerned about this minute is to tell you how you stand. And you stand in my power. But

there's more to it than a bodily blackmail – isn't there? –
because my power's the power of God, and that's what's
brought me here and all three of you with me. You know
my words and purposes – it's not just authority of the
orderly room, it's not just three stripes, it's not just given to
me by the reckoning of my mortal brain – well, *where* does
it come from?

He flings this question fiercely at HURST.

HURST (*trying to avoid it*). All right, I'm not arguing –
MUSGRAVE. *Where!*
HURST (*frantically defensive*). I don't believe in God!
MUSGRAVE. You don't? Then what's this!

He jabs his thumb into HURST'S *cheek and appears to scrape
something off it.*

HURST. Sweat.
MUSGRAVE. The coldest winter for I should think it's ten
years, and the man sweats like a bird-bath!
HURST (*driven in a moral corner*). Well, why not, because –
MUSGRAVE (*relentless*). Go on – because?
HURST (*browbeaten into incoherence*). All right, because I'm
afraid. 'Cos I thought when I met you, I thought we'd got
the same motives. To get out, get shut o' the Army – with
its 'treat-you-like-dirt-but-you-do-the-dirty-work' – 'kill
him, kill *them*, they're all bloody rebels, State of Emergency,
high standard of turnout, military bearin' – so *I* thought up
some killing, I said I'll get me own in. I thought o' the
Rights of Man. Rights o' the Rebels : that's *me*! Then I
went. And here's a serjeant on the road, he's took two men,
he's deserted same as me, he's got money, he can bribe a
civvy skipper to carry us to England . . . It's nowt to do wi'
God. I don't understand all that about God, why d'you
bring God into it! You've come here to tell the people and
then there'd be no more war –

MUSGRAVE (*taking him up with passionate affirmation*). Which *is* the word of God! Our message without God is a bad belch and a hiccup. You three of you, without me, are a bad belch and a hiccup. How d'you think you'd do it, if I wasn't here? Tell me, go on, tell me!

HURST (*still in his corner*). Why then I'd – I'd – I'd tell 'em, Sarnt Musgrave, I'd bloody stand, and tell 'em, and –

MUSGRAVE. Tell 'em *what*!

HURST (*made to appear more stupid than he really is*). All right : like, the war, the Army, colonial wars, we're treated like dirt, out there, and for to do the dirty work, and –

MUSGRAVE (*with withering scorn*). And they'd run you in and run you up afore the clock struck five! You don't understand about God! But you think, yourself, you, alone, stupid, without a gill of discipline, illiterate, ignorant of the Scriptures – you think you can make a whole town, a whole nation, understand the cruelty and greed of armies, what it means, and how to punish it! You hadn't even took the precaution to find the cash for your travel. I paid your fare!

HURST (*knuckling under*). All right. You paid . . . You're the Serjeant . . . All right. Tell us what to do.

MUSGRAVE (*the tension eased*). Then we'll sit down, and we'll be easy. It's cold atween these tombs, but its private. Sit down. Now : you can consider, and you can open your lugs and you can listen – ssh! Wait a minute . . .

The SLOW COLLIER *enters at one side, the* PUGNACIOUS *and* EARNEST COLLIERS *at the other. All three carry pick-hefts as clubs.*

SLOW COLLIER (*calls to the other two*). Four on 'em, you see. They're all here together.

PUGNACIOUS COLLIER. Setting in the graveyard, eh, like a coffin-load o' sick spooks.

EARNEST COLLIER (*coming towards the soldiers*). Which one's the Serjeant?

MUSGRAVE (*standing up*). Talk to me.

EARNEST COLLIER. Aye and I will too. There's a Union made at this colliery, and we're strong. When we say strike, we strike, all ends of us: that's fists, and it's pick-hefts and it's stones and it's feet. If you work in the coal-seam you carry iron on your clogs – see!

He thrusts up his foot menacingly.

PUGNACIOUS COLLIER. And you fight for your life when it's needed.

MUSGRAVE. So do some others of us.

EARNEST COLLIER. Ah, no, lobster, *you* fight for pay. You go sailing on what they call punitive expeditions, against what you call rebels, and you shoot men down in streets. But not here. These streets is *our* streets.

MUSGRAVE. Anything else?

EARNEST COLLIER. No. Not this evening. Just so as you know, that's all.

PUGNACIOUS COLLIER. Setting in the graveyard. Look at 'em, for Godsake. Waiting for a riot and then they'll have a murder. Why don't *we* have one *now*: it's dark enough, ent it?

EARNEST COLLIER. Shut up. It'll do when it's time. Just so as they know, that's all.

The COLLIERS *turn to go.*

MUSGRAVE. Wait a minute.

They pause.

Who told you we'd come to break the strike?

EARNEST COLLIER. Eh?

MUSGRAVE. Who told you?

EARNEST COLLIER. Nobody told us. We don't need to be told. You see a strike: you see soldiers: there's only one reason.

MUSGRAVE. Not this time there isn't. We haven't been sent
for –

PUGNACIOUS COLLIER. Get away wi' that –

MUSGRAVE. And all soldiers aren't alike, you know. Some of
us is human.

SLOW COLLIER   } Arrh –
PUGNACIOUS COLLIER   } (*laughs*)

MUSGRAVE. Now I'm in Mrs. Hitchcock's bar tonight until
such time as she closes it. There'll be my money on the
counter, and if you want to find what I'm doing here you
can come along and see. I speak fair; you take it fair. Right?

EARNEST COLLIER. No it's not right, Johnny Clever. These
streets is our streets, so you learn a warning . . . Come on,
leave 'em be, *we* know what they're after. Come on . . .

The COLLIERS *go, growling threateningly.*

ATTERCLIFFE. They hate us, Serjeant, don't they? Wouldn't
you say that's good?

MUSGRAVE. Because of the bad coal-trade they hate us; the
rest just follows. True, there's one man talks of shooting
rebels down in streets, but the others only think of bayonets
turned on pitmen, and that's no good. At the present, they
believe we've come to kill them. Soon they'll find we
haven't, so they'll stop hating. Maybe even some o' them'll
come and sign on. You'll see: His Worship's sovereigns –
they'll fall too damned heavy into these boys' pockets. But
we'll watch and take count, till we know the depth of the
corruption. 'Cos all that we know now is that we've had to
leave behind us a colonial war that is a war of sin and
unjust blood.

ATTERCLIFFE (*sharply*). All wars is sin, serjeant . . .

MUSGRAVE (*impatient*). I'm not discussing that. Single purpose at a single time : your generalities aren't material : this
is particular – one night's work in the streets of one city, and
it damned all four of us and the war it was part of. We're

each one guilty of particular blood. We've come to this town
to work that guilt back to where it began.

He turns to SPARKY.

Why to this town? Say it, say it!

SPARKY (*as with a conditioned reflex*). Billy. Billy's dead. He
wor my mucker, back end of the rear rank. He wor killed
dead. He came from this town.

MUSGRAVE (*relentless*). Go on.

SPARKY (*appealing*). Serjeant –

MUSGRAVE. Use your clear brain, man, and tell me what you're
doing here! Go on.

SPARKY (*incoherent with recollecting what he wants to forget*).
I'm doing here? I'm doing . . . Serjeant, you know it. 'Cos
he died. That wor Billy. I got drunk. Four days and four
nights. After work of one night. Absent. Not sober. Im-
properly dressed.

He tries to turn it into one of his jokes.

> Stick me in a cell, boys,
> Pull the prison bell
> Black Jack Musgrave
> To call the prison roll –

Sarnt, no offence – 'First ye'll serve your punishment' he
says. 'Then I'll show you how,' he says, the Serjeant. I says,
'You'll show me what?' He says, 'I'll show you how your
Billy can be paid for.' . . . I didn't want to pay for him –
what had I to care for a colonial war? . . .

He meets MUSGRAVE'S *eye and takes a grip on his motives.*

But I *did* want to pay for him, didn't I? 'Cos that's why I'm
here. 'You go down, I'll follow' . . . You, Serjeant, ent it?

> Black Jack Musgrave
> He always calls the roll.

He says:

> Go down to Billy's town
> Tell 'em how he died.

And that's what I'm doing here. The Serjeant pays the fare. Here I am, I'm paid for. Next turn's for Billy. Or all that's left of Billy. Who'll give me an offer for his bones? Sixpence for a bone, for a bone of my dead mucker . . .

He again avoids emotion by turning on HURST, *jeeringly.*

You didn't even know him when he lived, you weren't in his squad, what do *you* care that he's dead? To you he's like God, ent that the truth, you don't care and you're not bothered!

HURST (*angrily*). Hold your noise, you dirty turd! Who are you telling!

SPARKY. You. Oh you, me boy, you. A man and a soldier –

He meets MUSGRAVE'S *eye again, and his voice trails away.*

– a man and a soldier . . .

MUSGRAVE (*emphatically*). Aye. And *you're* a soldier. Don't forget that. You're my man and you'll hear me. You're not on any drunk now. Now you've got discipline. You've got grief, but good order, and its turned to the works of God!

SPARKY (*submissively*). Yes, Sarnt.

MUSGRAVE (*to* HURST). Turned to the works of God!

HURST (*submissively*). Yes, Sarnt.

MUSGRAVE (*in a more encouraging voice*). There was talk about danger. Well, I never heard of no danger yet that wasn't comparative. Compare it against your purposes. And compare it against my strategy. Remember: the roads are closed, the water's frozen, the telegraph wires are weighted down with snow, they haven't *built* the railway. We came here safe, and here we are, safe here. The winter's giving us one day, two days, three days even – that's clear safe for us to hold our time, take count of the corruption, then stand before

this people with our white shining word, and let it dance!
It's a hot coal, this town, despite that it's freezing – choose
your minute and blow: and whoosh, she's flamed your roof
off! They're trembling already into the strikers' riots. Well,
their riots and our war are the same one corruption. This
town is ours, it's ready for us: and its people, when they've
heard us, and the Word of God, crying the murders that
we've done – I'll tell you they'll turn to us, and they'll turn
against that war!

ATTERCLIFFE (*gravely*). All wars, Serjeant Musgrave. They've
got to turn against all wars. Colonial war, do we say, no war
of honour? I'm a private soldier, I never had no honour, I
went killing for the Queen, I did it for me wages, that wor
my life. But I've got a new life. There was one night's work,
and I said: no more killing.

HURST (*with excitement*). It's time we did our *own* killing.

ATTERCLIFFE. No, boy, it isn't.

HURST. Aye, and I mean it. We're all on the run, and we're all
of us deserters. We're wild-wood mad and raging. We caught
it overseas and now we've got to run around the English
streets biting every leg to give it *them* – that can't be done
without –

MUSGRAVE (*interrupting*). Listen to me!

HURST (*subsiding*). Serjeant.

MUSGRAVE (*with angry articulation*). We are here with a word.
That's all. That's particular. Let the word dance. That's all
that's material, this day and for the next. What happens
afterwards, the Lord God will provide. I am with you, He
said. Abide with Me in Power. A Pillar of Flame before the
people. What we show here'll lead forward forever, against
dishonour, and greed, and murder-for-greed! There is our
duty, the new, deserter's duty: God's dance on this earth:
and all that we are is His four strong legs to dance it . . .
Very well. That'll do. It's dark. We'll go in. Now we'll be
likely buying drinks around and so on, in the public tonight.

I don't want to see any o' you with more nor you can hold.
When there's danger, there's temptation. So keep it gay, but
that's all. Off you go now! Take 'em in.

ATTERCLIFFE (*as the senior*). All right then, smartly now,
walking up the street. Remember, we're recruiting. I'll give
you the time – left right left right.

They walk out briskly, leaving MUSGRAVE *alone. As they go,
the* BARGEE *enters, and gives them a parody salute in passing.*
MUSGRAVE *doesn't see him, walks downstage, crosses his hands
on his chest and stands to pray. The* BARGEE *parodies his
attitude behind his back.*

MUSGRAVE. God, my Lord God. Have You or have You not
delivered this town into my hands? All my life a soldier I've
made You prayers and made them straight, I've reared my
one true axe against the timber and I've launched it true.
My regiment was my duty, and I called Death honest,
killing by the book – but it all got scrawled and mucked
about and I could not think clear . . . Now I have my duties
different. I'm in this town to change all soldiers' duties. My
prayer is: keep my mind clear so I can weigh Judgement
against the Mercy and Judgement against the Blood, and
make this Dance as terrible as You have put it into my brain.
The Word alone is terrible: the Deed must be worse. But I
know it is Your Logic, and You will provide.

*He pauses for a moment, then turns sharply on his heel and
strides away after the soldiers. He still fails to see the* BARGEE.
The latter has whipped off his hat at the conclusion of MUS-
GRAVE'S *prayer, and now he stands looking solemnly up to
Heaven. He gives a sanctimonious smirk and breathes: 'Amen'.*

Act Two

SCENE ONE

The bar of the public house.

A scene of noise and conviviality, crowded confusion. MRS. HITCHCOCK *is seated behind the bar, drinking tea with brandy in it.* ANNIE *is going backwards and forwards in the room carrying drinks and empties.* MUSGRAVE *is sitting with a tankard, calmly watching.* SPARKY *is wearing his drum and alternately beating it and drinking and singing. The* SLOW *and* PUGNACIOUS COLLIERS, *well-oiled, are drinking and dancing. The* BARGEE *is drinking and dancing and playing a mouth-organ and beating time to the singing.* ATTERCLIFFE *is drinking and dancing and pinning cockades to the hats of the* COLLIERS. *At intervals one of the dancers grabs hold of* ANNIE *and swirls her around, but she retains a contemptuous aloofness and carries on with her work. As the scene opens the men* (save MUSGRAVE) *are all joining in the chorus:*

CHORUS. Blow your morning bugles
            Blow your calls ey-ho
            Form platoon and dress the ranks
            And blow, boys blow!

This chorus is sung (with progressively less correctness) by most of the men at the end of each verse of the song.

SPARKY *(singing).*

            When first I came to the barracks
            My heart it grieved full sore
            For leaving of my old true love
            That I would see no more.

chorus

SLOW COLLIER (*to* MUSGRAVE, *who is studying a notebook*).
   I'm not signing nowt. Provisional, I said, provisional.
MUSGRAVE. Aye, aye, provisional. No one makes it different.
SPARKY (*sings*).

> They made us drill and muster
> And stand our sentries round
> And I never thought I'd lay again
> A girl upon the ground.

chorus

PUGNACIOUS COLLIER (*to* ATTERCLIFFE). That's *my* point,
   my point, too . . . all right enlisting, aye . . . but I'm a
   married man –
SPARKY (*sings*).

> But soon we were paraded
> And marching to the war
> And in every town the girls lay down
> And cried out loud for more.

chorus

PUGNACIOUS COLLIER (*to* ATTERCLIFFE). I'm not so sure I
   like your looks, aye, *you*!
SPARKY. Me?
PUGNACIOUS COLLIER (*pointing to* ATTERCLIFFE). You!
SPARKY (*sings*).

> And when we'd lodge in billets
> We'd beer in every can
> And the landlord's wife and daughters learnt
> Just how to love a man.

chorus

PUGNACIOUS COLLIER (*going at* SPARKY). I'm a married
   man, bedamn, I've got a wife, I've got a wife, a wife . . .

SPARKY. No one's taking her from you.

PUGNACIOUS COLLIER. Not you?

SPARKY. No.

MUSGRAVE (*interrupting*). All right, steady, friend, *no one.*

SLOW COLLIER. *I'll* take her from you when you go to the war, I'll take her –

PUGNACIOUS COLLIER. You?

SLOW COLLIER. Me! Or no, no, no: I'll make do with our Annie!

He makes a drunken lurch at her which she more or less evades.

Come on then, mucker!

Foiled by ANNIE, *he seizes the* PUGNACIOUS COLLIER *and they do a clog dance together while the* BARGEE *plays. Chorus while they dance, and general cheer.*

BARGEE. Bring 'em in some more, Annie, it's all on the Queen tonight – how many have you listed, serjeant!

MUSGRAVE. I'm not listing no one tonight. (*He bangs with his tankard for silence*). Now then, boys, everybody –

BARGEE (*officiously*). Everybody listen!

A roll on the drum.

BARGEE. Listen!

MUSGRAVE (*expansively*). This is Her Majesty's hospitality – that's *all* that it is, boys, on a soldier's honour, so! Any man that drinks tonight –

BARGEE. Any man that drinks tonight –

MUSGRAVE. He drinks at the Queen's pleasure, and none of you need fear to find a shilling in your mug at end of it – that like o' lark's finished and gone with the old days – the Army only wants good men, that's free men, of your own true will for the Empire – so drink and welcome: and all men in this town –

BARGEE. All men in this town –

MUSGRAVE. When we hold our meeting and the drum beats
and we bring out our colours, then you can make your return
in the signing of your names – but only those men willing!
That's all : drink and away!

A roll on the drum.

BARGEE. Drink and away, me boys, hurray!

PUGNACIOUS COLLIER. Serjeant, you're a bleeding lobster,
but you're a man! Shake me by the hand!

The BARGEE *gives a whoop and starts to dance, playing a
mouth-organ. He stumbles, and everybody laughs.*

ANNIE (*scornfully*). And what regiment's *that* one, serjeant?
The Backwards-Mounted-Foot?

BARGEE. I'll tell you, me lovely, why not? The Queen's Own
Randy Chancers : or the Royal Facing-Both-Ways – hey, me
clever monkeys :

> Old Joe looks out for Joe
> Plots and plans and who lies low?
> But the Lord provides, says Crooked Old Joe.

MUSGRAVE (*looking sharply at him*). Eh?

The BARGEE *shrugs and grins.* MUSGRAVE *dismisses the
question.*

BARGEE. Just a little joke . . . little joke : little dog, I'll be with
you . . .

*He whistles 'Michael Finnegan' and ducks out of the pub.
Meanwhile* SPARKY *has taken off his drum and come downstage
to intercept* ANNIE. ATTERCLIFFE *is drinking with the*
COLLIERS *and one or other of these plays the drum at intervals.
The going of the* BARGEE *has made the room somewhat quieter
for a while.*

SPARKY (*to* ANNIE). Little dog – bow-wow, *I'm* a little dog,
any trick for a bit of biscuit, Annie, bit o' meat – look :

He takes a pack of cards out of his pocket and presents it.

Take one, go on, take one.

She obeys.

Well?

ANNIE. Queen o' Spades.

SPARKY (*laughing*). That's a hell of a card to take: I think there's treacle on it, sticks to all fingers out o' this pack, I call her Grandma, makes her gentle, y'see – hope she'll kiss me whiskers and leave it at that.

He has replaced the card and shuffles.

Now then, take first four cards on top. Tell me what they are.

ANNIE (*obeying*). Eight Nine Ten Jack, all spades.

SPARKY (*triumphantly*). Right, right, calls the roll straight up to the one you took, the Queen, and where's the one you took? On the bottom – take it!

ANNIE (*obeying*). It is the Queen and all!

SPARKY. 'Course it is: I *told* you. That's what I call life – it all turns up in the expected order, but not when you expect it. And that's what sets your two teeth laughing, click-clack, doesn't it, ha ha ha! Oh I'm a clever lad, you see, they call me Sparky, lots o' games, lots o' jokes . . .

ANNIE (*not impressed*). Lots of liquor too. Now get out of me road while I fetch some more – *I've* got *work*, you know.

SPARKY (*going after her and again intercepting her*). Hey, but lovey, listen: there was an Englishman, a Welshman and a bloody great Irish – all three of 'em on Defaulters, y'see, for drunk. Now the Orderly Sarnt, he says, 'One, Two, Three, all we want's a Scotchman.' And a voice in the guardroom-yard says: 'Hoots awa', man, I'm taking back the empties fairst.'

She avoids him and goes away to the bar, thus ruining the

climax of his tale. He tries to follow her up, but this time he is intercepted by MUSGRAVE. HURST *appears in the doorway.* ANNIE *looks up at him and follows him with her eyes for the rest of this dialogue.*

MUSGRAVE (*to* SPARKY). You've had enough.

SPARKY. I'm not drunk.

MUSGRAVE. No and you won't be neither. This is no time.

SPARKY (*pointing to* HURST). No – and *here* he comes, look at him.

MUSGRAVE (*striding angrily over to* HURST). Where have you been?

HURST (*surlily*). Down by the canal.

MUSGRAVE. Why?

HURST. All right, I'd got things on my mind. And I'll tell you this, Serjeant, it isn't enough.

MUSGRAVE. What isn't enough?

HURST. What you and that old cuckold are reckoning to do. It's all soft, it's all flat, it's all – God and the Word! Tchah! What good's a word, what good's a bloody word, they can *all* talk bloody words – it isn't enough : we've got to be strong!

MUSGRAVE. Leave it alone, boy. *I* hold the logic. *You* hold some beer and get on with your work.

MUSGRAVE *walks away from* HURST.

HURST (*shouts after him*). It isn't enough!

He turns to find ANNIE *standing at his elbow, looking into his face and handing him a tankard of beer. He takes it and drinks it rapidly, without looking at her.*

MRS. HITCHCOCK (*calling from the bar*). The Queen's in debt, Serjeant!

MUSGRAVE. Hello, ma'am?

MRS. HITCHCOCK. I said the Queen's in debt!

MUSGRAVE. Chalk it up Ma'am, and another round for us all.

MRS. HITCHCOCK. No more chalk.

MUSGRAVE. Easily found though.

He plunges his hand in his pocket and pulls out a quantity of money. He does a rapid count, whistles in consternation, and selects a few coins.

ATTERCLIFFE (*watching him*). Not so much of it left, is there?

MUSGRAVE. Easy, easy.

He goes over to the bar and pays. SPARKY *is now showing his card tricks to the* COLLIERS. ANNIE *plucks at the sleeve of the pensive* HURST.

ANNIE (*simply*). You're the best to look at of all the four, aren't you?

HURST. Eh? What's that?

ANNIE. Tell you again? Why? You know it, don't you?

HURST (*preoccupied*). I'd forgot it. I'd other matter beyond wondering what you'd think to our looks.

He studies her closer, and snaps out of his gloomy mood into an attitude of lady-killing arrogance.

Why, I don't need to think o' women. I let them think of *me.* I've knocked greasier ones than you between me porridge and me bacon. Don't flatter yourself.

ANNIE. I'm not, soldier: I'm flattering you. I'll come to you tonight.

HURST (*pleased, though trying not to show it*). Will you? That's a good choice, you've got sense.

ANNIE (*meaningly*). But you forget them other matters, eh?

HURST (*decidedly warming to her*). I'll try . . . I'd rather. I hope I can . . . Stand straight: let's see . . . Gay and greasy, like I like 'em! You're big, and you're bonny. A good shape, I'd call it. And you've got good hair, but wants a comb in it. You ought to wash your face. And your neck smells of soot, don't it?

ANNIE (*accepting this in the spirit in which it's meant*). I've been
    blowing up the fire.
HURST (*boastfully*). Ah, the last I had was a major's daughter.
    I've got standards. Lovely.

ATTERCLIFFE comes across to them.

ATTERCLIFFE. You said he was the best looker. I heard you.
    But it's not true.
ANNIE. Then who is? You?
ATTERCLIFFE. I'll tell you a tale about that. That pitman
    over there – he said to me he thought I'd steal his wife. By
    God, I'd sooner steal his nightsoil . . . I've got a wife. Ask
    me to tell you one o' these days.– Sparky'd make a joke of it –
    wouldn't you, Sparky!

The last phrases are shouted across the room.

SPARKY (*shouts back*). Not any more – we're all going too fast.

He turns back to the COLLIERS

    Down, down – any card, any card, mate – tell me its name –
    down.
PUGNACIOUS COLLIER. Six o' Hearts!
SPARKY. Right, right – *and* we shuffle and cut –

Enter the BARGEE.

BARGEE (*shouts*). Time, gennelmen please, everybody time,
    last orders everybody!
MRS. HITCHCOCK (*angrily*). Who's given *you* leave to do the
    calling here!
BARGEE (*singing*).

> Blow your morning bugles
> Blow your calls ey-ho –

    If it's not me and it's not you, there'll be somebody else –
    look!

Enter CONSTABLE.

CONSTABLE. All right, Mrs. Hitchcock, it's time you closed
your bar.

MRS. HITCHCOCK. What are you talking about!

CONSTABLE. Magistrates' orders, missus. All public houses to
close at nine o'clock sharp, pending settlement of colliery
dispute.

MRS. HITCHCOCK. It's the first I've heard of it.

SLOW COLLIER (*to the* CONSTABLE). Get out of it.

PUGNACIOUS COLLIER (*ditto*). Go home, you closhy bluebottle, and sweep your bloody chimney.

CONSTABLE. That'll do there.

MUSGRAVE. That'll do, lads, keep it easy.

PUGNACIOUS COLLIER (*to* MUSGRAVE). We're not in the
Army yet, y'know!

ATTERCLIFFE. Steady, matey, steady. All friends, y'know:
married men together.

PUGNACIOUS COLLIER. But, Serjeant, you're a man, and I'll
shake you by the hand.

CONSTABLE (*now things seem quiet again.*). Magistrates issued
the order only this evening, missus. I've let you stay open a
lot longer than the others – it's nigh on a quarter to ten
already – and I'm in my rights to allow an exception for this
house, on account of the Army. Question of facilities. I trust
you've made good use of the extra time, Sarnt Musgrave?

MUSGRAVE. H'm.

PUGNACIOUS COLLIER (*with great friendliness*). Have the last
drink on me, bluebottle!

CONSTABLE (*curtly*). The last drink's been had already. Close
your bar, please, missus.

PUGNACIOUS COLLIER (*an angry idea occurring to him*). Wait
a minute . . . Suppose I join your Army. Suppose I bloody
'list. What does my wife do?

BARGEE. Cock-a-doodle-do!

PUGNACIOUS COLLIER (*finding his own answer*). She goes to bed with the Peeler! I'll break his wooden head off.

He goes for the CONSTABLE *with a tankard, the* CONSTABLE *staggers backwards and falls, the* COLLIER *raises his tankard to smash it into his face.* ATTERCLIFFE *and* MUSGRAVE, *being nearest, jump to prevent him.*

ATTERCLIFFE (*pulling the* COLLIER *fiercely back*). Hey, ey, ey, ey-ey, hold it there, boy, hold it there! My God, you might ha' killed him. No...

ATTERCLIFFE *is trembling all over.*

SLOW COLLIER. Why shouldn't he if he wants to?

ATTERCLIFFE (*with great passion*). We've had enough o' that already – no more, no more, no more of it.

MUSGRAVE (*holding* ATTERCLIFFE *to quiet him*). Stop it there!

CONSTABLE (*getting up slowly*). Stand back, stand back. By God, it's *time* this place was closed. Turn out into the street, go on with you, get home. D'ye want me to whistle up me specials? Go on.

He hurls the COLLIERS *and* BARGEE *out of the pub.*

ATTERCLIFFE. He was going to, Serjeant. He would have, he'd have killed him. It's always here. Kill him. Kill.

MUSGRAVE (*roughly*). That'll do ... We've all had enough, Mr. Constable. I'll get this lot to bed.

CONSTABLE. All right then. And try and keep folk quiet. I know you've got to buy 'em drink and that – but ... *you* know – easy?

MUSGRAVE. Aye aye, easy. We know the trends. Don't you worry : *we* stand for law-and-order too, don't we?

CONSTABLE. Well, I hope so –

He goes to the door and calls into the street.

I said home, no loitering, go on, go on, or I'll run you in!

He comes back to MUSGRAVE *in a confidential conspiratorial sort of way.*

It's a sort of curfew, you see. I told His Worship : 'If there's trouble at night, you can't hold *me* responsible. I've done my best,' I said – I told him frank . . . Oh, and while we're on about His Worship, Serjeant, I might as well take occasion to discuss some names with you. There's a few like I could tell you as'd look very convenient on a regimental muster.

MUSGRAVE (*coldly*). I'm here for volunteers only, you know.

CONSTABLE (*insinuatingly*). Ah well, what's a volunteer? You, you, and you – the old Army custom – eh, Serjeant? Mrs. Hitchcock! A couple o' pints o' taddy for me and the Serjeant.

MRS. HITCHCOCK. We're closed.

CONSTABLE (*broad-mindedly*). That's all right, missus. Serve to the Serjeant : hotel-resident. All above the board.

MRS. HITCHCOCK (*to* ANNIE). So take 'em their drinks. Queen as pays.

She pours herself out another cup of tea. ANNIE *prepares the drinks and brings them to* MUSGRAVE *and the* CONSTABLE, *who gets into a huddle over a list the latter produces.*

SPARKY (*to the other two* SOLDIERS). Very commodious Queen. I say, a very commodious Queen, ha ha, if she'd drank all she paid for tonight, heh, Sponge By Appointment, they could swab out the Windsor Castle Guardhouse, ha ha, who'd be a Coldstream! I say, they could swab out –

ATTERCLIFFE. Oh shut up, man, for God's sake. We've had all we can take of your stinking patter.

SPARKY (*aggrieved*). Ey-ey, matey – ey-ey.

He withdraws, hurt.

HURST (*to* ATTERCLIFFE). Shut up yourself – what's got into you?

ATTERCLIFFE. Why, *you* were making enough carry-on earlier, weren't you? Are you so daft or so drunk you didn't see what just happened?

HURST. There was nowt happened. Couple o' pitmen three parts pissed? What's the matter wi' that? You were near as bad yourself – don't tell *me*. *You* were on about your *wife!*

ATTERCLIFFE. There was all but a man killed. We've come to stop it, not to start it – go on, sing to us.

He sings, with savage emphasis.

> Who'll give a penny to the poor blind man
> Holds out his hand with an old tin can.

– 'Cos that's all you are and it curdles up my bowels. I'm going to the coach-house.

HURST. The coach-house! What for?

ATTERCLIFFE. Where there's a man to talk to who don't talk like a fool.

He goes out of the door behind the bar.

SPARKY. Here, what d'you think to *him*? What sort o' talk does he reckon he'll get.

HURST. Keep your mind off that!

SPARKY (*wildly*). Rattling, clattering, old bones in a box? Billy used to sing, d'you think he'll have a sing-song?

HURST. I don't understand you. This don't make *me* laugh. It fair makes me sick.

SPARKY (*jeeringly*). Sick and bloody scared. Hey-ey, that's you, that's you truly.

HURST. Well, I've got things on my mind. If you can call it scared –

SPARKY. You and me, we're a pair, boy.

HURST (*savagely*). All right. But you'll learn. All *right*.

He turns abruptly away, and broods.

SPARKY (*beckoning* ANNIE, *who comes unenthusiastically*). I say, Annie – oh I'll tell you what, Annie, I don't know what I'm doing here.

She looks at him questioningly; he waves the point aside.

Aha, for that . . . Look, we've made us our beds up in the stables – ha, loose-box for every man, but the serjeant in the house.

ANNIE. Aye, I know.

SPARKY. We call it the Discipline, y'see. Yes-sarnt-no-sarnt, three-bags-full-sarnt – that's our merry lives. Ha ha. Third box from the end tonight, the fastest racehorse of 'em all. Oaks, Derby, I carry 'em away, boy: but I'm best at a steeple-chase – *hup* and *hover*, hedge and ditch, dear, and not by soldiers' numbers neither . . . Come for a gallop.

It is clear from the tone of the last phrase he is not joking.

ANNIE (*unemotionally*). Not tonight.

SPARKY. Oh . . . Go on, tonight.

ANNIE (*with something of a sneer*). Maybe next I will. I can't tell from day to day.

SPARKY. No more can I. You know, you've not yet give me one little laugh . . . But I'll contrive it: now y'see, there was a butcher, a baker, and a cats'-meat-man, all on the edge of the river. And down this river comes this dead dog, floating.

HURST (*whose head has dropped, suddenly jerks himself up again*). God, I was near asleep! I started a bad dream and it woke me.

MUSGRAVE (*to the* CONSTABLE). No, mister, it won't wash. We can't play pressgangs these days. If a man gets drunk and then signs, all right: but otherwise –

CONSTABLE (*vexed*). You're not over-co-operative, are you?

MUSGRAVE. I'm sorry. Oh, I'll see what I can do: but I won't promise more. Besides, agitators is agitators, in or out the Army. I'm not sure we want 'em. But I'll think. Good night.

He goes with the CONSTABLE *to the street door.*

CONSTABLE. Good night. Good night, missus.

Exit the CONSTABLE. MUSGRAVE *comes down to the* SOLDIERS.

MUSGRAVE (*calling* ANNIE). Lassie.

ANNIE. Hello.

MUSGRAVE. These are my men. They're here with their work to do. You will not distract them.

ANNIE. I won't?

MUSGRAVE. No. Because *they* know, whether you know it or not, that there's work is for women and there's work is for men : and let the two get mixed, you've anarchy.

ANNIE (*rather taken aback*). Oh? And what's anarchy? You, you clever grinder – words and three stripes –

MUSGRAVE. Look, lassie, anarchy : now, we're soldiers. Our work isn't easy, no and it's not soft : it's got a strong name – duty. And it's drawn out straight and black for us, a clear plan. But if you come to us with what you call your life or love – *I'd* call it your indulgence – and you scribble all over that plan, you make it crooked, dirty, idle, untidy, *bad* – there's anarchy. I'm a religious man. I know words, and I know deeds, and I know how to be strong. So do these men. You will not stand between them and their strength! Go on now : take yourself off.

ANNIE. A little bit of wind and a little bit of water –

MRS. HITCHCOCK. Annie –

ANNIE. But it drowned three score of sailors, and the King of Norway's daughter. (*She smiles for the first time in the play.*)

She sings:

>   O mother O mother
>   It hurts me so sore
>   Sing dody-eye-dodo
>   Then ye daft little bitch

> Ye should do it no more
> For you've never left off
> Since we sailed from the shore.

MRS. HITCHCOCK (*sharply*). Annie, get to bed.

MUSGRAVE (*to the* SOLDIERS). You two, get to bed. And pay heed to what I say.

ANNIE *goes out behind the bar, with a satirical curtsy.* MUSGRAVE *goes out by the street door.* HURST *makes a move as though to speak to him, but is too late. He stands reflective.*

SPARKY.

> To bed to bed says Sleepy-head
> Tarry a while says Slow
> Open the book, says the wise old Rook
> We'll have prayers before we go.

He sways a little tipsily, and laughs.

SCENE TWO

A street. Night.

The PUGNACIOUS *and* SLOW COLLIERS *enter, drunk and marching, the* BARGEE *drilling them. (This is a kind of 'Fred Karno' sequence which must be kept completely under control. At each command each of the three carries out, smartly, a drill-movement; but each drill movement is different for each man, and none of them performs the movement shouted. They must not be so drunk that they cannot appear erect and alertly jerking. The effect should be, not so much of three incompetents pretending to be soldiers, but of three trained soldiers gone mad.) The* COLLIERS *carry pickhefts as rifles, and the* BARGEE *an oar.*

MUSGRAVE *enters, and stands quietly watching.*

BARGEE. Right turn. Forward march. Left right left right left right left.

PUGNACIOUS COLLIER. To the front present. Halt.

BARGEE. About turn.

SLOW COLLIER. One two three four.

BARGEE. Order arms.

PUGNACIOUS COLLIER. Present and correct. By the right, number.

SLOW COLLIER. One two three four.

They are now at attention, together.

PUGNACIOUS COLLIER. Present and correct.

BARGEE (*this order is properly obeyed*). Stand-at-ease. Easy . . .

PUGNACIOUS COLLIER (*breaking the spell*). I'll tell you what, we're bloody good.

BARGEE (*with enthusiasm*). Eh. Lordy, mucker – good! By, I've never seen the like – y'know, if you signed on they'd excuse you three weeks' drill on the spot. You make that serjeant look like Old-Mother-Bunch-in-the-Popshop, alongside o' you – love you, mucker, you're *born* to it!

PUGNACIOUS COLLIER. Well, why didn't I think on it afore?

SLOW COLLIER (*still on parade*). One two three four.

PUGNACIOUS COLLIER. I'd not ha' got wed if I'd known!

SLOW COLLIER (*suddenly coming to attention and starting off*). Quick march. One two three –

He bumps against WALSH, *who has just entered.*

Arh and be damned.

WALSH. Where the hell are you going to?

MUSGRAVE *starts to go out. He passes* WALSH, *who stops him with a hand on his chest.*

WALSH. So we was mistook, eh? You're not here for no riots after all, but catching up men: that's it, in'it? Guineas?

MUSGRAVE. Sovereigns.

PUGNACIOUS COLLIER (*suddenly indicating* MUSGRAVE *to* WALSH). Here. This one: three stripes, but he's a man.

WALSH. Aye? And what are you? Drunk on *his* money: marching and drilling like a pack o' nit-headed kids at a barrack-gate!

PUGNACIOUS COLLIER. Better nor bloody starve for no coal-owners, any road!

WALSH (*with passion*). I'll tell you, I'm that ashamed, I could spew.

MUSGRAVE (*gripping* WALSH *by the lapel and drawing him away*). Now listen here. I can see you, and see *you* what you are. I wasn't given these – (*he touches his stripes*) – for not knowing men from ninepins. Now I'm telling you one word and I'm telling you two, and that's all. (*He lowers his voice.*) You and me is brothers –

WALSH (*in high irony*). Eh begod! A Radical Socialist! Careful, soldier, careful. D'ye want to be hanged?

MUSGRAVE (*very seriously*). No jokes. I mean this. I mean it. Brothers in God –

WALSH (*even more scornful*). Oh, hoho, *that* –

MUSGRAVE. – And brothers in truth. So watch. And wait. I said, *wait*.

WALSH (*jeering*). Brothers in God.

> Gentle Jesus send us rest
> Surely the bosses knows what's best!

Get along with yer –

MUSGRAVE (*calmly*). Well: I said, wait. You'll see.

Exit MUSGRAVE.

SLOW COLLIER (*who has been marking time since his collision, now mutters*).

> One two three four
> Where's the man as lives next door?
> Five six seven eight
> Come on in, he's working late.

WALSH (*looking at him in disgust*). Holy God, I'd never ha'
dreamt it.

SLOW COLLIER (*his muttering rising in volume*).

> Nine ten eleven twelve
> Take his place and help yourself,
> Thirteen fourteen fifteen sixteen –

PUGNACIOUS COLLIER (*with a stupid laugh*). He's talking
about my wife.

SLOW COLLIER (*annoyed at being interrupted*).

> Thirteen fourteen fifteen sixteen
> Into the bed and there we'll fix him!

PUGNACIOUS COLLIER (*in rising rage*). I couldn't do it to the
soldiers, I couldn't do it to the Peeler, but by, I'll do it to
you! I'll break your bloody head.

He goes for SLOW COLLIER, *who hits him in the belly, lets off
a yell and runs out.* PUGNACIOUS COLLIER *follows with a
roar.*

BARGEE (*calling after them in glee*). Watch out for the Constable! Heh heh heh.

WALSH. Holy God! My mates! My brothers!

BARGEE (*kindly*). Ah well, they're drunk.

WALSH. I know they're drunk, and I know who's helped 'em
to it.

BARGEE. I could help *you* to summat, and all.

WALSH. What's that?

BARGEE. They won't stay drunk all week. Oh the soldiers gives
'em sport, they *need* a bit o' sport, cold, hungry . . . When
you want 'em, they'll be there. Crooked Joe, he's *here*.

WALSH. Aye?

BARGEE. Could you shoot a Gatling gun?

WALSH (*looking at him sideways*). I don't know.

BARGEE. If you really want a riot, why don't you go at it

proper? Come on, I'll tell you . . . (*He hops out, whistling 'Michael Finnegan' and looking back invitingly.*)

WALSH (*considering*). Aye, aye? Crooked, clever, keelman, eh? . . . Well – all right – then *tell* me!

He hurries after him.

SCENE THREE

Interior of the pub (stable and bedroom).

Night. The stage is divided into two distinct acting-areas. The downstage area represents the stable, and is supposed to be divided into three loose boxes. If it is not practicable for the partitions between these to be built, it should be sufficient to suggest them by the three mattresses which are laid parallel, feet to the audience. The actors must not appear to be able to see each other from box to box. The forestage represents the central passage of the stable and is the only access to the boxes. Entry to the forestage can be from both wings (one side leads to the house, the other to the yard and coach-house).

The upstage area, raised up at least a couple of feet, represents a bedroom in the house. It is only large enough to contain a brass-knobbed bedstead with a small table or other support for a candle. The two areas must be treated as completely separate. Access to the bedroom area should be from the rear, and the audience must not be allowed to think that the actors can see from one area to the other (except as regards the light in the window, which is supposed to be seen as if from across the yard).

MUSGRAVE, *in shirt and trousers, is sitting on the bed, reading by candlelight. His tunic etc. lies folded beside the bed.*

HURST *and* SPARKY *come into the stable from the house carrying palliasses and blankets. They proceed to make up their beds (in the two end boxes, leaving the middle one empty.* SPARKY *is at the house end,* HURST *next to the yard). They also undress to their shirts (of grey flannel) and their (long woollen) underpants and socks. Their clothes are laid out neatly beside the beds.*

SPARKY (*as he prepares for bed*). I say . . . I say, can you hear me?

HURST (*uninterested*). I can.

SPARKY. You know, I'll tell you: I'm a bit pissed tonight.

HURST. Uh. What of it?

SPARKY. What's that?

HURST. I said what of it? We all are, aren't we? *I* want an hour or two's sleep, I don't know about *you,* so let's have less o' your gab.

SPARKY. I say, there's a light on still in Black Jack's window.
HURST grunts.

MUSGRAVE *has now lain down on top of his blanket, but has not taken off his trousers, or put out his candle.*

SPARKY. Aye, aye. God's awake. Ha, Ha! Not only God neither. Y'know, I think there might be some of us mortal, even yet . . . I said God's awake!

HURST. I *heard* you, and be damned.

A pause.

SPARKY. Hour or two's sleep . . . What do you want to *sleep* for, and a fine fat tart all promised and ready!

HURST (*who has got undressed and under his blanket*). That'll do. Now shut your row, can't ye, when you're asked! I said I wanted to sleep, so let me.

SPARKY. Why, it's you she's promised, y'see – *you,* not me – wake up, mucker, wake up. She'll soon be here, y'see. She'll soon be here! (*He blows 'reveille' with his lips, then gets under his blanket.*) You, boy, *you,* not me! . . . Shall I sing you a song?

HURST (*almost asleep, and woken again*). Eh, what? Are you going to shut up, or aren't you!

SPARKY. Well, are *you* going to shut up or aren't you, when she comes? It's all right the best-looker loving the girl, but his two mates along the row wi' nowt but a bit o' wainscot atween – hey-ey-ey, it'll be agony for *us* tonight, y'know – so keep it quiet.

A pause.

(*He starts to sing, softly*).

> She came to me at midnight
> With the moonshine on her arms
> And I told her not to make no noise
> Nor cause no wild alarms.
> But her savage husband he awoke
> And up the stairs did climb
> To catch her in her very deed :
> So fell my fatal crime . . .

While he is singing, ANNIE *enters from the house, carrying a candle. She goes gently to* HURST'S *box and stands looking down at him. When she speaks, he sticks his head out of the bedclothes and looks at her.*
In the bedroom, MUSGRAVE *sits up, blows out his light, and goes to sleep.*

ANNIE (*with tender humour*). Here I come. Hello. I'm cold. I'm a blue ghost come to haunt you. Brr. Come on, boy, warm me up. You'll not catch cold off *me*.
HURST (*getting up*). No . . . I daresay not . . .

They put their arms round each other.

But what about the morning?
ANNIE. Ah, the morning's different, ent it? I'll not say nowt about mornings, 'cos then we'll *all* be cold. Cold and alone. Like, stand in a crowd but every one alone. One thousand men makes a regiment, you'd say?
HURST. Near enough.

ANNIE. But for all that, when you're with them, you're still alone. Ent that right? So huggle me into the warm, boy, now. Keep out the wind. It's late. Dark.

HURST (*suddenly breaking away from her*). No, I won't. I don't care what I said afore, it's all done, ended, capped – get away. Go on. Leave me be.

ANNIE (*astonished and hurt*). What is it? What's the matter? Lovey –

HURST (*with violence*). Go on. As far as *my* mind goes, it's morning already. Every one alone – that's all. You want me to lose my life inside of you –

ANNIE. No. No. But just for five hours, boy, six –

HURST. You heard Black Jack say what's right. Straight, clear, dark strokes, no scrawling, I was wrong afore, I didn't trust him. He talked about God, so I thought he wor just nowt. But what he said about *you*: there, that was truth. He's going to be *strong!*

ANNIE (*scornfully*). So *you* take note of Black Jack, do you?

HURST. Aye, and I do. It's too late tonight for anything else. He's got to be trusted, got to be strong, we've got no alternative!

ANNIE (*standing a little away from him*). My Christ then, they *have* found him a brother! It was only this evening, warn't it, *I* saw you, down by the canal, all alone and wretched –

She sings with fierce emphasis:

> All round his hat he wore the green willow – !

HURST. All right.

ANNIE (*not letting him off*). But it can't have been you, can it? 'Cos now you're just the same as the rest of 'em – the Hungry Army! You eat and you drink and you go. Though *you* won't even eat when it's offered, will you? So *sprawl* yourself on the straw without me, get up to your work tomorrow, drum 'em in and write 'em down, infect 'em all and bury 'em! I don't care.

HURST. What are you on about, what's the matter, why don't you go when you're told? Godsake, Godsake, leave a man to his sleep!

ANNIE. You know what they call me?

HURST. I'd call you a bloody whoor –

ANNIE (*savagely ironical*). Oh, not just a whoor – *I'm* a whoor-to-the-soldiers – it's a class by itself.

ATTERCLIFFE *has entered from the yard with his bedding. They do not notice him yet.* ANNIE *turns to pleading again.*

ANNIE. Christ, let me stay with you. He called me life and love, boy, just you think on *that* a little.

HURST *pushes her away with a cry. She falls against* ATTERCLIFFE.

ATTERCLIFFE (*holding her up*). Life and love, is it? I'm an old soldier, girly, a dirty old bastard, me, and *I've* seen it all. Here.

He grips her and kisses her violently all over face and neck. He sneers at HURST.

Hey-up there, son, get in your manger and sleep, and leave this to the men.

HURST. All right . . . and you're welcome.

He goes to his box and lies down again, huffily, trying to sleep.

ATTERCLIFFE (*still holding* ANNIE, *with a sort of tenderness*). Now then, what'll I do to you, eh? How d'you reckon you're going to quench *me*? Good strong girly with a heart like a horsecollar, open it up and let 'em all in. And it still wouldn't do no good.

ANNIE (*hard and hostile*). Wouldn't it? Try.

ATTERCLIFFE. Ah, no. Not tonight. What would *you* know of soldiers?

ANNIE. More'n you'd think I'd know, maybe.

ATTERCLIFFE. I doubt it. Our Black Jack'd say it's not material. He'd say there's blood on these two hands. (*He looks at his hands with distaste.*) You can wipe 'em as often as you want on a bit o' yellow hair, but it still comes blood the next time so why bother, *he'd* say. And *I'd* say it too. Here. (*He kisses her again and lets her go.*) There you are, girly: I've given you all you should get from a soldier. Say 'Thank you, boy', and that's that.

ANNIE (*still hard*). Thank you boy . . . You know it, don't you? All I should get. All I ever have got. Why should I want more? You stand up honest, you do, and it's a good thing too, 'cos you're old enough.

ATTERCLIFFE (*with a wry smile*). H'm. I am and all. Good night.

He starts making up his bed and undressing. SPARKY has sat up and is listening. As ANNIE is standing still, ATTERCLIFFE starts talking to her again.

ATTERCLIFFE. Girly. When I was a young lad I got married to a wife. And she slept with a greengrocer. He was the best looker (like *he's* the best looker) – (*he points towards* HURST'S *box*) – or any road that's what *she* said. *I* saw him four foot ten inch tall and he looked like a rat grinning through a brush; but he sold good green apples and he fed the people and he fed my wife. I didn't do neither. So now I'm a dirty old bastard in a red coat and blue breeches and that's all about it. Blood, y'see: killing. Good night.

He has now undressed and lies down to sleep immediately.
ANNIE *stands for a minute, then subsides to a crouching position, in tears.*
SPARKY *creeps out of his box.*

SPARKY. Tst tst tst, Annie. Stop crying: come here.

ANNIE. Don't talk to me, go to bed, I can't bear wi' no more of you.

SPARKY. Annie, Annie, look now, I want to talk. I'm not deaf, y'know, and I'm not that drunk, I mean I've been drunker, I mean I can stand, ha ha, one foot and all, I'm a stork, look at me – (*He tries to balance on one foot*). Him at the far end – don't you worry for *him*, Annie – why, he's not mortal any more, he's like God, ent he? And God – (*He looks towards* MUSGRAVE'S *light*) – hello, God's asleep.

ANNIE. God?

SPARKY. He's put his light out. Look,

ANNIE. That's where the serjeant is.

SPARKY. That's right. I never thought he'd sleep. *I* can't sleep . . . what have you got against me?

ANNIE (*surprised*). Nowt that I know.

SPARKY. But you didn't come to me, did you? I mean, you asked *him* and he said no, I asked *you* and you said no. That's all wrong. I mean, you know what the Black Musgrave'd call that, don't you – *he'd* say anarchy!

ANNIE. *He'd say*? He?

MUSGRAVE *groans in his bed.*

Every one of you swaggering lobsters, that serjeant squats in your gobs like an old wife stuck in a fireplace. What's the matter with you all!

SPARKY. Ssh ssh, keep it quiet. Come down here . . .

He leads her as far as possible from the other two.

Listen.

ANNIE. What for?

SPARKY. Snoring. Him? Him? Good, two snorings. They're asleep . . . I told you in the bar, y'know, they call me Sparky – name and nature – Sparky has his laugh. . . . A man can laugh, because or else he might well howl – and howling's not for men but for dogs, wolves, seagulls – like o' that, ent it?

ANNIE. You mean that you're frightened?

SPARKY (*with a sort of nervous self-realisation*). Aye, begod, d'you know: I am. God's not here, he's put his light out: so I can tell you, love: I *am*. Hey, not of the war, bullets in the far Empire, that's not the reason, don't think it. They even give me a medal, silver, to prove so. But I'll tell you, I'm – here, kiss me, will you, quickly, I oughtn't to be talking . . . I think I've gone daft.

ANNIE (*who is looking at him curiously but fascinated*). All right, I will . . .

She kisses him, and he holds her.

MUSGRAVE (*in clear categorical tones, though in his sleep*). Twenty-five men. Nine women. Twenty-five men. No children. No.

ANNIE (*in a sudden uprush*). Look, boy, there was a time *I* had a soldier, he made jokes, he sang songs and all – ah, *he* lived yes-sarnt no-sarnt three-bags-full-serjeant, but he called it one damned joke. God damn you, he was killed! Aye, and in your desert Empire – so what did *that* make?

SPARKY. I don't know . . .

ANNIE. It made a twisted little thing dead that nobody laughed at. A little withered clover – three in one it made. There was me, and there was him: and a baby in the ground. Bad shape. Dead.

She can say nothing more and he comforts her silently a moment.

SPARKY (*his mind working*). Why, Annie . . . Annie . . . you as well: another one not paid for . . . O, I wish *I* could pay. Say, suppose I paid for yours; why, maybe you could pay for mine.

ANNIE. I don't understand.

SPARKY (*following his thought in great disturbance of mind*). It *wouldn't* be anarchy, you know; he can't be right there! All it would be, is : *you* live and *I* live – we don't need his duty, we don't need his Word – a dead man's a dead man! We could call it *all* paid for! Your life and my life – make our *own* road, we don't follow nobody.

ANNIE. What are you talking about?

SPARKY (*relapsing into his despair again*). Oh God, I don't know. God's gone to sleep, but when he wakes up again –

ANNIE (*bewildered but compassionate*). Oh quiet, boy, be quiet, easy, easy.

She stoops over him, where he has crumpled into a corner, and they embrace again with passion.

MUSGRAVE (*now shouting in his sleep*). Fire, fire! Fire, fire, London's burning, London's burning!

MRS. HITCHCOCK, *in a nightdress and robe, and carrying a tumbler, hurries into his bedroom.*

MRS. HITCHCOCK. What's the matter?

She lights his candle.

MUSGRAVE (*sitting up and talking very clearly as if it made sense*). Burning. Burning. One minute from now, and you carry out your orders – get *that* one! *Get* her! Who says she's a child! We've got her in the book, she's old enough to kill! You will carry out your orders. Thirty seconds. Count the time. (*He is looking at his watch.*) Twenty-six . . . twenty-three . . .

MRS. HITCHCOCK (*very alarmed*). Serjeant – Serjeant –

MUSGRAVE. Be quiet. Twenty . . . Eighteen . . . I'm on duty, woman. I'm timing the end of the world. Ten more seconds, sir . . . Five . . . three . . . two . . . one.

He lets out a great cry of agony and falls back on the bed.
All in the stable hear and take notice. ATTERCLIFFE *turns over again to sleep.* HURST *sits up in alarm.* ANNIE *and* SPARKY *stand apart from each other in surprise.*

ANNIE. Sparky, it's your God. He's hurt.

SPARKY *sits staring and gasping, till* ANNIE *pulls him to her again.*

MRS. HITCHCOCK. What are you playing at – you'll wake up the town!

MUSGRAVE *shivers and moans.*

MRS. HITCHCOCK (*shaking him gently*). Come on – it's a nightmare. Wake up and let's get rid of it. Come on, come on.

MUSGRAVE. Leave me alone. I wasn't asleep.

MRS. HITCHCOCK. You warn't awake, any road.

MUSGRAVE. Mind your own business.

MRS. HITCHCOCK. I thought you might be poorly.

MUSGRAVE. No . . . No . . . (*Suddenly*) But it *will* come, won't it?

MRS. HITCHCOCK. What will?

MUSGRAVE. The end of the world? You'll tell me it's not material, but if you could come to it, in control ; I mean, numbers and order, like so many ranks this side, so many that, properly dressed, steadiness on parade, so that whether you knew you was right, or you knew you was wrong – you'd know it, and you'd stand. (*He shivers.*) Get me summat to eat.

MRS. HITCHCOCK. I got you a hot grog. Here. (*She gives him a tumbler.*)

MUSGRAVE. What – what . . .?

MRS. HITCHCOCK. I take it at nights for me bad back. I heard you calling so I brought it in. Have a biscuit.

She gives him a biscuit from her dressing gown pocket.

MUSGRAVE. Aye, I will . . . (*He eats and drinks.*) That's better . . . You *do* understand me, don't you? Look, if you're the right-marker to the Company and you're marching to the right, you can't see the others, so you follow the orders you can hear and hope you hear them true. When I was a recruit

I found myself once half across the square alone – *they'd*
marched the other way and I'd never heard the word!

MRS. HITCHCOCK. You ought to lie down. You *are* poorly, I
can tell. Easy, Serjeant, easy.

MUSGRAVE (*relaxing again*). Easy . . . easy . . .

She draws the blanket over him and sits soothing him to sleep.

SPARKY (*with a sudden access of resolution*). Annie, I don't care.
Let him wake when he wants to. All I'll do this time is to
stand and *really* laugh. Listen to this one, because here's
what I'll be laughing at. There was these four lads, y'see,
and they made it out they'd have a strong night all night in
the town, each boozer in turn, pay-day. And the first one in
the first boozer, he says : 'Each man drinks my choice,' he
says. 'One sup of arsenic to every man's glass' – and *that's*
what they've to drink. Well, one of them, he drinks and he
dies, next man drinks and *he* dies, what about the third?
Has he to drink to that rule? 'Cos they'd *made* it a rule –
each man to the first man's choice.

HURST *has left his box and crept up and is now listening to this.*

ANNIE. I don't know –

SPARKY. Neither do I. But I can tell you what *I'd* do.

ANNIE. What?

SPARKY (*with a switch to hard seriousness*). I'd get out of it,
quick. Aye, and with you. Look, love, its snowing, we can't
leave the town now. But you could bed me down some-
wheres, I mean, like, hide; bide *with* me while it's all
over, and then get me some clothes and we'd go – I mean,
like, go to London? What about London? You've never
been to London?

ANNIE. Bide hid while *what's* all over? What's going to
happen?

SPARKY. Eh, that's the question. I wish I could tell you. It's
Black Jack's work, not mine.

ANNIE. Bad work, likely?

SPARKY. Likely . . . I don't know. D'you know, I never *asked!* You see, he's like God, and it's as if *we* were like angels – *angels*, ha, ha! But that's no joke no more for me. This is funnier nor *I* can laugh at, Annie, and if I bide longer here, I'm *really* wild-wood mad. So get me out of it, quick!

ANNIE (*decisively*). I will. I'm frightened. Pull your clothes on, Sparky. I'll hide you.

SPARKY. Good love, good –

ANNIE. But you'll not leave me behind?

He has started dressing, very confusedly, putting his tunic on first.

SPARKY. No.

ANNIE. Swear it.

He has his trousers ready to step into. He lets them fall while he takes her for a moment in his arms:

SPARKY. Sworn.

HURST *nips in and seizes the trousers.*

(*Releasing* ANNIE) Now then, sharp. Hey, where's me trousers?

HURST. Here!

SPARKY. What's the goddamn – give 'em back, you dirty –

HURST (*triumphantly*). Come and get 'em, Sparky! Heh, you'll be the grand deserter, won't you, running bare-arsed over the moor in six-foot drifts of snow!

SPARKY. Give me them!

He grabs one end of the trousers and a farcical tug-o'-war begins.

HURST (*in high malice*). A man and a soldier! Jump, natter, twitch, like a clockwork puppet for three parts of the night, but the last night of all, you *run*! You little closhy coward.

ATTERCLIFFE *has woken and tries to intervene.*

ATTERCLIFFE. What the hell's the row – easy, easy, *hold* it!
SPARKY. He's got my bloody trousers!

He gives a great tug on the trousers and pulls them away,
HURST *falling down.*

HURST. I'm going to *do* you, Sparky.

His hand falls on SPARKY'S *belt, with bayonet scabbard
attached, which is lying on the floor. He gets up, drawing the
bayonet.*

ANNIE. No, no, stop him!
ATTERCLIFFE. Drop that bayonet!

ANNIE *mixes in, seizing* HURST'S *wrist and biting it. The
bayonet drops to the floor.* ATTERCLIFFE *snatches it and*
HURST *jumps upon him. Together they fall against* SPARKY
and all three crash to the floor. SPARKY *gives a terrifying,
choking cry.*
MUSGRAVE *leaps up in the bedroom. Those on the forestage
all draw back, appalled, from* SPARKY'S *dead body.*

MUSGRAVE (*to* MRS. HITCHCOCK). Stay where you are.

He leaves the bedroom.

HURST. He's dead. He's dead. *I* didn't do it. Not me. No.
ATTERCLIFFE. Dead?
HURST. Of course he's dead. He's stuck in the gut. That's you.
    Your hand. You killed him.
ATTERCLIFFE. I can't have.
HURST. You did.
ATTERCLIFFE (*stupidly*). I've got the bayonet.
HURST. Aye, and you've killed him.
ATTERCLIFFE. O Holy God!

MUSGRAVE *enters from the house.* MRS. HITCHCOCK *has left the bedroom.*

MUSGRAVE. What going on?

HURST. Sparky's been killed.

MUSGRAVE. *What!* How?

HURST. His own bayonet. He was deserting. I tried to stop him. Then *he* –

He points to ATTERCLIFFE.

MUSGRAVE (*to* ATTERCLIFFE). Well?

ATTERCLIFFE (*hopelessly*). Here's the bayonet. I got holding it, Serjeant. I did. It's always me. You can call it an accident. But *I* know what that means, it means that it –

MUSGRAVE. Shut up. You said deserting?

HURST *nods.*

What's *she* doing here? Was she with him?

HURST *nods.*

Aye, aye . . . Desertion. Fornication. It's not material. He's dead. Hide him away.

HURST. Where?

MUSGRAVE. In the midden at back of the yard. And don't show no lights while you're doing it. Hurry.

HURST (*to* ATTERCLIFFE). Come on.

ATTERCLIFFE. Holy God, Holy God!

They carry the body out.

MUSGRAVE (*to* ANNIE, *unpleasantly*). Oh, you can shake, you can quiver, you can open your mouth like a quicksand and all – blubbering and trouble – but *I've* got to think, and *I've* got to do.

MRS. HITCHCOCK *enters from the house. She is carrying* MUSGRAVE'S *tunic, hat, and boots, which she puts down.*

Missus, come here. There's things going wrong, but don't ask me what. Will you trust me?

She looks at him searchingly and gives a short nod.

Get hold of this lassie, take her upstairs, lock her in a cupboard, and keep quiet about it. I've got a right reason : you'll know it in good time. Do as I tell you and you won't take no harm.

MRS. HITCHCOCK. The end of the world, already.

MUSGRAVE. What's that? D'ye hear what I say?

MRS. HITCHCOCK. Oh aye, I heard you.

She takes the shuddering ANNIE *by the hand, and then looks sharply at her fingers.*

Hey-ey-ey, this here, it's blood.

MUSGRAVE. I know. I repeat it : don't ask me.

ANNIE *looks at* MUSGRAVE *and at* MRS. HITCHCOCK, *then licks her hand, laughing in a childish fashion.*

MRS. HITCHCOCK. Come away in, Annie . . . Aye, I'll go and lock her up . . . It might be the best thing. I've got to trust you, haven't I? I've always praised religion.

She takes ANNIE *away, into the house.* MUSGRAVE *sits down suddenly, with his head in his hands. The* BARGEE *creeps in from the yard and sits beside him, in a similar attitude.*

BARGEE (*singing softly*).

> Here we set like birds in the wilderness,
>   birds in the –

MUSGRAVE *sits up, looks at him, realises who it is, and grabs him by the throat.*

BARGEE (*struggling free*). It's all right, bully, it's only Old Joe.

MUSGRAVE (*relaxing, but still menacing*). Oh it is, is it? Well?

BARGEE (*significantly*). I was thinking, like, if I wor you, *I* wouldn't just set down in a stable, not now I wouldn't, no.

MUSGRAVE. Why not?

BARGEE. *I* see your jolly muckers, over there, mucking in the muck-pile, eh? But if they turned theirselves around and looked at the coach-house –

MUSGRAVE *leaps up in alarm.*

MUSGRAVE. What about the coach-house?

BARGEE. There's bars at its windows : and there's a crowbar at the bars – listen!

A crash of glass offstage from the yard.

That's the glass gone now! If you're quick, you can catch 'em!

MUSGRAVE *has run to the yard side of the stage.*

MUSGRAVE (*calling to offstage*). Get to the coach-house, get round the back! Quick! Quick!

He runs off in great excitement.
More crashes of glass, shouting and banging.
The BARGEE *watches what is happening in the yard, leaping up and down in high delight.*

BARGEE. Go on, catch 'em, two to the back and the serjeant to the door, open the padlock, swing back the wicket – one little laddie, he's trapped in the window – head in, feet out – pull him down, Serjeant, pull him down, soldiers – boot up, fist down, tie him in a bundle – oh me pretty roses, oh me blood-red flowers o' beauty!

The two SOLDIERS *hurry back, with* WALSH *frogmarched between them, his hands bunched up and tied behind his back.* MUSGRAVE *follows. All are panting. They throw* WALSH *down.*

MUSGRAVE. What about the others?

HURST. Run away, Serjeant.

ATTERCLIFFE. Nigh on a dozen of 'em.

HURST. Ran down the alley.

MUSGRAVE. Let's have a look at this one! Oho, so it's *you!* What were you after?

WALSH (*grinning*). What d'you think, lobster?

MUSGRAVE. Our little Gatling? Isn't that right?

WALSH. That's right, boy, you're sharp.

MUSGRAVE (*quieter*). But *you're* not sharp, brother, and I'm going to tell you why.

Shouting and shrill whistles, off.

HURST. It's that Constable's out, and his Specials and all – listen! Hey, we'd better get dressed.

He starts huddling on his tunic and trousers.

MUSGRAVE (*to* WALSH). Chasing your friends. He'll be coming here, shortly.

Whistles again.

CONSTABLE (*offstage, in the house*). Open up, Mrs. Hitchcock, open up – name of the Law!

MUSGRAVE. Ah, here he is. Now he asked me this evening to kidnap you for the Army. But *I* told you we was brothers, didn't I? So watch while I prove it. (*To* HURST.) Take him out and hide him.

HURST (*taken aback*). Him in the midden too?

MUSGRAVE. Don't be a fool. Do as you're told.

WALSH. Wait – wait a minute.

MUSGRAVE (*furiously*). Go with him, you damned nignog. Would ye rather trust the Constable?

WALSH (*very puzzled*). What are you on, for God's sake?

MUSGRAVE. Don't waste time! (*He pushes* WALSH *and barks*

at HURST.) Get him in that woodshed. God, what a shower o' tortoises!

HURST *hustles* WALSH *out to the yard.* MUSGRAVE *turns on* ATTERCLIFFE.

You get your trousers on.

ATTERCLIFFE *obeys.* MRS. HITCHCOCK *comes in, very agitated.*

MRS. HITCHCOCK. The Constable's here, he's running through the house.

MUSGRAVE. Then send him to me! It's in control, in control, woman. I *know* all about it!

MRS. HITCHCOCK *goes back into the house.*

ATTERCLIFFE. Musgrave, what are you doing?

MUSGRAVE. I'm doing what comes next and that's all I've got time for.

ATTERCLIFFE (*in a gush of despair*). But he was killed, you see, killed. Musgrave, don't you see, that wipes the whole thing out, wiped out, washed out, finished.

MUSGRAVE. *No!*

MRS. HITCHCOCK *and the* CONSTABLE *hurry in from the house.*

CONSTABLE. Ah, Serjeant, what's happened? Saw a gang breaking in at the back of this coach-house. What's kept in the coach-house? (*To* MRS. HITCHCOCK.)

MRS. HITCHCOCK. The Serjeant's got his –

MUSGRAVE. I've got my gear.

MRS. HITCHCOCK. Hello, here's the Parson.

The PARSON *hurries in from the house.*

PARSON. Constable, what's going on?

CONSTABLE. I think it's beginning, sir. I think it's the riots.

PARSON. At this hour of the morning?

CONSTABLE. I've sent word to the Mayor.

He starts making a rapid report to the PARSON. *The* BARGEE *sidles up to* MUSGRAVE.

BARGEE. Don't forget Old Joe. I brought the warning. Let me in on a share of it, go on, there's a bully.

MUSGRAVE. Get out, or you'll get hurt!

The MAYOR *hurries in from the house.*

MAYOR. This is bad, it's bloody bad. How did it start? Never mind that now. What steps have you taken?

CONSTABLE. Me Deputy-Specials all around the streets, but I've not got enough of 'em and they're frightened – that's frank. I *warned* you, Your Worship.

MAYOR. Question is this: can you hold the town safe while twelve o'clock mid-day?

CONSTABLE. Nay I don't know.

MAYOR. The telegraph's working.

MUSGRAVE. The telegraph!

MAYOR. Aye, there's a thaw begun. Thank God for that: they've mended the broken wire on top of the moor. So I sent word for the Dragoons. They'll come as fast as they can, but not afore twelve I shouldn't think, so we've *got* to hold this town!

MUSGRAVE. Six hours, thereabouts. Keep 'em quiet now, they may bide. Mr. Mayor, I'll do it for you.

MAYOR. How?

MUSGRAVE. I'll do what I'm paid for : start a recruiting-meeting. Look, we had 'em last night as merry as Christmas in here, why not this morning? Flags, drums, shillings, sovereigns – hey, start the drum! Top o' the market-place, make a jolly speech to 'em!

MAYOR. Me?

HURST *begins beating the drum outside in the yard.*

MUSGRAVE. You! You, Parson, too. Mrs. Hitchcock, free beer
to the crowd!

PARSON. No!

MAYOR (*catching the idea*). *Aye*, missus, bring it! *I'll* pay for it
and all!

MUSGRAVE (*to the* BARGEE). *You*, if you want to help, you can
carry a flag. (*To* ATTERCLIFFE.) Get <u>him</u> a flag!

Exit ATTERCLIFFE. *Enter* HURST, *drumming furiously.*

We'll *all* carry flags. Fetch me me tunic.

MRS. HITCHCOCK. Here it is, I brought it.

MUSGRAVE (*quite wild with excitement*). Flags, ribbons, bunches
o' ribbons, glamourise 'em, glory!

ATTERCLIFFE *hurries in from the yard, with his arms full of
colours. He hands these out all round.*

BARGEE. Rosebuds of Old England!

MAYOR. Loyal hearts and true!

PARSON. The Lord mighty in battle!

MUSGRAVE. GOD SAVE THE QUEEN!

General noise, bustle and confusion.

Act Three

The market-place.

*Early morning. In the centre of the stage is a practicable feature –
the centre-piece of the market-place. It is a sort of Victorian
clock-tower-cum-lamppost-cum-market-cross, and stands on a
raised plinth. There is a ladder leaning against it. On the plinth
are the soldiers' boxes and a coil of rope. The front of the plinth is
draped with bunting, and other colours are leaning against the
centre-piece in an impressive disposition.*

*When the scene opens, the stage is filled with noise and movement
HURST is beating his drum, the MAYOR, the PARSON and
MUSGRAVE are mounting the plinth, and ATTERCLIFFE is up
already, making the last arrangements. The CONSTABLE takes
up his stand beside the centre-piece, as does HURST. The BARGEE
is hopping about on the forestage.*

*The SOLDIERS are all now properly dressed, the MAYOR has put
on his cocked hat and red robe and chain, and the PARSON his
gown and bands, and carries a Bible. They are all wearing bright
cockades.*

*The role of the BARGEE in this scene is important. As there is no
crowd, the speeches are delivered straight out to the audience, and
the BARGEE acts as a kind of fugleman to create the crowd-
reactions. Noises-off indicated in the dialogue are rather unrealistic
– as it were, token-noises only.*

At one side of the stage there is an upper-storey window.

BARGEE (*casting his cap*).
> Hip hip hooroar
> Hark hark the drums do bark
> The Hungry Army's coming to town
> Lead 'em in with a Holy Book
> A golden chain and a scarlet gown.

Here they are on a winter's morning, you've got six kids at home crying out for bread, you've got a sour cold wife and no fire and no breakfast: and you're too damn miserable even to fight – if there's owt else at all to take your mind off it – so here you are, you lucky people, in your own old market-place, a real live lovely circus, with real live golden sovereigns in somebody's pocket and real live taddy ale to be doled out to the bunch of you!

MRS. HITCHCOCK *enters, trundling a beer-barrel.*

Oh, it's for free, you can be certain o' that, there's no strings to this packet – let's lend you a hand wi' that, missus!

He helps her roll the barrel to one side of the centre-piece, where she chocks it level and sits down on it. She also has a hand-basket full of tankards. The BARGEE *comes back downstage.*

There we are, then. And here *you* are, the streets is filling, roll up, roll up, and wallow in the lot! I'll tell you the word when to cheer.

The platform party is now all in place. The drum gives a final roll. The MAYOR *steps forward.*

CONSTABLE. Silence for the Mayor!

BARGEE. Long live His Worship, who gives us food and clothing and never spares to meet the people with a smile! Hooroar!

Three boos, off.

Boo, boo, boo? Don't be so previous, now; he'll surprise us

all yet, boys. Benevolence and responsibility. Silence for the
Mayor!

MAYOR. All right. Now then. It's been a hard winter. I know
there's a bit of a thaw this morning, but it's not over yet,
there may be worse to come. Although you might not think
it, I'm as keen and eager as any o' you to get the pits working again, so we can all settle down in peace to a good roast
and baked 'taters and a good pudding and the rest of it. But
I'm not here to talk strikes today.

A noise off.

BARGEE (*interpreting*). He says: 'Who says strikes, it's a bloody
lockout.'

CONSTABLE. Silence for the Mayor!

BARGEE. Silence for His Worship!

MAYOR. I said I'm not up here to talk on that today. Serjeant
Musgrave, on my right, has come to town to find men for
the Queen. Now that's a good opportunity – it's a *grand*
opportunity. It's up to you to take it. By God, if I was a
young lad in a town without work, you'd not catch me
thinking twice –

BARGEE. He says: 'There's only one man drives the work
away in this town.'

The CONSTABLE *steps forward, but the* BARGEE *forestalls
him.*

Silence for the Mayor!

MAYOR. All right. You think I'm playing it crooked all the
time – *I* know.

A cheer off.

But listen to this: (*He holds up a jingling money-bag.*) Here's
real gold. It rings true to me, it rings true to you, and
there's one o' these for every lad as volunteers. That's
straight. It's from the shoulder. It pulls no punches. Take

it or throw it away – I'm set up here and waiting. (Parson, tell 'em *your* piece now.) And keep quiet while the Rector's at you : he talks good sense and you need it. If you can't give *me* credit, at least you can give *him* some, for considering what's best for the community. Go on, Parson : tell 'em.

He retires and the PARSON *steps forward.*

PARSON. 'And Jesus said, I come not to bring peace but a sword.' I know very well that the times are difficult. As your minister of religion, and as a magistrate, it is my business to be aware of these matters. But we must remember that this town is only one very small locality in our great country.

BARGEE. Very true, very true.

Two cheers, off.

PARSON. And if our country is great, and I for one am sure that it *is* great, it is great because of the greatness of its responsibilities. They are world wide. They are noble. They are the responsibilities of a first-class power.

BARGEE. Keep 'em there, Reverend! First-class for ever! Give a cheer, you boys!

Three cheers, very perfunctory.

And the crowd roars! Every hat in the air, you've struck 'em in the running nerve, hooroar!

PARSON. Therefore, I say, therefore : when called to shoulder our country's burdens we should do it with a glancing eye and a leaping heart, to draw the sword with gladness, thinking nothing of our petty differences and grievances – but all united under one brave flag, going forth in Christian resolution, and showing a manly spirit! The Empire calls! Greatness is at hand! Serjeant Musgrave will take down the names of any men willing, if you'll file on to the platform in an orderly fashion, in the name of the Father, the Son and mumble mumble mumble . . .

He retires. There is a pause.

MUSGRAVE. Perhaps, Mr. Mayor, before we start enrolling
names, it might be as well if I was to say a few words first,
like, outlining the type of service the lads is likely to find,
overseas, and so forth?

The SLOW COLLIER *slouches in, and up to the base of the
plinth.*

SLOW COLLIER. Have you got my name down?

MUSGRAVE. No. Not yet.

SLOW COLLIER. Are you sure of that ?

MUSGRAVE. Aye, I'm sure. D'you want me to take it?

SLOW COLLIER. Some of us was a bit full, like, last night in the
boozer.

MUSGRAVE. A man's pleasuring, friend, that's all. No harm in
that?

SLOW COLLIER (*thrusting forward his hat with the cockade in
it*). Then what's this? Eh? Someone gave me this.

MUSGRAVE (*laughs*). Oh I'll tell you what that means : you
drank along of me – that's all that it means – and you
promised you'd come and hear me this morning. Well, here
you are.

SLOW COLLIER. Ah. Provisional. Aye. I thought that's what it
was. Provisional.

The PUGNACIOUS COLLIER *slouchse in.*

PUGNACIOUS COLLIER. Provisional or not, we're not signing
nowt without we've heard more. So go on then, soldier, tell
us. Prove it's better to be shot nor starve, *we'll* listen to you,
man, 'cos we're ready to believe. And more of us and all.

CRIES OFF. Aye. Aye. Aye. Tell us.

BARGEE. Go on, Serjeant, tell us. It's a long strong tale, quiet
while he tells it – quiet!

MUSGRAVE. Now there's more tales than one about the Army,

and a lot of funny jokers to run around and spread 'em, too. Aye, aye, we've all heard of 'em, we know all about 'em, and it's not my job this morning to swear to you what's true and what's not true. O' *course* you'll find there's an RSM here or a Provost-sarnt there what makes you cut the grass wi' nail-scissors, or dust the parade-ground with a toothbrush. It's all the bull, it's all in the game – but it's not what sends me here and it's not what put *these* on my arm, and it's nowt at all to do with *my* life, or these two with me, or any o' yours. So easy, me boys, don't think it. (*To the* COLLIERS.) There was another lad wi' *you*, in and out last night. He ought to be here. (*To the* BARGEE.) Go and fetch him, will you? You know where he is.

BARGEE (*finger to nose*). Ah. Ha ha. Aye aye.

He slips out conspiratorily.

MUSGRAVE (*continues his speech*). I said, easy me boys, and don't think it. Because there's *work* in the Army, and bull's not right work, you can believe me on that – it's just foolery – any smart squaddy can carry it away like a tuppenny-ha'penny jam jar. So I'll tell you what the *work* is – open it up!

ATTERCLIFFE *flings open one of the boxes. It is packed with rifles. He takes one out and tosses it to* MUSGRAVE.

MUSGRAVE. Now this is the rifle. This is what we term the butt of the rifle. This is the barrel. This here's the magazine. And this – (*he indicates the trigger*) – you should know what *this is*, you should know what it does . . . Well, the rifle's a good weapon, it's new, quick, accurate. This is the bayonet – (*he fixes his bayonet*) – it kills men smart, it's good and it's beautiful. But I've more to show than a rifle. Open it up!

ATTERCLIFFE *opens a second case. It contains a Gatling gun and tripod mounting.*

This is the newest, this is the smartest, call it the most beautiful. It's a Gatling gun, this. Watch how it works!

ATTERCLIFFE *secures the gun to its mounting.*

ATTERCLIFFE. The rounds are fed to the chambers, which are arranged in a radial fashion, by means of a hopper-shaped aperture, *here.* Now pay attention while I go through the preliminary process of loading.

He goes through the preliminary process of loading.

MUSGRAVE (*his urgency increasing all the time*). The point being that here we've got a gun that doesn't shoot like: *Bang*, rattle-click-up-the-spout-what're-we-waiting-for, *bang!* But: Bang-bang-bang-bang-bang-bang-bang-bang-*bang* – and there's not a man alive in the whole of this market-place. Modern times. Progress. Three hundred and fifty rounds in one minute – *flat!*

The BARGEE *re-enters, soft-footed.*

MUSGRAVE (*quickly to him*). Is he coming?

The BARGEE *nods, finger to lips.*

ATTERCLIFFE. Now then, you see, the gun's loaded.
MUSGRAVE. It didn't take long, you see.
ATTERCLIFFE. No.

HURST *gives a roll on the drums.*
ATTERCLIFFE *swivels the gun to face out into the audience.*
MUSGRAVE *loads his rifle with a clip of cartridges.*

MUSGRAVE (*his voice very taut and hard*). The question remains as to the *use* of these weapons! (*He pushes his rifle-bolt home.*) You'll ask me: what's their purpose? Seeing we've beat the Russians in the Crimea, there's no war with France (there *may* be, but there isn't yet), and Germany's our friend, who do we have to fight? *Well*, the Reverend

answered *that* for you, in his good short words. Me and my
three lads – two lads, I'd say rather – we belong to a regiment
is a few thousand miles from here, in a little country without
much importance except from the point of view that there's
a Union Jack flies over it and the people of that country can
write British Subject after their names. And that makes us
proud!

ATTERCLIFFE. I tell you it makes us proud!

HURST. We live in tattered tents in the rain, we eat rotten food,
there's knives in the dark streets and blood on the floors of
the hospitals, but we stand tall and proud: because of why
we are there.

ATTERCLIFFE. Because we're there to serve our duty.

MUSGRAVE. A soldier's duty is a soldier's life.

WALSH *enters at the extreme rear of the stage and walks
slowly up behind the others and listens.*
A roll on the drum.

MUSGRAVE. A soldier's life is to lay it down, against the
enemies of his Queen,

A roll on the drum.

against the invaders of his home,

A roll on the drum.

against slavery, cruelty, tyrants.

A roll on the drum.

HURST. You put on the uniform and you give your life away,
and who do you give it to?

ATTERCLIFFE. You give it to your duty.

MUSGRAVE. And you give it to your people, for peace, and for
honesty.

A roll on the drum.

MUSGRAVE. That's *my* book. (*He turns on the* MAYOR.)
What's *yours?*

MAYOR (*very taken aback*). Eh? What? I'm not a reading
man, but it *sounds* all right . . . strong. Strong . . .

MUSGRAVE (*to the* PARSON). What about *yours?*

PARSON (*dubiously*). You speak with enthusiasm, yes. I hope
you'll be listened to.

MUSGRAVE (*at the top of his passion*). By God, I hope I am!
D'ye hear me, d'ye hear me, d'ye hear me – I'm the Queen
of England's man, and I'm wearing her coat and I know her
Book backwards. I'm Black Jack Musgrave, me, the hardest
serjeant of the line – I work my life to bugle and drum, for
eighteen years I fought for one flag only, salute it in the
morning, can you haul it down at dark? The Last Post of
a living life? Look – I'll show it to you all. And I'll *dance* for
you beneath it – hoist up the flag, boy – up, up, *up!*

ATTERCLIFFE *has nipped up the ladder, holding the rope. He
loops the rope over the cross-bar of the lamp-bracket, drops to
the plinth again, flings open the lid of the big box, and hauls on
the rope.*

HURST *beats frantically on his drum. The rope is attached to
the contents of the box, and these are jerked up to the cross-bar
and reveal themselves as an articulated skeleton dressed in a
soldier's tunic and trousers, the rope noosed round the neck.
The* PEOPLE *draw back in horror.* MUSGRAVE *begins to dance,
waving his rifle, his face contorted with demoniac fury.*

MUSGRAVE (*as he dances, sings, with mounting emphasis*).

> Up he goes and no one knows
> How to bring him downwards
> Dead man's feet
> Over the street
> Riding the roofs
> And crying down your chimneys

Up he goes and no one knows
Who it was that rose him
But white and red
He waves his head
He sits on your back
And you'll never never lose him
Up he goes and no one knows
How to bring him downwards.

He breaks off at the climax of the song, and stands panting. The drum stops.

That'll do. That'll do for *that*. (*He beckons gently to the* PEOPLE.) You can come back. Come back. Come back. We're all quiet now. But nobody move out of this market-place. You saw the gun loaded. Well, it's on a very quick swivel and the man behind it's well trained. (*He gestures with his rifle towards the platform party.*) And *I've* won a regimental cup four year running for small-arms marksmanship. So be good, and be gentle, *all* of you.

That checks the BARGEE, *who made a move. The* MAYOR *seems to be about to speak.*

Right, Mr. Mayor – I'll explain the whole business.

PARSON (*in a smaller voice than usual*). Business? What business, sir? Do you intend to imply you are *threatening* us with these weapons?

MAYOR. The man's gone balmy. Constable, do summat, grab him, quick!

The CONSTABLE *makes an indecisive move.*

MUSGRAVE. Be *quiet*. I shan't warn agen. (*To the* MAYOR *and the* PARSON.) You two. Get down there! Constable, *there!*

He gestures peremptorily and the three of them obey him, moving downstage to stand facing the platform and covered by the gun.

Now I said I'll explain. So listen. (*He points to the skeleton.*)
This, up here, was a comrade of mine – of ours. At least, he
was till a few months since. He was killed, being there for
his duty, in the country I was telling you about, where the
regiment is stationed. It's not right a colony, you know, it's
a sort of Protectorate, but British, y'know, British. This, up
here, he was walking down a street latish at night, he'd
been to the opera – *you've* got a choral society in this town, I
daresay – well, he was only a soldier, but North Country, he
was full of music, so he goes to the opera. And on his way
again to camp he was shot in the back. And it's not surprising, neither : there was patriots abroad, anti-British,
subversive ; like they didn't dare to shoot him to his face. He
was daft to be out alone, wasn't he? Out of bounds, after
curfew.

ATTERCLIFFE (*with suppressed frenzy*). Get on to the words as
matter, serjeant!

MUSGRAVE (*turning on him fiercely*). *I'm* talking now ; you wait
your turn! . . . So we *come* to the words as matter. He was the
third to be shot that week. He was the fifteenth that month.
In the back and all. Add to which he was young, he was
liked, he sang songs, they say, and he joked and he laughed
– he was a good soldier, too, else *I'd* not have bothered (we'll
leave out his sliding off to the opera WOL, but by and large
good, and I've got standards). So at twelve o'clock at night
they beat up the drums and sounded the calls and called
out the guard and the guard calls us *all* out, and the road
is red and slippery, and every soldier in the camp no longer
in the camp but in the streets of that city, rifle-butts,
bayonets, every street cut off for eight blocks north and west
the opera-house. And that's how it began.

HURST (*the frenzy rising*). The streets is empty, but the houses
is full. He says, 'no undue measures, minimum violence', he
says. 'But bring in the killers.'

ATTERCLIFFE.The killers are gone, they've gone miles off in

that time – *sporting* away, right up in the mountains, I told
you at the time.

MUSGRAVE. That's not material, there's one man is dead, but
there's *everyone's* responsible.

HURST. So bring the *lot* in! It's easy, they're all in bed, kick
the front doors down, knock 'em on the head, boys, chuck
'em in the wagons.

ATTERCLIFFE. I didn't know she was only a little kid, there
was scores of 'em on that staircase, pitch-dark, trampling,
screaming, they're all of 'em screaming, what are we to do?

HURST. Knock 'em on the head, boy, chuck 'em in the
wagons.

ATTERCLIFFE. How was I to tell she was only a little kid?

MUSGRAVE (*bringing it to an end*). THAT'S NOT
MATERIAL! You were told to bring 'em in. If you killed
her, you killed her! She was just one, and who cares a damn
for that! Stay in your place and keep your hands on that
Gatling. We've got to have order here, whatever there was
there; and I can tell you it wasn't order . . . (*To* HURST.)
You, take a rifle. Leave your drum down.

HURST *jumps on the plinth, takes a rifle and loads.*

We've *got* to have order. So I'll just tell you quietly how
many there were was put down as injured – that's badly
hurt, hospital, we don't count knocks and bruises, any o'
that. Twenty-five men. Nine women. *No* children, whatever
he says. She was a fully grown girl, and she had a known
record as an associate of terrorists. That was her. Then four
men, one of them elderly, turned out to have died too.
Making five. Not so very many. Dark streets. Natural surge
of rage.

HURST. We didn't find the killers.

MUSGRAVE. Of course we didn't find 'em. Not *then* we didn't,
any road. We didn't even know 'em. But *I* know 'em, now.

(*He turns on* WALSH.) So what's *your* opinion?

MAYOR. He's not balmy, he's mad, he's stark off his nut.

PARSON. Why doesn't somebody do something, Constable?

Noises off.

MUSGRAVE (*indicates* WALSH). I'm talking to *him*.

CONSTABLE (*very shakily*). I shall have to ask you to – to come down off this platform, Sarnt Musgrave. It looks to me like your – your meeting's got out of hand.

HURST (*covering the* CONSTABLE). Aye, it has.

MUSGRAVE (*to* WALSH). Go on, brother. Tell us.

WALSH *climbs up at the back of the plinth.*

WALSH (*with a certain levity*). *My* opinion, eh? I don't know why you need it. You've got *him*, haven't you? (*He waggles the skeleton's foot familiarly.*) What more d'you want? (*He comes forward and sits on the front of the plinth, looking at the other two* COLLIERS.) Aye, or you too, with your natty little nosegays dandled in your hatbands. Take 'em out, sharp! He's learnt you the truth, hasn't he?

They remove their cockades, shamefacedly.

PUGNACIOUS COLLIER. All right, *that'll* do.

WALSH. Will it, matey, will it? If it helps you to remember what we've been fighting for, I daresay it will. Trade Unions aren't formed, you know, so we can all have beer-ups on the Army.

SLOW COLLIER. He said that'll do. I'm sick and bloody tired – I don't know *what* it's all about.

WALSH (*drops down to the forestage*). Come home and I'll tell you. The circus is over. Come on.

MUSGRAVE. Oh no it's not. Just bide still a while. There's more to be said yet. When I asked you your opinion I meant about them we was talking about – them as did *this*, up here.

WALSH. Well, *what* about them – brother? Clear enough to me. You go for a soldier, you find yourself in someone else's country, you deserve all you get. *I'd* say it stands to reason.

MUSGRAVE. And that's *all* you would say? I'd thought better of you.

WALSH (*irritated*). Now look, look here, what *are* you trying to get? You come to this place all hollering for sympathy, oh you've been beating and murdering and following your trade boo-hoo: but we're not bloody interested! You mend your own heartache and leave us to sort with ours – we've enough and to spare!

MUSGRAVE (*very intensely*). This *is* for your heart. Take another look at *him*. (*Points to skeleton.*) Go on, man, both eyes, and carefully. Because you all used to know him: or most of you did. Private Billy Hicks, late of this parish, welcome him back from the wars, he's bronzed and he's fit, with many a tall tale of distant campaigning to spin round the fireside – ah, *you* used to know him, *didn't* you, Mrs. Hitchcock!

MRS. HITCHCOCK *has risen in great alarm.*

SLOW COLLIER. That's never Billy Hicks, ye dirty liar.

PUGNACIOUS COLLIER. He wor my putter for two year, when I hewed coal in number five – he hewed there hisself for nigh on a year alongside o' my brother.

SLOW COLLIER. He left his clogs to me when he went to join up – that's never our Billy.

NOISES OFF. Never Billy. Never Billy.

BARGEE. 'Never Billy Hicks' – 'Never Billy Hicks' – they don't dare believe it. You've knocked 'em to the root, boy. Oh the white faces!

MRS. HITCHCOCK. She ought to be told. She's got a right to know.

MUSGRAVE. Go along then and tell her.

HURST (*to* MUSGRAVE). You letting her go?

MUSGRAVE. Yes.

HURST. But –

MUSGRAVE (*curtly*). Attend to your orders.

MRS. HITCHCOCK *goes out.*

When I say it's Billy Hicks, you can believe me it's true.

WALSH. Aye, I'll believe you. And you know what I think – it's downright indecent!

MUSGRAVE. Aye, aye? But wait. Because here is the reason. I'm a religious man, and I see the causes of the Almighty in every human work.

PARSON. That is absolute blasphemy!

MAYOR. This won't do you a pennorth o' good, you know.

MUSGRAVE. Not to me, no. But maybe to you? Now as I understand the workings of God, through greed and the world, this man didn't die because he went alone to the opera, he was killed because he had to be – it being decided ; that now the people in that city was worked right up to killing soldiers, then more and more soldiers should be sent for them to kill, and the soldiers in turn should kill the people in that city, more and more, always – that's what I said to you : four men, one girl, then the twenty-five and the nine – *and* it'll go on, there or elsewhere, and it can't be stopped neither, except there's someone finds out Logic and brings the wheel round. You see, the Queen's Book, which eighteen years I've lived, it's turned inside out for *me*. There used to be my duty: now there's a disease –

HURST. Wild-wood mad.

MUSGRAVE. Wild-wood mad we are ; and so we've fetched it home. You've had Moses and the Prophets – that's *him* – (*He points at* WALSH.) – 'cos he told you. But you were all for enlisting, it'd still have gone on. Moses and the Prophets, what good did they do?

He sits down and broods. There is a pause.

WALSH (*awkwardly*). There's no one from this town be over

keen to join up now. You've preached your little gospel: I daresay we can go home?

MUSGRAVE *makes no reply. The* SOLDIERS *look at one another doubtfully.*

HURST. What do we do now?
ATTERCLIFFE. Wait.
HURST. Serjeant –
ATTERCLIFFE (*shushing him*). Ssh-ssh!

A pause. Restive noises, off.

HURST. Serjeant –
ATTERCLIFFE. Serjeant – they've heard your message, they'll none of them forget it. Haven't we done what we came for?
HURST (*astonished, to* ATTERCLIFFE). Done what we came for?

ATTERCLIFFE *shushes him again as* MUSGRAVE *stirs.*

MUSGRAVE (*as though to himself*). One man, and for him five. Therefore, for five of them we multiply out, *and* we find it five-and-twenty. . . . So, as I understand Logic and Logic to me is the mechanism of God – that means that today there's twenty-five persons will have to be –

ATTERCLIFFE *jumps up in horror.* ANNIE *and* MRS. HITCH-COCK *appear at the upper window. When she sees the skeleton* ANNIE *gasps and seems about to scream.*

MUSGRAVE (*cutting her short*). It's true. It's him. You don't need to cry out; you knew it when he left you.
ANNIE. Take him down. Let me have him. I'll come down for him now.
BARGEE. Away down, me strong Annie. I'll carry you a golden staircase – aha, she's the royal champion, stand by as she comes down.
As he speaks he jumps on to the plinth, takes away the ladder, nips across the stage and props it under the window.

MUSGRAVE. No! Let her wait up there. I said: wait! . . . Now then, who's with me! Twenty-five to die and the Logic is worked out. Who'll help me? You? (*He points to* WALSH.) I made sure that you would: you're a man like the Black Musgrave, you: you have purposes, and you can lead. Join along with my madness, friend. I brought it back to England but I've brought the cure too – to turn it on to them that sent it out of this country – way-out-ay they sent it, where they hoped that only soldiers could catch it and rave! Well here's three redcoat ravers on their own kitchen hearthstone! Who do we start with? These? (*He turns on the* MAYOR.) 'Loyal hearts and true, every man jack of us.' (*To the* PARSON.) 'Draw the sword with gladness.' Why, *swords* is for honour, carry 'em on church parade, a *sword'll* never offer you three hundred and fifty bullets in a minute – and it was no bright sword neither finished *his* life in a back street! (*He points to* BILLY, *and then at the* CONSTABLE.) Or what about the Peeler? If we'd left it to *him*, *you'd* ha' been boxed away to barracks six or eight hours ago! Come on now, let's have you, you know I'm telling you truth!

WALSH. Nay: it won't do.

HURST. It won't do? Why not?

WALSH. I'm not over clear why not. Last night there was me and some others tried to whip away that Gatling. And we'd ha' used it and all: by God, there was need. But that's one thing, y'see, and this is another – ent it, you tell me?

He appeals to the COLLIERS.

PUGNACIOUS COLLIER. Nay, I don't know.

SLOW COLLIER. I think they're all balmy, the whole damn capful's arse-over-tip –

WALSH. No it's not. *I'm* not. And it comes to this wi' me: *he's* still in uniform, and he's still got his Book. He's doing his duty. Well, I take no duties from no bloody lobsters. This town lives by collieries. That's coal-owners and it's pitmen

– aye, and they battle, and the pitmen'll win. But not wi' no
soldier-boys to order our fight for us. Remember their trade:
you give 'em one smell of a broken town, you'll never get
'em out!

MUSGRAVE (*with growing desperation*). But you don't understand me – all of you, listen! I told you we could *cure* –

ATTERCLIFFE. I don't think you can.

MUSGRAVE (*flabbergasted*). Eh? What's that? Stay by your
weapon!

ATTERCLIFFE. No. (*He stands away from the gun.*)

HURST *rapidly takes his place.*

HURST (*to the crowd*). Keep still, the lot of you!

ATTERCLIFFE. It won't do, Black Jack. You swore there'd be
no killing.

MUSGRAVE. No I did not.

ATTERCLIFFE. You gave us to believe. We've done what we
came for, and it's there we should have ended. *I've* ended.
No killing.

*He deliberately gets down from the platform, and squats on the
ground.* MUSGRAVE *looks around him, appealing and appalled.*

BARGEE. I'm with you, general!

MUSGRAVE. You?

BARGEE. Nobody else! I'll serve you a lovely gun! Rapine and
riot! (*He scrambles on to the plinth, picks up a rifle from the box
and loads it.*) When do we start breaking open the boozers?
Or the pawnshops and all – who's for a loot?

MUSGRAVE. None of you at all? Come on, come on, why, he
was your Billy, wasn't he? That you knew and you worked
with – don't you want to revenge him?

ANNIE. Somebody hold the ladder. I'm going to come down.

The SLOW COLLIER *does so.*

MUSGRAVE (*urgently, to her*). Billy Hicks, lassie : here : he used

to be yours! Tell them what they've got to do: tell them the
truth!

ANNIE *has started to come down the ladder. When she is
down, the* COLLIER *lowers it to the ground.*

HURST. Wait a minute, serjeant, leave me to talk to them!
We've not got time bothering wi' no squalling tarts.

MUSGRAVE. Keep you your place.

HURST (*furiously*). I'm in my bloody place! And I'll tell you
this straight, if we lose this crowd now, we've lost all the
work, for ever! And remember summat else. There's
Dragoons on the road!

General sensation. Shouts off: 'Dragoons'.

HURST (*to the crowd*). So you've just got five minutes to make
up your minds.

He grabs his rifle up, and motions the BARGEE *violently to the
Gatling. The* BARGEE *takes over, and* HURST *leaps off the
plinth and talks straight into the* COLLIERS' *faces and at the
audience.*

We've earned our living by beating and killing folk like
yourselves in the streets of their own city. Well, it's drove us
mad – and so we come back here to tell you how and to
show you what it's like. The ones we want to deal with
aren't, for a change, you and your mates, but a bit higher up.
The ones as never get hurt. (*He points at the* MAYOR,
PARSON *and* CONSTABLE.) Him. Him. Him. You hurt them
hard, and they'll not hurt you again. And they'll not send *us*
to hurt you neither. But if you let 'em be, then us three'll be
killed – aye and worse, we'll be forgotten – and the whole
bloody lot'll start all over again!

He climbs back and takes over the gun.

MUSGRAVE. For God's sake stand with us. We've *got* to be
remembered!

SLOW COLLIER. We ought to, you know. He might be right.

WALSH. I don't know. I don't trust it.

PUGNACIOUS COLLIER. Ahr and be damned, these are just like the same as us. Why don't we stand with 'em?

WALSH (*obstinately*). I've not yet got this clear.

ANNIE. To me it's quite clear. He asked me to tell you the truth. My truth's an easy tale, it's old true-love gone twisted, like they called it 'malformed'– they put part in the ground, and hang the rest on a pillar here, and expect me to sit under it making up song-ballads. All right.

> My true love is a scarecrow
> Of rotted rag and bone
> Ask him : where are the birds, Billy?
> Where have they all gone?

He says: Unbutton my jacket, and they'll all fly out of the ribs – oh, oh, I'm not mad, though you told us that *you* were – let's have that bundle!

MRS. HITCHCOCK *throws down a bundle.* ANNIE *shakes it out, revealing* SPARKY'S *tunic.*

Take a sight o' this, you hearty colliers : see what they've brought you. You can match it up with Billy's. Last night there were four o' these walking, weren't there? Well, this morning there's three. They buried the other one in Ma Hitchcock's midden. Go on, ask 'em why!

HURST. He's a deserter, is why!

ANNIE (*holding up the tunic*). Hey, here's the little hole where they let in the bayonet. Eee, aie, easily in. His blood's on my tongue, so hear what it says. A bayonet is a raven's beak. This tunic's a collier's jacket. That scarecrow's a birdcage. What more do you want!

WALSH. Is this what she says true? Where *is* he, the fourth of you?

MUSGRAVE. He was killed, and that's all. By an accident
killed. It's barely materi –

ATTERCLIFFE. Oh, it's material. And no goddamned accident.
I said it to you, Musgrave, it washes it all out.

WALSH. It bloody does and all, as far as I go. (*He turns to the*
other COLLIERS.) If you want to stand by 'em when they've
done for their own mucker and not one of the bastards can
tell ye the same tale, well, you're at your damned liberty and
take it and go!

The COLLIERS *murmur dubiously.*

HURST (*frantic*). I'm going to start shooting!

General reaction of fear: he clearly means it. He spits at
MUSGRAVE.

You and your everlasting Word – you've pulled your own
roof down! But *I'll* prop your timber for you – I'll give a
One, Two, and a Three : and I'm opening fire!

ATTERCLIFFE. No.

He jumps up and stands on the step of the plinth, below the gun
and facing it, with his arms spread out so that the muzzle is
against his breast.

HURST (*distorted with rage*). Get down! Get down off it, you old
cuckold, I don't care who you are. I'll put the first one
through you! I *swear* it, I will! One! Two! . . .

MAYOR (*to the* CONSTABLE). Go for that gun.

The CONSTABLE *is making a cautious move towards the gun,*
but he is forestalled by MUSGRAVE, *who flings himself at*
HURST *and knocks him away from the breach. There is a*
moment's tense struggle behind the gun.

MUSGRAVE (*as he struggles*). The wrong way. The wrong way.
You're trying to do it without Logic.

Then HURST *gives way and falls back down the steps of the plinth. He recovers himself.*

HURST (*panting with excitement*). All right then, Black Jack. All right, it's finished. The lot. You've lost it. I'm off!

MUSGRAVE (*stunned*). Come back here. You'll come back, you'll obey orders.

HURST *makes a grab forward, snatches his rifle from the platform and jumps back clear.*

HURST (*to the crowd*). Get out o' my road!

At the very instant he turns towards the wings to run away, a shot is fired offstage. His quick turn changes into a grotesque leap as the bullet hits him, and he collapses on the stage. A bugle blares from offstage.

VOICES OFF. Dragoons!

Orders shouted and general noise of cavalry coming to a halt and dismounting.

MAYOR   ⎫ (*one after another, rapidly.*)
CONSTABLE ⎬ The Dragoons! The Dragoons!
PARSON   ⎭ Saved! Saved! Saved!
VOICES OFF. Saved! Saved! Saved!

MUSGRAVE *is standing beside the gun, temporarily at a loss.* ATTERCLIFFE *has jumped down beside* HURST *and lifted his head. Everyone else stands amazed.*
Suddenly MUSGRAVE *swings the gun to point toward the Dragoons. The* BARGEE *ups with his rifle and sticks it into* MUSGRAVE'S *back.*

BARGEE. Serjeant, put your hands up!

MUSGRAVE *is pushed forward by the rifle, but he does not obey. The* TROOPER *enters, clicking the bolt of his smoking carbine, and shouting.*

TROOPER. Everybody stand where you are! You, put your hands up!

MUSGRAVE *does so.*

BARGEE. I've got him, soldier! I've got him! Crooked Joe's got him, Mr. Mayor.

The OFFICER *strides in, drawing his sabre.*

Give a cheer – hooroar!

Cheers off.
The OFFICER *comes to attention before the* MAYOR *and salutes with his sabre.*

OFFICER. Mr. Mayor, are we in time?

MAYOR. Aye, you're in time. You're *just* in bloody time.

OFFICER (*seeing* MUSGRAVE). 22128480 Serjeant Musgrave, J.?

MUSGRAVE. My name.

OFFICER. We heard word you'd come here. You are under arrest. Robbery and desertion. There were *three* who came with you.

ATTERCLIFFE (*getting up from* HURST, *whose head falls back.*) You can count me for one of them. One other's dead already. Here's the third.

OFFICER. You're under arrest.

CONSTABLE. Hold out your hands.

He takes out two pairs of handcuffs and fetters them.

OFFICER. Mr. Mayor, my troopers are at your disposal. What do you require of us?

MAYOR. Well, I'd say it was about all over by now, young man – wouldn't you?

OFFICER. Law and order is established?

PARSON. Wiser counsels have prevailed, Captain.

BARGEE. *I* caught him, *I* caught him, *I* used me strategy!

OFFICER. My congratulations, all.

WALSH (*with great bitterness*). The community's been saved. Peace and prosperity rules. We're all friends and neighbours for the rest of today. We're all sorted out. We're back where we were. So what do we do?

BARGEE.

Free beer. It's still here.
No more thinking. Easy drinking.
End of a bad bad dream. Gush forth the foaming stream.

He takes the bung out of the barrel and starts filling tankards.

OFFICER. The winter's broken up. Let normal life begin again.

BARGEE. Aye, aye, *begin* again!

He is handing the mugs to the people. He starts singing, and they all join in, by degrees.

There was an old man called Michael Finnegan
He had whiskers on his chin-egan
The wind came out and blew them in agen
Poor old Michael Finnegan –
Begin agen –

There was an old man etcetera . . .

He gives out mugs in the following order: the MAYOR, *the* PARSON, *the* SLOW COLLIER, *the* PUGNACIOUS COLLIER, *the* CONSTABLE. *Each man takes his drink, swigs a large gulp, then links wrists with the previous one, until all are dancing round the centre-piece in a chain, singing.*

ANNIE *has climbed the plinth and lowers the skeleton. She sits with it on her knees. The* DRAGOONS *remain standing at the side of the stage.* MUSGRAVE *and* ATTERCLIFFE *come slowly downstage. The* BARGEE *fills the last two tankards and hands one to* WALSH, *who turns his back angrily. The* BARGEE *empties one mug, and joins the tail of the dance, still holding the other. After one more round he again beckons* WALSH. *This time the latter thinks for a moment, then bitterly throws his hat on the ground, snarls into the impassive face of the* DRAGOON, *and joins in the dance, taking the beer.*

The scene closes, leaving MUSGRAVE *and* ATTERCLIFFE *on the forestage.* MRS. HITCHCOCK *retires from the window.*

SCENE TWO

A prison cell.

This scene is achieved by a barred wall descending in front of the dancers of the previous scene. After a while the sound dies away, and the lights change so that we can no longer see past the bars.

MUSGRAVE *remains standing, looking into the distance with his back to the audience.* ATTERCLIFFE *sighs and sits down gingerly on the floor.*

ATTERCLIFFE. Sit down and rest yourself, serjeant. That's all there is left . . . Go on, man, sit down . . . Then stand and the devil take you! It's *your* legs, not mine. It's my *hands* is what matters. They finished Sparky and that finished me, and Sparky finished you. Holy God save us, why warn't I a greengrocer, then I'd never ha' been cuckolded, never gone for no soldier, never no dead Sparky, and never none of this. Go on, serjeant, talk to me. I'm an old old stupid bastard and I've nowt to do now but fret out the runs of the consequence; and the whole croaking work it's finished and done. Go on, serjeant, talk.

MUSGRAVE *does not move.*

A pause.

MRS. HITCHCOCK *enters, carrying a glass.*

MRS. HITCHCOCK (*to* MUSGRAVE). It's port with a bit o'

lemon. I often take it of a morning; like it settles me stummick for the day. The officer said I could see you, if I warn't no more nor five minutes. Sit down and I'll give it to your mouth – them wrist-irons makes it difficult, I daresay.

MUSGRAVE (*without looking at her*). Give it to him. I don't want it.

MRS. HITCHCOCK. He can have half of it. You take a sup first.

MUSGRAVE *shakes his head.*

All right. How you like.

She goes to ATTERCLIFFE *and puts the glass to his mouth.*

ATTERCLIFFE. I'm obliged to you, missus.

MRS. HITCHCOCK. It's on the house, this one. Change from the Queen, ent it?

MUSGRAVE. Numbers and order. According to Logic. I had worked it out for months.

He swings round to MRS. HITCHCOCK.

What made it break down!

MRS. HITCHCOCK. Ah, there's the moral of it. You ask our Annie.

MUSGRAVE (*furiously*). He was killed by pure accident! It had nothing to do –

ATTERCLIFFE. Oh by God, it had.

MRS. HITCHCOCK. The noisy one, warn't he? Pack o' cards and all the patter. You asked me to trust you – (*her voice rises with rage and emotion*) – he was only a young lad, for gracious goodness Christ, he'd a voice like a sawmill – what did you want to do it for, you gormless great gawk!

ATTERCLIFFE. *He* didn't do it.

MRS. HITCHCOCK. He did, oh he did! And he broke his own neck.

MUSGRAVE. What's the matter with you, woman!

MRS. HITCHCOCK. All wrong, you poured it out all wrong! I

could ha' told you last night if only I'd known – the end of
the world and you thought you could call a parade. In control – *you!*

MUSGRAVE (*very agitated*). Don't talk like that. You're talking
about my duty. Good order and the discipline : it's the only
road I know. Why can't you see it?

MRS. HITCHCOCK. All I can see is Crooked Joe Bludgeon
having his dance out in the middle of fifty Dragoons! It's
time you learnt your life, you big proud serjeant. Listen : last
evening you told all about this anarchy and where it came
from – like, scribble all over with life or love, and that makes
anarchy. Right?

MUSGRAVE. Go on.

MRS. HITCHCOCK. Then *use* your Logic – if you can. Look at
it this road : here we are, and we'd got life and love. Then
you came in and you did your scribbling where nobody
asked you. Aye, it's arsy-versey to what you said, but it's
still an anarchy, isn't it? And it's all your work.

MUSGRAVE. Don't tell me there was life or love in this town.

MRS. HITCHCOCK. There was. There was hungry men, too –
fighting for their food. But *you* brought in a different war.

MUSGRAVE. I brought it in to end it.

ATTERCLIFFE. To end it by its own rules: no bloody good.
She's right, you're wrong. You can't cure the pox by further
whoring. Sparky died of those damned rules. And so did the
other one.

MUSGRAVE. That's not the truth. (*He looks at them both in
appeal, but they nod.*) That's not the truth. God was with
me . . . God . . . (*He makes a strange animal noise of despair,
a sort of sob that is choked off suddenly, before it can develop
into a full howl.*) – and all they dancing – all of them – there.

MRS. HITCHCOCK. Ah, not for long. And it's not a dance of
joy. Those men are hungry, so they've got no time for *you*.
One day they'll be full, though, and the Dragoons'll be gone,
and then they'll remember.

MUSGRAVE (*shaking his head*). No.

MRS. HITCHCOCK. Let's hope it, any road, Eh?

She presents the glass to his lips. This time he accepts it and drinks, and remains silent.

ATTERCLIFFE (*melancholy but quiet*). That running tyke of a Sparky, he reckoned he wor the only bastard in the barracks had a voice. Well, he warn't. There's other men can sing when he's not here. So listen at this.

He sings.

> I plucked a blood-red rose-flower down
> And gave it to my dear.
> I set my foot out across the sea
> And she never wept a tear.
>
> I came back home as gay as a bird
> I sought her out and in :
> And I found her at last in a little attic room
> With a napkin round her chin.

At her dinner, you see. Very neat and convenient.

He sings.

> Oh are you eating meat, I said,
> Or are you eating fish?
> I'm eating an apple was given me today,
> The sweetest I could wish.

So I asked her where she got it, and by God the tune changed then. Listen at what she told me.

He sings to a more heavily accented version of the tune.

> Your blood-red rose is withered and gone
> And fallen on the floor :
> And he who brought the apple down
> Shall be my darling dear.

For the apple holds a seed will grow
In live and lengthy joy
To raise a flourishing tree of fruit
For ever and a day.
With fal-la-la-the-dee, toor-a-ley,
For ever and a day.

They're going to hang us up a length higher nor most apple-trees grow, Serjeant. D'you reckon we can start an orchard?

The Workhouse Donkey

A VULGAR MELO-DRAMA

FOR TAMARA

This cool sweet moon (now defeated by night
   Which crossed her with raincloud and mirk)
Had, under her first rising, sent momentary light
   Through every tree in the park.
Every bush, every pool, every thicket abhorrent
Remain to my blind sight apparent:
   And I can walk yet without danger or fright.

Themusic for this play, by John Addison,
is available upon application to the composer's agents:
London Management, 235/241 Regent St, London WIA 2JT

Author's Preface

I have called this play a melo-drama: a term I intend to be understood in its original sense of a play with a musical accompaniment. In the Chichester production, Mr Addison's score provided not only settings for the several songs but also a background for much of the dialogue, and linking passages between the scenes. The band was seated on an upper balcony of the stage and remained in view of the audience throughout the action. As the play is strictly a play and not a musical or a light opera, I dare say it would be possible to present it without instrumental accompaniment, but unless economy imperatively demands it, I do not recommend that this should be done.

The Workhouse Donkey was originally commissioned for the Royal Court Theatre, and it was necessary to adapt it somewhat for the open stage at Chichester. The directions in this printed text will, it is hoped, prove applicable to any of the more usual types of auditorium. For productions within a proscenium-arch it is essential that décor be kept to a minimum and that the action be allowed to flow from one scene into the next with the least possible delay. Both costumes and settings may have a certain air of caricature: but as the play is basically accurate and realistic (indeed, a great deal of it is conscientiously historical), the limits of visual extravagance normally adhered to by the artists of seaside picture-postcards should not be exceeded.

I had considerable difficulty in preparing *The Workhouse Donkey* for the stage. My chosen subject-matter proved both labyrinthine and intractable, and I do not think I could ever have condensed it into the bounds of conventional acting time without the assistance, advice, collaboration, criticism, and frequently expressed bewilderment of:

> Mr Lindsay Anderson
> Mr Stuart Burge
> Miss Margaretta D'Arcy
> Mr George Devine
> Sir Laurence Olivier
> and nearly everyone employed upon or connected with the production at Chichester.

I am, however, still uncertain how valuable our combined

efforts have been. Two-and-a-half or three hours is normally regarded as the maximum permissible length for a new play, and under the conditions at present prevalent in our theatres it is not easy to dispute this. But I would have been happy had it been possible for *The Workhouse Donkey* to have lasted, say, six or seven or thirteen hours (excluding intervals), and for the audience to come and go throughout the performance, assisted perhaps by a printed synopsis of the play from which they could deduce those scenes or episodes which would interest them particularly, and those which they could afford to miss. A theatre presenting such an entertainment would, of course, need to offer rival attractions as well, and would in fact take on some of the characteristics of a fairground or amusement park; with restaurants, bars, sideshows, bandstands and so forth, all grouped round a central playhouse. The design of the playhouse itself would need careful consideration, as clearly members of an audience continually moving to and from their seats in a conventional building will cause intolerable distraction. But I am convinced that if what we laughably call 'vital theatre' is ever to live up to its name, some such casual or 'prom-concert' conception must eventually be arrived at.* It will not suit every play, and every play should not be compelled to suit itself to it: the theatre must be catholic. But it never will be catholic if we do not grant pride of place to the old essential attributes of Dionysus:

> noise
> disorder
> drunkenness
> lasciviousness
> nudity
> generosity
> corruption
> fertility
> and
> ease.

The Comic Theatre was formed expressly to celebrate them: and whenever they have been forgotten our art has betrayed itself and our generally accessible and agreeable god has hidden his face.

* Miss Joan Littlewood has already put forward a similar and apparently highly practicable proposition. I hope she will be enabled to carry it out.

The personality of the late Mr Joseph D'Arcy of Dublin inspired much of the play.

The personality of my native town of Barnsley also inspired a great deal of it: but I have carefully avoided the imitation of the personalities of individual inhabitants. Thus the curiosity of the malicious will go ungratified.

In view of the fact that this play was first performed in a southern county, the speeches used as prologue and epilogue were directed towards the probable audience in such a place. In productions north of the Trent these speeches should be replaced by those given on pages 235 and 236.

*   *   *

Some Critics said:
This Arden baffles us and makes us mad:
His play's uncouth, confused, lax, muddled, bad.

Said Arden:
Why do you accuse me and abuse me
And your polite society refuse me,
Merely because I wear no belt nor braces?
There would be reason for the wry mouths in your faces
And reason for your uncommitted halting speeches
If you would but admit I wore no bloody breeches.

J.A.

The Workhouse Donkey was first performed at the Chichester Festival Theatre on 8 July 1963, with the following cast:

Labour

ALDERMAN BOOCOCK, the Mayor	Dudley Foster
MRS BOOCOCK, the Mayoress	Fay Compton
ALDERMAN BUTTERTHWAITE, his friend and Ex-Mayor	Frank Finlay
HOPEFAST ⎫	Peter Russell
HARDNUT ⎬ Borough Councillors	Harry Lomax
HICKLETON ⎭	Peter O'Shaughnessy

Conservative

ALDERMAN SIR HAROLD SWEETMAN, a wealthy brewer	Martin Boddey
LADY SWEETMAN, his wife	Alison Leggatt
MAURICE SWEETMAN, his son	Jeremy Brett
F. J., his friend: Industrialist and Borough Councillor	Peter Cellier

The Police

COLONEL FENG, Chief Constable	Anthony Nicholls
SUPERINTENDENT WIPER	Robert Stephens
SERGEANT LUMBER	Robert Lang
PC LIVERSEDGE	Derek Jacobi
PC LEFTWICH, retired from active duty: Mayoral Mace-Bearer and Town Hall Factotum	Keith Marsh
TWO POLICEMEN	Terence Knapp, Raymond Clarke

The Electorate

DR WELLINGTON BLOMAX, a physician	Norman Rossington
WELLESLEY, his daughter	Mary Miller
GLORIA, Manageress of the Copacabana Club	Marion Mathie
STONE MASONS	Michael Turner, Michael Rothwell
GUESTS, at the Sweetmans'	Raymond Clarke, Rowena Cooper, Marika Mann, Jean Rodgers
MAID, at the Sweetmans'	Louise Purnell
LANDLORD, of the Victoria and Albert	Dan Meaden

BARMAID		Elizabeth Burger
ASSISTANT BAR BOY		John Rogers
DRINKERS		Reginald Green, Terence Knapp,
		Michael Rothwell, Michael Turner
NURSE, at Dr Blomax's		Rowena Cooper
DOORMAN		Terence Knapp
HOSTESS		Irene Sutcliffe
WAITRESSES	at the	Rowena Cooper
	Copacabana Club	Marika Mann
DANCERS		Elizabeth Burger, Rowena Cooper,
		Jeanne Hepple, Louise Purnell,
		Jean Rogers, Michael Rothwell
SPECIALITY		Jeanette Landis
NUMBERS		
JOURNALISTS		Richard Hampton,
		Michael Rothwell, Michael Turner
PARK ATTENDANT		Reginald Green
LOVERS		John Rogers, Louise Purnell
WAITRESS, in a Tea Shop		Jeanne Hepple
DEMONSTRATORS		Elizabeth Burger,
		Reginald Green, Jeanne Hepple,
		Jeanette Landis, Michael Rothwell

Produced by Stuart Burge
Music by John Addison
Décor by Roger Furse
Lighting by Richard Pilbrow
Dances arranged by Eleanor Fazan

The action of the play takes place in a Yorkshire industrial town: somewhere between Sheffield and Leeds.
The action takes place in the early 1960s.

Act One

A building site.
Foundation stone ready in position for lowering.

Enter BLOMAX.

BLOMAX.
Ladies and gentlemen: let us suppose we go
From St Pancras to Sheffield,
To Doncaster from King's Cross:
By either route to Leeds.

Enter MASONS

Not very far to go, for us or the flight of a crow
But involving geographically an appreciable mutation,
(I mean, in landscape, climate, odours, voices, food.)
I put it to you that such a journey needs
In the realm of morality an equal alteration.

Enter WIPER, LUMBER *and* PCs *as Guard of Honour.*

I mean, is there anything you really believe to be bad?
If you come to the North you might well think it good.
You might well think, as I do,
That you should change the shape of your faces
Or even double their number
When you travel between two places.

Enter civic procession. It includes BOOCOCK, MRS BOO-
COCK (LEFTWICH *with mace preceding them*), SWEET-
MAN, F. J., *Labour Councillors, and* BUTTERTHWAITE.
*Aldermen and Mayor in robes of office, etc. Also Conserva-
tive Ladies and* YOUNG SWEETMAN, *and several Citizens.*

The values of other people
Are not quite as you understand them.
I would not overpraise them,
I would not recommend them,
I am certainly not here to offer to condemn them.
From the beginning to the end
Each man is bound to act
According to his nature
And the nature of his land.
Their land is different from yours.
Why, it has its own music.

Band plays 'Ilkley Moor'. BLOMAX *greets* WIPER, *receives a curt nod in reply, and withdraws; enter* WELLESLEY, *meets* BLOMAX *and stands with him.* WIPER *salutes the* MAYOR.

WIPER. Guard of honour present and ready for your inspection, Mr Mayor.

BOOCOCK. Good afternoon. Superintendent, it is my privilege to present to you your new chief constable, Colonel Feng. Colonel Feng, Superintendent Wiper, who has during the interregnum been very ably conducting . . .

FENG. Good afternoon, Superintendent.

WIPER. Good afternoon, sir.

FENG. Shall we have a look at the Guard of Honour, Mr Mayor?

BOOCOCK. Right we are, sir. After you.

FENG. Superintendent . . .

The band plays 'Ilkley Moor' while they inspect the Constables. BUTTERTHWAITE *detaches himself from the official group and comes down to the Masons. He holds an unlighted cigarette in an ivory holder.*

BUTTERTHWAITE. Eh, begod: the old blue marching bull. Brass bound and bloody minded. What a way to greet a lovely day. Have you got such a thing as a light, Jack?

1ST MASON. Here you are, Alderman.

BUTTERTHWAITE. Alderman? You ought to know me better nor that, lad!

1ST MASON. All right then, Charlie, no offence intended.

BUTTERTHWAITE. That's a bit more like.

He indicates his Alderman's robe.

We may be garnished up like the roast beef of old England, but we haven't quite forgotten all realities yet, I hope. Blimey, look at that! Left right, left right, one two three, and how long have you been in the force, my fine fellow? Jolly good. Jolly good, give that man three stripes! Eh, the police force: we can't do without 'em, but my God how we hate 'em!

The inspection is now over and the MAYOR *takes his place by the stone.*

Watch it: here we go!

BOOCOCK. Fellow townsmen, ladies and gentlemen, er, voters. This afternoon's little ceremony is, as you might say, a double one. Clapping as it were two birds wi't 'yah billet. Firstly, we are laying the foundation stone for our new police headquarters: and secondly, we are paying a very hearty welcome indeed to our new chief constable: Colonel Feng. Both of these innovations will no doubt impinge upon our way of life in manifold directions.

MRS BOOCOCK. Most of these, I hope, pleasant. But I also hope to some of us unpleasant. And justly so!

Laughter.

BOOCOCK. Colonel Feng comes to us by the unanimous choice of the Borough Watch Committee.

BUTTERTHWAITE (*aside*). *He* said that. *I* didn't. Why, I wasn't even there at the time.

BOOCOCK. I am happy to say that the Conservative Members of that Committee, under the respected leadership of Sir Harold Sweetman –

He and SWEETMAN *exchange bows.* BUTTERTHWAITE *grinds his teeth.*

– have concurred entirely with the opinions of us, the majority party. This being a benevolent augury, I will now request the Chief Constable to say a few words. Colonel Feng.

FENG. Mr Mayor, Madam Mayoress, Aldermen, Councillors, ladies and gentlemen. I am not, I confess, a Northern man by birth, nor yet by upbringing. I trust this will be forgiven me.

Laughter.

My last post as Chief Constable was in an extremely different locality, where the prevalence of violent crime was such that only the firmest of firm hands would serve to eliminate it. It has been eliminated. We live in an age of overthrown moral standards. The criminal today is coddled and cosseted by the fantastic jargon of mountebank psychiatry. Yet I ask you, ladies and gentlemen, do these sentimental social pundits ever pause to reflect upon the agony literally suffered night after night by the women of this country who watch their menfolk go out to earn their daily bread; and they wonder (yes they do): 'Will he come home safe and sound, unbroken and unmaimed?' With God's help, ladies and gentlemen, I will put their minds at rest. Thank you.

Applause. BUTTERTHWAITE *gives a long low private whistle.*

BOOCOCK. And thank *you*, Colonel Feng. There will be many a loud hear hear to that, I dare well say . . . Now then: the laying of the stone. Who better can we ask to carry this out than the man whom I might justly call the most honoured of our leading citizens; Chairman of the Regional Branch of the Labour Party, Secretary of the Local Mineworkers' Union, controlling spirit of one-hundred-and-one hard-working committees: and perhaps above all, the man who has held the office of Mayor of this borough not fewer than nine times altogether, which is, I believe, a national record!

2ND MASON (*aside to* BUTTERTHWAITE). In other words, the only man in town who really pumps the oil. Am I right, Charlie?

BUTTERTHWAITE (*aside to him*). You are.

BOOCOCK. Ladies and gentlemen, Alderman Charlie Butterthwaite. Give him a big hand. Come on, Charlie, you've a job o' work to do here.

CHEERS. Three times three for Charlie B. Hooray, 'ray, 'ray . . .

> *Band plays 'See the Conquering Hero'.*

BOOCOCK. By gummy. I can tell you, when I'm set up here in *these* – (*He indicates his robes.*) alongside of old Charlie, I can't help the feeling like I'm under false colours. They've all but got his name wrote on the tab at back!

> *Laughter.*

BUTTERTHWAITE. There he is again, nicking my gags. I'll tell Colonel Feng on you for petty larceny! . . . You know, if anyone o' you had come up to me a few years ago and told me that this afternoon I'd find meself all set to trowel the mortar for a new house for t' coppers, why, I'd ha' sent him off to t'looney-bin with a good boot up his rump! But it circles, you know, it all circles round. And as far as this town goes, *we're* t' masters now. It warn't so easy to credit that in 1897 when your old uncle Charlie first saw the light of day in the lying-in ward of the Municipal Workhouse. And 1926 I call to my memory as a year of some bitterness, too. I fancy

Sir Harold Sweetman bears those days in mind. He and his confederates. They beat us at the time. But we fought and fought again, and in the end we won. And that's the end o' that. All that's left atween us now, is a few small political differences – overweighed (at least off duty) by an abiding sense of gratitude for Sir Harold's present enterprise. The Brewery Industry! Why, think of us without it! We'd be a dehydrated nation. And the frogs and the jerries, they could sweep us up like sawdust! Right: now where's this bit o' bricklaying? I've not got me union card, but I dare say we can accommodate any question o' demarcation troubles. Mortar mixed all right, Jack, is it?

1ST MASON. Aye, it's mixed.

BUTTERTHWAITE. What's your consistency?

1ST MASON. Twelve parts fine crushed stone: three parts lime putty: one part Portland cement.

BUTTERTHWAITE. Not bad at all. I like to see good workmanship. Trowel? Right. Any young lass down there want the icing smoothed over her wedding cake? She's only to say the word. I'm ready and willing for t' usual consideration.

He smacks a kiss or two towards the audience.

Nobody? All right. Here we go . . . send it down, David.

The stone is lowered on to the mortar he has spread.

It gives me great pleasure to declare this stone well and truly laid. (*He taps the corners with his trowel.*) Knock, knock, knock and it's done. Any more for any more?

BOOCOCK (*restraining him*). Wait up, Charlie. Steady . . .

All stiffen as the band breaks into the National Anthem. Then the group begins to break up and converse in knots.

LUMBER. Guard of Honour, right turn. To your duties: quick march!

He marches out with the Constables. Citizens disperse.
WIPER *bumps into* BUTTERTHWAITE.

BUTTERTHWAITE. After you, Mr Wiper.
WIPER. After you, Mr Butterthwaite.
BUTTERTHWAITE. Alderman Butterthwaite, *if* you please.

LADY SWEETMAN *and* YOUNG SWEETMAN *enter and talk with* SWEETMAN. F. J., BLOMAX *and* WELLESLEY *also come back on stage, and* BUTTERTHWAITE *sees him.*

Hello, Wellington. Is that you? I think that wor one o' my better efforts. Don't you agree?
BLOMAX. Oh, very good. Very lively, Charlie.
BUTTERTHWAITE. I'll be there at ten sharp, at the usual table.

BUTTERTHWAITE *moves away towards his Labour Councillors.*

BLOMAX. As great Bonaparte wishes . . . What he meant to say was: that this evening at ten o'clock there will be an extraordinary meeting of the working caucus committee of the Labour Party at the east end of the saloon bar of the Victoria and Albert Hotel. Alderman Butterthwaite will be in the chair. And everybody else is to hang upon his words, as is usual: as is dutiful: as is after all only convenient. Does it appear to you strange a professional man like me should hail this clown as Bonaparte? The Napoleon of the North, as we matily describe him up here? Well, professional or not, I am a corrupted individual: for every emperor needs to have his dark occult councillor: if you like, his fixer, his manipulator – me. I do it because I enjoy it. I have also in my time enjoyed the delights of carnality – a less anti-social corruption perhaps, but in my case very often a swollen carbuncle of unexpected peril. You see, I am a doctor. My name is Wellington Blomax. I have not yet been struck off the register, but as you will find, it's been a pretty close thing.

(*He introduces* WELLESLEY *to the audience.*) Here I am confronted by the fruits of my loose studenthood. This poor girl without a mother is my own daughter: Wellesley. She came back home only a day or two ago after a sufficiently long absence. She works for her living and her education (I may say: at my expense) has been regrettably incompetent. Really, we hardly know each other.

WELLESLEY *gives a short laugh. So does he.*

But I conceive it my duty to introduce her at once to the local opportunities and make up for what she's missed.

BUTTERTHWAITE (*on the way out with Labour Councillors*). I think I've told everybody, but in case I missed one out, just confirm it, will you ?

BLOMAX. I'll attend to it, Charlie.

Exit BUTTERTHWAITE, *etc.*

WELLESLEY. Would you say he was one of them ?
BLOMAX. One of what ?
WELLESLEY. The Local Opportunities.
BLOMAX. Oh, my dearie, no. He's on my National Health, but
. . . no, no, no, what *you* want, my sweetheart, is the altogether opposite aspect of this deplorable townscape.

BLOMAX *points to* SWEETMAN.

Now the heavy gentleman over there . . .
WELLESLEY. Who's the young one with him ?
BLOMAX. His son and heir, my sweetheart. Sweetman's Amalgamated Brewery and Corn Products – enormous – luxurious . . .
WELLESLEY. I've already met him, thank you very much. We shared a compartment on the way down from Penrith.

YOUNG SWEETMAN *sees her and comes over.*

YOUNG SWEETMAN. Hello there.

WELLESLEY. Hello.

He leads her away from her father.

YOUNG SWEETMAN. You know, I knew perfectly well we were going to see each other again within less than three days. Now this time you are most definitely going to tell me who you are and what you are doing here and what I have to do to get to know you better . . .

The CONSERVATIVES *group together with* FENG. WELLESLEY *in conversation with* YOUNG SWEETMAN. *A* MAID *brings in a tray of drinks and the group becomes a cocktail party.*

SCENE TWO

Sweetman's House. SWEETMAN, LADY SWEETMAN, YOUNG SWEETMAN, FENG, F. J., TWO LADIES, WELLESLEY, MAID; BLOMAX *still on stage in foreground.*

BLOMAX.
Aha, does she not show a very pretty accomplishment?
A long-neglectful father need not scruple to hide
The trickling down of a tear of pride?

Exit BLOMAX.

SWEETMAN. Yes, Colonel Feng, what you saw and heard today is by no means unusual.

F. J. He does it all the time.

SWEETMAN. Yes. He was born in the workhouse: he conducted and ruined single-handed the General Strike: and he's everybody's Uncle Charlie and will remain so till he dies.

LADY SWEETMAN. Or until he's voted out. I'm quite sure it's not impossible. You talk about him all the time as though he were . . .

SWEETMAN. We are talking, my dear, about the man whose Napoleonic organization of the Socialist party machine . . .

F. J. Particularly in regard to the disposition of ward boundaries . . .

SWEETMAN. Yes, ward boundaries. It's all organized, you see. Overriding majority: organised by gerrymandering, and intended to continue. Such – Colonel Feng – is the lamentable framework into which, you will discover, you will have to accommodate yourself speedily, or else you will be . . .

1ST LADY. What do you think of it, Colonel Feng?

FENG. I have really no opinion, dear lady. I represent the force of law. I can have no opinion of political matters.

SWEETMAN. Yes. You will discover.

2ND LADY. Of course, the people do enjoy his speeches. You do have to laugh at them.

1ST LADY. Laugh at naughty children.

F. J. He rehearses it, of course.

LADY SWEETMAN. But, of course, we have to smack them.

WELLESLEY. Really have to smack? I mean, for providing entertainment? I mean, is the town really so badly misgoverned?

A pause.

YOUNG SWEETMAN. Misgoverned? Oh, it's not exactly misgoverned. It's just the wrong lot are the governors, that's all.

WELLESLEY. You see, if Colonel Feng says 'no politics' and yet he sees the town misgoverned, I mean really misgoverned . . . what do you do then, Colonel?

FENG. I rely, my dear young lady, upon the integrity of the British policeman. We live in an age of overthrown moral standards, and . . .

WELLESLEY. You said that at the ceremony.

FENG. So I did.

WELLESLEY. What about the moral standards of the British policeman? Are his overthrown as well?

LADY SWEETMAN. I suppose really the trouble is, we women, we see the personal side. While all the men all the time are looking for points of principle. But what I so dislike about people like Butterthwaite, they are not only so vulgar themselves but they expect everybody else to live at the same level. I don't see why I should. I cannot forgive them the way they deprived this town of our art gallery. It was a very nice little gallery, Colonel Feng – old masters, quite well spoken of. A genuine Titian, and there were 'Cows in a Field'. They gave it to Cuyp, but I believe it could be a Rembrandt. I have always been something of a connoisseur myself. In a small way, a collector. And so has Sir Harold.

SWEETMAN. Yes, moderns, mostly.

LADY SWEETMAN (*to* WELLESLEY). You must tell me all about yourself, my dear. My boy tells me he met you on a train . . .

SWEETMAN. Who is she?

YOUNG SWEETMAN. I met her the other day. Her father's a doctor.

SWEETMAN. And what does *she* do?

YOUNG SWEETMAN. She works in the forest.

SWEETMAN. Works in the what?

YOUNG SWEETMAN. The Forestry Commission. They plant trees in Westmorland.

SWEETMAN. A doctor, you said. Do I know him?

YOUNG SWEETMAN. I don't know. His name is Blomax.

SWEETMAN. Yes. He's a rogue and the crony of rogues. Did you ever meet her mother? She was as black as your hat.

YOUNG SWEETMAN. I don't believe you.

SWEETMAN. Yes. She was a Maltese. You will discover.

F. J. Is she one of that young crowd of yours at the Copacabana Club?

YOUNG SWEETMAN. Ha, ha. Oh no, not her.

SWEETMAN. The Copacabana? I didn't know you went there? Well, don't you go again. It's a sort of a dinner and dancing establishment, Colonel Feng. Nothing very horrifying.

F. J. Pretty tame compared to London.

SWEETMAN. Yes, and pretty trivial too . . . Of course, Colonel Feng, you might say all forms of pleasuring are pretty trivial when it comes down to it. All it usually comes down to in this town is the bottom of a pint pot—

YOUNG SWEETMAN. The bottom of half a dozen pint pots.

SWEETMAN. Half a dozen? Two dozen. Three dozen. Four. Drink themselves sick.

F. J.
And not uncommonly after licensed hours.

SWEETMAN.
An instructive experiment that you might well try
To sound the ground for your new job, I mean . . .

F. J.
Why don't you – Colonel – send a man or two
To the Victoria and Albert at half past eleven?

SWEETMAN.
Tonight perhaps.

F. J.
Tonight most suitable.

SWEETMAN.
Yes.

FENG.
A public house?

SWEETMAN.
Hotel.

YOUNG SWEETMAN.
Not one
Of ours, of course. A free house. *We* don't go there.

FENG.
You wish to lay an information, do you,
Sir Harold?

SWEETMAN.
No. Emphatically no.

We speak (in passing) of our town folks' pleasure
And – what was it she said – misgovernment ?
Monopoly and party have controlled
This town for thirty years. Consider it
And consider, sir, the grave unlikelihood
That you can live and serve here and yet hold
Upon our politics no opinion, sir.

FENG.

I think, Sir Harold, I discern your working.

SWEETMAN.

Yes . . .

FENG.

Then I will tell you *mine*. I am here
To keep the law. And therefore must begin
By testing at all points the law you keep
Already, and how you keep it. Public houses
Are indeed one point. But only one. And who
Frequent such public houses, or such clubs,
Or hotels if you call them so, or what
Or where – is neither here nor there ! Provided
That the law is kept. And where not kept
I should be glad of relevant information,
Or none at all. I do not know you, sir.
I do not know this people. And I must test
The whole community according to
The rigid statutes and the statutes only.
I can assure you now without vainglory
My testing will be thorough.

SWEETMAN.

Yes.

The MAID *whispers to* LADY SWEETMAN.

LADY SWEETMAN.

Dinner is served. Shall we go in ?
Colonel ?

FENG.
    Delighted, madam. After you.
YOUNG SWEETMAN (*to his father*).
    Are you quite sure he's ours?
SWEETMAN.
    What d'you mean?
    Go in to dinner . . . After you, F. J.
F. J.
    No, no, H. S. I follow after *you* . . .

> *Exeunt.*

SCENE THREE

Saloon bar of the Victoria and Albert.
    Enter BLOMAX *and several drinkers.*
    LANDLORD *behind his bar.*

BLOMAX. Big-hearted Arthur!
1ST DRINKER. No, no, no . . . Of course that horse is going to run . . .
2ND DRINKER. It's going to run at Beverley Races: there's no question about it . . .
3RD DRINKER. It was said very clearly . . .
BLOMAX. Big-hearted Arthur will be a non-starter! The information is confidential, but the oracle has delivered it. Alarm and despondency now spread like wildfire through celebrated Northern turf circles . . . Who's going to fill me?
4TH DRINKER (*handing him a glass*). Here you are, Doctor.
BLOMAX (*looking at him sharply*). Hello, hello, hello, I don't know you. You're not one o' my patients?
4TH DRINKER. Not exactly, no . . . but I dare say I *could* be?
1ST DRINKER. I dare say he *could* be. I'll vouch for him, Doctor.
BLOMAX (*clearing a space on a table, takes a pad of forms out*).

Very well then, so be it. Always carry me blank forms ready.
You see . . . Name, address and previous medical adviser?

4TH DRINKER *whispers in his ear.*

(*Writing.*) Now sign on the line, sir . . . Now then, what's
the trouble? And how can I cure it? A little matter of a
certificate perhaps? Easily arranged . . .

4TH DRINKER *whispers again.*

Aha, you were down with a runny tummy, were you, so you
couldn't possibly have been out burgling? Couldn't you? I
wonder . . . No, it won't do. I steer very clear of courts of
law, my dear sir. If it had to come up anywhere else, I would
do your documents with pleasure . . . but . . .

4TH DRINKER *shoves some money over to him.*

All right, I will consider it. But I'm very very doubtful . . .

GLORIA *enters and comes up to* BLOMAX.

GLORIA. For the sake of old times, can we have a little word?
BLOMAX. Gloria! Good gracious me! We don't expect to find
you these days slumming it in the midst of the town in this
dreary old boozing-ken! Gentlemen, you all know Gloria! –
Get her a drink! – I am surprised, my dear Gloria, that you
can tear yourself away from that expensive establishment of
yours out there on the bypass . . . (*He addresses the audience.*)
. . . known for your information as the Copacabana Club.
And this most elegant and most gorgeous lady – who was for
a space my very close friend – is now the manageress. There
you are: You all know Gloria. What you don't know – I
fancy – is where the money comes from that keeps that club
going. *I* don't know it either.
GLORIA. *I'm* not going to tell you.
BLOMAX. What *are* you going to tell me?
GLORIA. I want professional advice of a rather private nature.

Are you acquainted with Superintendent Wiper of our local police?

BLOMAX. How d'you do, in public. Not much else beyond that.

GLORIA. This isn't for in public. Let's go to the back.

She moves upstage. BLOMAX *is about to follow her when* BUTTERTHWAITE, BOOCOCK *and* LABOUR COUNCILLORS *all come in.*

BLOMAX. Wait a moment, we're interrupted! The processional entrance. They need to have a tune! Charlie, Mr Mayor, how are you? How are you?

BUTTERTHWAITE. We need to have a tune. And some words to it and all. Dr Wellington, oblige.

BLOMAX (*sings*).
When Bonaparte assumed his crown
He put it on himself.
He was sole author of his power
And he piled his private wealth.
He kept his throne with sword and gun,
Dragoon and Cuirassier,
He marched with cannon at either flank
And bayonets in his rear.

BUTTERTHWAITE (*sings*).
But I am not the same as that:
I bow to the public voice.
My best endeavours are bent thereto
As befits the people's choice—

He sees BLOMAX *is going out after* GLORIA.

Hey, what about the rest of it?

BLOMAX. You'll have to do it for yourself. I'm temporarily prevented. (*He joins* GLORIA.)

BUTTERTHWAITE (*shouting after him*). I wish you were temporarily prevented from one or two other activities.

BLOMAX returns and takes BUTTERTHWAITE *aside.*

BLOMAX. Which reminds me. Do you know what won the three-forty?

BUTTERTHWAITE. It did come to my ears. And I should like to know why, when you recommend a horse, it always develops spavins afore it reaches t'starting-gate. I gave you that money to put on for me on what you swore was a dead cert.

BLOMAX. Correction, Charlie. Twice. All you gave me was one of your promises: and as usual you chose to override my considered recommendation in favour of what you were told by some half-cock informant at the Miners' Union offices. I'm no bookie's runner, you know: but even if I was, I'd need to be paid for it.

BUTTERTHWAITE. You can't be paid today. Are you being pressed for t'cash?

BLOMAX. No, not exactly, but . . .

BUTTERTHWAITE. And what'd you expect me to do for you if you were? Burgle t'town hall?

BLOMAX. Why not? You're the great dictator, aren't you?

BUTTERTHWAITE. Get away with you, go on!

> BLOMAX *retires with* GLORIA. BUTTERTHWAITE *and party sit down round a table and the other drinkers move politely away from their vicinity. The* LANDLORD *brings their drinks.*

Barney, you have now seen the new Chief Constable. Both publicly ceremonious and privately confidential over the well-oiled social harmony of the Mayor's parlour. What do you think of him?

BOOCOCK. He's a change from t'last one, isn't he? He's got integrity; he's got energy; he's got a power of command. Of course, there won't be much for him to do.

BUTTERTHWAITE. That's just the trouble, ain't it?

HICKLETON. What do you mean?

BUTTERTHWAITE. A compendium of all the qualities Mr Mayor has just named, if he finds himself idle he looks for a job o' work. What I ask is: where?

BOOCOCK. I could indicate a few places. You remember what he said about overthrown moral standards? Now, you take that new club that's opened up on the bypass. The Coco . . . Capoco . . . the . . . er . . .

BUTTERTHWAITE. The Cocoa-banana?

BOOCOCK. Or whatever it might be. I believe it is described as a nightclub-cum-roadhouse. I'd call it an expense-account brothel.

HOPEFAST. There's no proof of that, is there?

BOOCOCK. There isn't. But in my opinion that licence should never have been issued without a few more searching questions. I've been hearing stories. There's dancing there, you know. And a great deal of it is in the nude.

BUTTERTHWAITE. Who's in the nude?

BOOCOCK. I've been hearing stories. It's come in from London, and it's not what we're used to.

HARDNUTT. Whose money's at back of it?

BOOCOCK. I don't know and I don't care. But young Sweetman and his debutantey riff-raff have been frequenting it pretty frequent. And you're not telling me *their* tastes are all in the nature of an advanced class in metallurgy at the technical college. I have already passed the word to Colonel Feng and I hope he takes a look.

BUTTERTHWAITE. Ah, we don't want to interfere with the pleasures of our gilded youth, Barney. They're an ornament to the town.

BOOCOCK. The late-night traffic accident reports are an ornament to the town and all – by – if I had my way I'd set some o' them gilded youth to a couple 'years down t'pit. But then I never do have my way. So what's the bloody odds?

GLORIA *moves towards the door,* BLOMAX *trotting behind her.*

GLORIA. All right then, I'm off. I'll waste no more time. If you won't do it, you won't.

BLOMAX. I didn't say I wouldn't.

HICKLETON (*watching her*). Oho, ho, ho!

BUTTERTHWAITE (*watching her*). Well now, I'm looking at a very privileged old divorcé indeed.

BLOMAX (*to* GLORIA). I said only what I always say. I'm promising nothing . . .

GLORIA *sweeps out.*

HICKLETON. You know who she is, don't you?

BUTTERTHWAITE. No. Who is she?

HICKLETON. What Barney wor just talking about. She runs the bloody place.

BUTTERTHWAITE. Oh! Dr Blomax, come here!

BLOMAX *obeys him.*

HICKLETON. We're all admiring your taste, lad. May we make so bold as to poke in our noses and ask . . .

BOOCOCK. We don't want to interfere, but . . .

BUTTERTHWAITE. But our attention has been drawn to what we might call the pursuits of your fair lady companion.

BOOCOCK. And I am sure you will agree with me, Doctor, that the immorality in this town has got to be very firmly checked.

BLOMAX. Mr Mayor, all I know of the lady is that she is a patient. She is under the seal of the oath of Hippocrates, which is not the same thing as the French word for hypocrites. I'm sorry, there it is.

BUTTERTHWAITE. Eh dear, we're getting ethical. We *do* stand rebuked. Come on, take a seat. Now, to return to business. We have been discussing the character of our latest public servant. And I regret to inform you our opinions are divided. When that appointment was made, I was flat on me back in the Municipal Hospital with me mortifying gallstones. But if I'd known they'd agreed on *him*, I'd ha' dragged meself up and come down on that Watch Committee and vetoed the whole bang shoot!

BOOCOCK. If you had, you'd ha' been a fool There is not a shadow of reason . . .

BUTTERTHWAITE (*thumping his belly*). I don't need reasons. I *know* it in here!

BLOMAX. I wouldn't go so far as to say you weren't right.

BUTTERTHWAITE. Why? Have you heard summat? Come on, what's Feng been up to?

BLOMAX. Nothing very significant. But I *have* been given the word that tonight he is taking his dinner with His Majesty, Lord Sweetman. Her Ladyship in attendance very gracious over the braised lamb, and innumerable assistance provided by members of the entourage.

BOOCOCK. Well, what's so strange about that? He's entitled to eat his dinners where he wants, I suppose?

BUTTERTHWAITE. I wouldn't be too sure. A Chief Constable is maintained to be a non-political office. If the first thing he does when he comes into a town is to huddle over his grub with a pack of roaring Tories, I claim he wants watching. What you're going to find is an insidious partisan: And if that's the road it turns out, *I'm* not going to dry your eyes for you. Why couldn't you have invited him to dinner yersen?

BOOCOCK. He's welcome any time to tek a sup o'tea wi' me and Mrs Boocock, but . . .

BUTTERTHWAITE. Oh Barney, Barney, Barney, you've no bloody notion, have you? All right, but you'll discover, as somebody might put it . . . Any particular problems due up at t'next Council Sessions?

LANDLORD. Last orders, everybody. Last orders, if you please.

BOOCOCK. I'm sorry to say that it's the same old perennial. The future of the art gallery.

BUTTERTHWAITE. Oh my gracious God.

BOOCOCK. Sweetman wants to make it an issue.

BUTTERTHWAITE. No, look, now look here! I'm sick to bloody death of that art gallery. In 1939 we took it over as an emergency annexe to the Municipal Hospital. There wor no opposition. Since then it's proved its necessity one hundred and ten per cent. Every single meeting of the Hospital Management Committee has confirmed the state of affairs. Dammit, the Chairman is my cousin's brother-in-law. I ought to know. And what about my gallstones? Wellington, bear testimony!

BLOMAX *nods agreement.*

BOOCOCK. Sweetman lays claim we could afford a new hospital and return the art gallery to its original function. What's more, he says he has some pictures of his own he wants to donate.

BUTTERTHWAITE. There is a regular diesel service on the hour every hour into Wakefield and Leeds, and good art galleries in both places. If people want pictures, let them go there. There is no demand for art in this town.

BOOCOCK. It could be an election issue.

BUTTERTHWAITE. Do you seriously imagine the ratepayers are going to stand to be plucked for a new bloody hospital? Godsake, have some common!

BOOCOCK. It ought to be considered, though.

BUTTERTHWAITE. Considered who by?

BOOCOCK. The Ways and Means Committee for a start. I've got it marked down for the agenda on Tuesday.

BUTTERTHWAITE. There's a pair o' Sweetman's pensioners w' seats on that Committee. They could use it to make trouble and hold up other business.

LANDLORD. Time, gentlemen, please.

BOOCOCK. I would like it attended to, Charlie.

BUTTERTHWAITE. All right. I'll attend to it.

LANDLORD (*putting some lights out*). Gennelmen, *if* you please. Closing time, gennelmen. Time if you please!

BOOCOCK. Right. Well, we'd best be off home. Are you coming along?

BUTTERTHWAITE. No. I've got a chap I want to see down the Pontefract Road. I'll see you tomorrow.

BOOCOCK. Goodnight to you, Charlie.

BUTTERTHWAITE. Night night, me old Barney . . .

DRINKERS (*going out*). Night, Mr Mayor . . . Night, Charlie. Night, Frank . . . (*etc.*)

> *The stage empties except for* COUNCILLORS, BUTTER- THWAITE, LANDLORD *and* BLOMAX.

BUTTERTHWAITE. Let's have another round, Frank.

LANDLORD. Wait up a minute. I've got to draw me curtains . . .

BUTTERTHWAITE. Who's on the beat tonight? PC Liversedge?

LANDLORD. Should be by rights.

BUTTERTHWAITE. Grand. We're all clear then.

> *The drinks are brought as they resume their seats round the table.*

Now look here, I'm not having it. If everybody in this Council was to dilly-dally around after Barney Boocock's formalities, nowt'd get done. Nowt. Who have we got here belonging to the Ways and Means? One, two, three. Right. There's enough for a quorum. Alderman Butterthwaite i't'chair, Councillors Hopefast, Hardnutt and Hickleton present in committee – er – Doctor Wellington Blomax, Deputy Secretary. I declare the Committee in session.

HOPEFAST. I move that the minutes of the previous meeting be taken as read.

HARDNUTT. Seconded.

BUTTERTHWAITE. Votes? All right. Passed. So the motion

before this Committee is that the time is not yet ripe for consideration of the reversal of the Municipal Hospital Annexe to its original function.

HICKLETON. Seconded.

BUTTERTHWAITE. Right. Anybody agen it? I should bloody well hope there's nobody agen it . . . All right. Very good. Motion passed, nem con. And our flash Harry Sweetman can wear that in the brim of his Anthony Eden and go to church with it . . .

Enter PC LIVERSEDGE.

LIVERSEDGE. Ha, h'm.

BUTTERTHWAITE. Evening, Liversedge. How are you? Have a pint of ale. It's on the Corporation.

LIVERSEDGE. Are you aware, sir, that it is after permitted hours?

HOPEFAST. Don't talk so daft.

LIVERSEDGE. You'll have to excuse me, Councillor. But I have my duty to perform.

BUTTERTHWAITE. You have your *what*? Look, lad. We're discussing local government business in here. You ought to be aware of that by now. What the hell d'you think you're playing at?

LIVERSEDGE. Alderman, I'm sorry, but it's very particular orders.

BUTTERTHWAITE. Orders. Whose orders?

LIVERSEDGE. There's been summat of a shake-up. You see, it . . .

Enter LUMBER *and another* PC.

LUMBER. Right, Liversedge. Who have you found? Oh! I might have guessed it.

HARDNUTT. Come on then, Sergeant. Where's the handcuffs?

LUMBER. Now, Councillor, you know it's not a matter for

handcuffs. But I *shall* have to ask you gentlemen for your names and addresses.

BUTTERTHWAITE. Oh for Godsake, flatfoot, go and get stuffed! If you don't know who we are, *I'm* not going to bloody tell you! I remember the days in 1926 I'd ha' took twelve o' you bluebottles on wi' nowt but me two boots and a twist o' barbed wire round me pick heft. What were *you* doing then?

LUMBER. When?

BUTTERTHWAITE. The General Strike 1926 I'm talking about! I know what you were doing. You warn't even wetting on your poor mother's apron. You wor nowt but a dirty thought atween your dad and his beer. . . . There's no question this is Feng! Wellington, go round to the station tomorrow and see that slimy Wiper. Find out what's happening and how serious it is. (*To the police.*) Get out o' my road.

BLOMAX (*to the police as he leaves*). Quis custodiot ipses custodias? Good night to the lot of you . . .

    Exeunt

SCENE FOUR

A street.
Enter WELLESLEY *and* YOUNG SWEETMAN.

WELLESLEY. Was I not dressed well enough to suit you?

YOUNG SWEETMAN. You were beautifully dressed.

WELLESLEY. But you say that to all the girls you bring home with you to dinner.

YOUNG SWEETMAN. I don't bring all the girls home.

WELLESLEY. Then why did you bring me? I would much rather you'd taken me out to an expensive restaurant or something.

YOUNG SWEETMAN. There *are* no expensive restaurants.

WELLESLEY. Yes, there are. In Leeds. And what about that club?

YOUNG SWEETMAN. The Copacabana? It's not really the sort of place . . .

WELLESLEY. It's very expensive.

YOUNG SWEETMAN. In any case I had to be at home this evening. Because of the Chief Constable and all the family prestige and so on. And I wasn't going to let you escape from me again like you did at the station. There's another thing, if we bring a girl home round here . . . it means that we want to . . .

WELLESLEY. To present her to the authorities as a future associate? You ought to have told me that before. You could even have proposed before. In a respectable formal fashion. Now it's too late. You tell me I didn't find favour. I wasn't dressed well enough.

YOUNG SWEETMAN. Wellesley, I have said you were beautifully dressed!

WELLESLEY. Describe me, if you please.

YOUNG SWEETMAN. Now, Wellesley, look here . . .

WELLESLEY. Go on, Maurice. Describe me. Let me hear if you still mean it.

BLOMAX *enters. The other two do not notice him.*

YOUNG SWEETMAN.

> As I was lying on my bed
> And my eyelids blue with sleep
> I thought I saw my true love enter,
> Golden and dusty were her feet.
> Her gown of green, it let be seen
> Her shoulders white and brown,
> Her hair was tied in a high tight ribbon
> As sleek as a pool of trout
> And her earlobes like the Connemara Marble
> Moved quietly up and about.

WELLESLEY. As I breathed, I suppose?

YOUNG SWEETMAN. As you breathed, and as you were eating. I mean, that was the impression.

WELLESLEY. Then why can't I go there again?

YOUNG SWEETMAN. Oh, Wellesley, for God's sake . . . I have been trying to explain to you. You should have given me a different name. Your father – *you* ought to know it. For God's sake how could I? They don't tell me all the scandal. He is not persona grata, at my father's or anywhere else.

BLOMAX (*coming forward*). Indeed, and why not?

YOUNG SWEETMAN. Oh, we're overheard. I wasn't talking to you.

BLOMAX. You were talking *about* me. I may very well be a corrupted individual, but let me inform you I am a graduate of Edinburgh University, which is not to be squirted at, and I clap MD to the rear quarters of my name . . . with very high honours. What's the matter with that?

YOUNG SWEETMAN. To put it quite bluntly, sir: You don't have enough money. You're a resident of this town; you don't need me to tell you the sine qua non.

BLOMAX. Ho, the 'gracilis puer perfusus liquidis odoribus sub antro'! Don't you try and blind me with your hic haec hoc, young man! I've heard about *you* . . . and I'm not at all sure you're a fit companion for my beautiful daughter. (*He tries to put his arm round* WELLESLEY, *but she shrugs him off.*) To whom I have a manifest duty, she being in her origins an unfortunate mistake; as was also her dear mother, now – alas – divorced and forgotten, but traumatic in my history.

(*Sings.*)

> I married my wife because I had to
> Diddle di doo: Di doo doo-doo
> My wedding day in the month of May
> The honeymoon in flaming June
> A babe of shame of such ill fame

          All it wants is an honest name
          I married my wife because I had to
          Diddle di doo: di doo doo-doo . . .
Now sir, be off . . . before I ask you your intentions.

YOUNG SWEETMAN. Oh my God . . . Wellesley . . . I . . .

WELLESLEY. I think you'd better go. You're only making things worse.

YOUNG SWEETMAN. All right. But it's not finished.

WELLESLEY. Isn't it?

YOUNG SWEETMAN. No. I mean . . . no, it's not finished . . .

    Exit YOUNG SWEETMAN.

WELLESLEY. Thank you very much. I'm sure it was well intended.

BLOMAX. All I am doing is to pursue my way of life. I put you on to him. It's up to you to hold him. If my reputation is a stumbling-block, I might very well remind you that half of that reputation is caused by what caused *you*. So why don't you go home and wipe off those tears? Go along now, whoops! I've got business in hand . . .

    Exit WELLESLEY (*who has shed no tears*). BLOMAX *addresses the audience.*

Far too much business, as a matter of fact. But the Emperor has commanded: I must follow his behests.

    He leaves the stage to re-enter directly.

SCENE FIVE

The Police headquarters.
Stage divided into inner and outer offices. LUMBER *and the* PCS *occupy the outer office.*

    WIPER *enters the inner office* (*from within*), *takes off his coat,*

sits down, covers his face with a red handkerchief and goes to sleep.
BLOMAX *enters the outer office.*

BLOMAX. Hello, hello, hello, Sergeant Lumber, here we are again. Another day dawns and a lovely day for all.

LUMBER. Is it? I may say I'm extremely surprised to see *you* here, Dr Blomax. I've just been getting out a summons in your name. You've saved me the effort of sending a man round with it. Here you are, take it.

BLOMAX. Thank you very much . . . I'm going back by way of the Town Hall; I'll take the others as well, if you like, and save you some more effort.

LUMBER. Take what others, Dr Blomax? There's only one other – for the landlord of the Victoria and Albert, and it's already been served.

BLOMAX. Ah . . .

LUMBER. You might very well say 'Ah'.

BLOMAX (*gesturing towards the inner door*). Will he see me?

LUMBER. He won't.

BLOMAX. Ah . . . if I was to walk through, would you stop me by force?

LUMBER. I might have a try.

BLOMAX. I'm a stronger man than you are, and I can show you the proof.

He takes a banknote out of his pocket, furtively, taking care that the PCs cannot see it.

LUMBER. Oh no you can't. I wor proper insulted last night and my uniform humiliated. It's not that easy forgotten.

WIPER. Lumber!

LUMBER. Sir?

WIPER. I thought I told you I wasn't to be disturbed!

BLOMAX (*sings*).

        I married my wife because I had to
        Diddle di doo, di doo doo-doo . . .

WIPER *comes to the door.*

WIPER. I've nowt to say to you. I don't know who you are.

BLOMAX (*showing him the summons*). Oh yes, you do, Alfred. Because you've written me a letter. Why, I've got it in my hand. Look.

He slips past into the inner office.

WIPER (*coming in after him*). Sergeant Lumber, will you ask the Doctor to remove himself, please.

BLOMAX. Oh no, no, Alfred. We must look at this strategically.

He shuts the door. LUMBER *and the* PCs *withdraw into their own office.*

WIPER. Well?

BLOMAX. Only two summonses, Alfred . . .

WIPER. How many more did you want?

BLOMAX. Another couple o' pair might not have been inappropriate.

WIPER. They've sent you down here to find out the odds, isn't that so? Well, I can tell you straight now: the odds is black dangerous. And it doesn't please me any more than it does you. You talk about strategy: I've been using *tactics* – at the risk of my career – to save a few faces. I've been compelled to issue that one: and the one for the landlord, as a means of a cover . . . but look how I've worked it. Who do you think's going to be on the bench when you come up afore it?

BLOMAX. I dunno, who is?

WIPER. It *could* be Sir Harold Sweetman, and then you'd be i' t' cart . . . but as it so happens it'll be Alderman Butterthwaite. You're both going to plead guilty. You'll both be let off with a conditional discharge, and no further questions. There you are, tell your pals that, and bring me back their gratitude.

BLOMAX. Oh, very good, Alfred. Very tactical indeed. But it's not quite enough. They want to know in the Town Hall how far this is going and what it portends. In other words, they know your Colonel Feng is a most intrepid pioneer, but who gave him the notion that the best place to demonstrate his sterling British pluck was the Victoria and Albert on Uncle Charlie's Committee night.

WIPER. I don't believe that anybody gave it him.

BLOMAX. Oh yes, they did. We find ourselves here, sir, at a most surgical crux. We probe into it and we cut . . .

WIPER. And all that we discover is a magnificent backbone!

BLOMAX. You mean that he's entirely impartial!

WIPER. I am very sorry to tell you he is – absolutely impartial. A pub is a pub, a man is a drunken fornicator, and an Act of Parliament is divinity!

BLOMAX. Does that make you happy?

WIPER. It does not. For one thing, although I can't call myself an enthusiastic adherent of your horny-handed gang of trade-union oligarchs, at least for some years I have managed to retain a reasonably comfortable relationship with them. That is to say, I never interfered with their evening arrangements, and they never interfered with me.

BLOMAX. Until in walked the backbone . . . eh?

(*He sings.*)

> There came a ramrod vertebrae
> And its name was Colonel Feng.
> It pointed neither left nor right
> But strictly in between,
> And like a rattling bren gun, sir,
> This song he used to sing,
> That he cared for nobody, no, not he,
> And nobody cared for him!

WIPER. Do you have to do that in here?

BLOMAX. Of course, me dear Alfred, the comfort of your relationship has not been entirely confined to the trade-union oligarchs, has it ? The word 'fornicator' was significant. What about the Copacabana Club ?

WIPER. I do not understand you.

BLOMAX. No ? If you were an honest law-man, you'd have closed that libidinous knocking-shop a long long time ago. Instead of which you've been paid to let it wriggle on. And who have you been paid by ? The manageress. And how has she paid you ? In kind, my dear Alfred. And very likely in cash. Though maybe not her own cash. It would be nice to know whose ? I'm going to do it again, same tune, different words:

(*He sings.*)

> Big Gloria is a gorgeous girl
> And keeps many more employed
> Whose gorgeous curves for gorgeous money
> Are frequently enjoyed,
> And where and how that money goes
> Is fruitless to inquire,
> For bare and fruitless ever must be
> The fruits of man's desire.

WIPER. *Don't* start on a third stanza.

BLOMAX. You see, our Gloria herself's a patient of mine. She came to me last night for an abortion. *Your abortion*, Alfred . . . If she'd read her calendar correctly. But not being unaware of me medical ethics, I refused her request . . . at least for the time being. I never act precipitately. I always prefer to know just how it all sets up.

WIPER. I'll tell you how it all sets up. I'm a married man!

BLOMAX. Oh yes, I know that . . .

WIPER. And by God, why couldn't the stupid strumpet keep her purple mouth shut!

BLOMAX. Gloria and I are very old friends. And let me inform you, Alfred, she feels badly done to. However, however, keep your spirits hearty. It's not at all a bad thing I should know about all this, because I fancy I can help you.

LUMBER (*looking in briefly*). Excuse me, sir. You said to warn you, it's nearly ten to twelve.

He withdraws again.

WIPER. What! Oh, good heavens, get out of here quick! I'm expecting the Chief Constable at dead on the hour. If he should find you . . .

BLOMAX. No, no, no. Wait, Alfred. You and I are comfortable men, and we don't want to be disrupted. But if Colonel Feng is as impartial as you make out, and the Victoria and Albert was raided last night, not to embarrass the Labour Party, but out of pure zeal for good order: then he's not going to stop at embarrassing his own police force, nor yet the good people who pay for your inactivity. He's going to get you caught, and Gloria caught, and what's more her mysterious backers – who I'll bet are *not* disciples of Karl Marx or Keir Hardie.

WIPER. Aye, very likely. But I've not got time now. Will you please go, before we get trapped!

BLOMAX. But supposing – now listen, I am strategical – supposing Charlie Butterthwaite was to come to believe that Feng is *not* impartial, but a creature of Sweetman's, that he sent your lads to the pub to stir a political stink, then Charlie and his comrades are going to set right about and commence their *own* stirring. There will really be a stink, Feng will be sacked, or else forced to resign, and all disruption will be concluded before it touches *you*.

WIPER. It's a point, it's a point, I'll grant you it's a point . . . but will you please . . .

BLOMAX. It's a point well worth making . . .

VOICE (*off*). Ten-shun!

FENG (*off*). Good morning. Carry on, if you please.

LUMBER. Oh my Lord, he's here. Sir, sir, he's here!

FENG *enters the outer office.*

FENG. Good morning, Sergeant. Carry on. Superintendent in?

LUMBER. Oh yessir, he's in, but . . .

FENG *passes through into the inner office.*

WIPER. Good morning, sir.

FENG. Good morning, Superintendent. I'm sorry if I'm a little early. Carry on, if you please.

WIPER. The gentleman's just going, sir.

BLOMAX (*singing to himself*).

> A babe of shame of such ill fame
> All it wants is an honest name
> Diddle di doo, di doo doo-doo . . .

He tips his hat to FENG *and goes out through the outer office.*

FENG. Who the devil's that?

WIPER. Dr Wellington Blomax.

FENG. Who?

WIPER. Dr Wellington Blomax, sir . . . A very brilliant practitioner, I believe . . . but of late years perhaps . . . er, h'm, he sometimes does our medical work for us.

FENG. Really?

WIPER. Only occasionally, of course, when the regular man's away . . .

FENG. Superintendent, what steps are you taking to control the growth of organized vice in the borough.

WIPER. Fortunately very few, sir . . . I mean there are very few to take . . . We closed down a show at the Theatre Royal last year, the odd naughty girl still tries to advertise in the newsagent's windows, but we keep a close check. By and large, it's a clean community. The North of England, you know, the old puritanical traditions . . .

FENG. Good. I have a few notions of my own that it might be as well to look into, one of these days . . . quite soon, in fact. Yes. What about next Monday?

WIPER. Next Monday, sir? What . . . ?

FENG. Yes. Monday night. Send two or three plain clothes men to that place they call the Copacabana and find out what goes on . . . Any results of interest from your pub crawl, by the way?

WIPER. Nothing of importance, sir, no . . . we've issued a couple of summonses . . . it is as well, however, to keep people reminded?

FENG. It most certainly is, Superintendent. I know no attitude more corrupting to an efficient police force than that of complacency. I detect certain traces of it in your conversation; extirpate them, sir, extirpate them root and branch.

Exit FENG *through* WIPER's *inner door.*

WIPER. It can't be done, there's no time . . . besides, I don't trust that Doctor. I mean, I ask you, would *you*? I shall have to *work* it on Monday. I shall have to work it the old way – that means by forewarning them – and it's never a safe way. I don't know what . . .

FENG (*within*). Superintendent?

WIPER. Sir?

FENG (*within*). Will you bring me the file upon last year's crimes of violence, please?

WIPER. Sir, right away . . .

FENG (*within*). *And* the year before that, Superintendent, if you please . . .

Exeunt

SCENE SIX

BLOMAX's *surgery.*

Enter BLOMAX *and* GLORIA.

BLOMAX (*to audience*). I see very little reason why I should help

Alfred Wiper out of his self-created midden. Except my permanent necessity to have at least *one* copper bound to me by an obligation. And besides: I'm fond of Gloria.

(*He sings*):

The days they have been in the green of my garden
When between us was neither a 'beg your pardon'
Nor a 'stop it', nor 'give over': but 'here I am, here',
'Oh my dove and my dear', 'so close and so near'.
The days they have been, without forethought nor fear.

I'm sorry to keep you waiting, but I thought it'd be better to leave it till all the other patients were finished with. Tact, you know, discretion . . .

He examines her, cursorily, while talking.

GLORIA. Well, have you changed your mind? Are you going to arrange it then?

BLOMAX. Oh dear me, no. With this unprecedented Feng, a-prowling round the tent of Midian, illegal operations are very definitely *out*.

GLORIA. I see.

BLOMAX. Now look here, Gloria. Tell me truly. Who wants it? You or Wiper?

GLORIA. I thought you would ha' realized. I'm in a difficult position. I hold this job on a very tight contract and one of the clauses states that I must remain a woman of good reputation.

BLOMAX. Good reputation, in a joint like yours?

GLORIA. Of course. It's a capital investment. It's got to be safeguarded.

BLOMAX. Any more dizzy spells, by the way? Little vomitings? Any o' that?

GLORIA. No.

BLOMAX. Good girl, if you have a recurrence, take two o' these in water . . . (*He gives her some pills.*) But I just wish you could tell me whose capital it is.

GLORIA. Why?

BLOMAX. Because I think I ought to know. I need full possession of the facts. I'm trying to organize a political embrangle-
ment with the principal motive of keeping you out of jail. I
tell you, Feng's prowling! The father of the son is a somewhat haunted Superintendent just at present, and he's afraid
that he may not be able to give you value for your money for
very much longer. He and I between us will do our level best
to keep the flat feet of the law from pulverizing your terrazzo.
But if we can't work it . . . be ready, and be warned.

GLORIA. You mean, I suppose, he'll have to raid the club.

BLOMAX. Something after that fashion. But no doubt he'll give
you notice. All I say is: be ready.

GLORIA. Principal motive, eh? Keep me out of jail? Oh no,
come clean. What is it you're after?

BLOMAX. After? But I *told* you—

GLORIA. I've known you too long. You *enjoy* your embrangle-
ments, don't you. You set them up on purpose. Just like with
Charlie Butterthwaite and all them bets you let him lose, but
you wouldn't dream of foreclosing. So long as all your friends
are still standing under obligations to you, you've got something to live for . . . I don't want this baby. All right. What's
to happen?

BLOMAX. What indeed? Oh dearie me, what indeed, indeed . . .

> It is not alone my friends
> Who stand under an obligation,
> I too have a duty, Gloria,
> In view of our past relation.
> You wish me to preserve it,
> And I will: your reputation:
> It runs tick-tock, tick-tock,
> At the core of my cogitation.

It's only a matter of days now, I have to go to Beverley to the
races. Why don't you come with me?

GLORIA. I wouldn't be seen dead.

BLOMAX. At least as far as Doncaster. I can fix it up at the Office there. I know a man in the Office . . .

GLORIA. What Office?

BLOMAX. In Doncaster. You'll find out. Oh dearie me, what a curious prescription. But legal, I think it's legal . . . Come on, cheery-up . . . and the corners of your mouth, dear, let them lift, let them lift!

He breaks into a song and forces her to dance with him. She does so unwillingly at first, but then laughs and they are gay.

> I look to the left
> And I look to the right
> I'm a dirty old devil
> Alone in the notions
>
> Of politics and progress
> And high-minded soaring
> With a little bit to drink
> And a slice of good hope
>
> For my patients
> And a smile and bright word
> And don't you go thinking
> You can call me a tortoise
>
> And a dormouse
> And a ostrich in sand
> If it ever gets too hot
> I can pull out my hand
> I can pull out my hand
> I can pull out my hand . . .

Exeunt

SCENE SEVEN

A room in the Town Hall.

LEFTWICH *enters with a loaded tea trolley and starts arranging cups and saucers.* BLOMAX *enters from the side opposite his last exit, carrying a black bag.*

BLOMAX. Good afternoon, Constable Leftwich retired.

LEFTWICH. Afternoon, Doctor.

BLOMAX. The Town Hall seems strangely empty. Is it not three o'clock yet?

LEFTWICH. Five minutes after. Town Planning Committee's in session today. As you know, His Worship takes a very close interest there, and he never were the swiftest to elucidate a technical agenda.

BLOMAX. Aye . . . How's his leg?

LEFTWICH. Nay . . .

BLOMAX. I thought so. I've brought the doings. (*He lays his bag on the trolley.*) What about Uncle Charlie? Is he at the Town Planning?

LEFTWICH. He isn't. He's down at t'Rates Office. Creating with the clerks. One of the accountants discovered a discrepancy and there's a fair foaming fury going on about it, I can tell you.

BLOMAX. That could be very timely. I'll nip down and intercept him before he cools off.

He is about to go out when he is prevented by the entrance of MRS BOOCOCK. *He makes a leg.*

Good afternoon, Madam Mayoress. Once again the sun rises upon our matutinal gloom and fog, and once again in your presence . . .

MRS BOOCOCK. Good afternoon, Dr Blomax. Herbert, where's the Mayor? Is he still wi' t'Town Planning?

Exit BLOMAX *disappointed.*

LEFTWICH. They should be out for a breather any time now.

MRS BOOCOCK. They'd better be. They've been stuck wi' that traffic roundabout for the best part of two months.

LEFTWICH. Here they are, they're coming. . .

Enter BOOCOCK *and* LABOUR COUNCILLORS. *They sit down, exhausted, to their tea.*

BOOCOCK. Ah . . . hello, Sarah love. How are you? Well, at last we look like coming to some sort of conclusion. But the amount o' vested interest involved in this one item . . . Oh, I do wish Charlie wor sitting in on this. *He'd* sort us out all right. What's happened to him today?

LEFTWICH. Rates Office.

BOOCOCK. Oh, that . . .

HARDNUTT. What's he got to do wi' t'Rates Office, for God-sake? It's none o' his department. He can't keep his nose out, can he?

HOPEFAST. I thought we paid a permanent staff to deal with all that.

BOOCOCK. The permanent staff are responsible to the democratic representatives.

HOPEFAST. All right, Barney, we know. But some of them representatives sometimes seem to forget that they bloody well *are* democratic.

HICKLETON. I don't think we should begrudge him his little investigations. He's only cooking up the books for his summer holidays, I dare say.

BOOCOCK. He's *what*?

HICKLETON. Just a joke . . .

BOOCOCK. Well, I don't call it funny. That's the sort of humour, fellow Councillor, that gets reported out of walls. Remember there's men in this town . . . aye, and in this building . . . if we give them so much as one crook of a

finger they will turn it back on to us like a bloody harpoon.
And that's not what we're chosen for.

> I will not have it dreamed or thought
> Or even in a whisper told
> That any man of our good men
> Can wear the shameful label:
> 'Bought and Sold'.
> We're up here to show the Tories
> How honest men can rule.
> We've a built a playground for the little children
> And a comprehensive school.
> We lead the whole West Riding
> In our public schemes of housing,
> And for the drainage of the town,
> In pre-stressed concrete firm and strong
> That not an H-bomb can ding down,
> The Borough Engineer's contrived
> A revolutionary outfall:
> And add to that we've built
> This splendid new Town Hall.

He sits down in pain.

> It comes a rugged reflection
> To a rude old man like me
> Who's had no ease to his efforts
> Nor helpful education:
> That in the hour of his honour
> And the heaping of red robes
> And gold chains of his glory
> He sets up a strong staircase
> For to stride up in his pride:
> And reaches nowt but rheumatics
> Nosing theirselves northward
> From his knee to his ribcage!

MRS BOOCOCK. He's often short of money. I've heard that for a fact.

BOOCOCK. We're all often short.

MRS BOOCOCK. Oh no, not *you*. Economically regulated, aye, but you can't say I keep you short.

BOOCOCK. That's not to the purpose. We're talking about Charlie.

MRS BOOCOCK. Aye, the famous nine-times Mayor . . . or are you sure it isn't ten?

BOOCOCK. I am the Mayor, Sarah.

MRS BOOCOCK. You wear the chain.

BOOCOCK. I hold the office!

MRS BOOCOCK. The office of what? He's selected you this season to play the centre-forward in his own private football team, but don't you imagine that gives you any control over fixture-lists, transfer-fees, or owt else o' t'manager's business!

BOOCOCK. My God, she's never been to a football match in her life.

MRS BOOCOCK. All right and I haven't. They call me Madam Mayoress and I belong in t'kitchen to mash you your tea and fry up your bacon, but happen I might wonder who really owns the belly where it lodges on its road. That's all, I say no more . . .

Enter BUTTERTHWAITE *and* BLOMAX.

BUTTERTHWAITE. I *knew* it. I knew it in here! (*He thumps his belly.*) The predictable result is this of not consulting *me*! My gallstones weren't that bad, I could ha' . . .

BLOMAX. Alfred Wiper said to me . . .

BUTTERTHWAITE. Don't you talk to me about Wiper. There's only one thing fit to be wiped off by that wedge o' greasy gammon and that's his own fat clarted . . . ha, h'm, watch our language . . .

MRS BOOCOCK. Gammon, bacon, or ham: it's time it were took off its hook. It's oversmoked and downright nasty.

    Exit MRS BOOCOCK.

BUTTERTHWAITE. Have you heard what Wellington said, Barney?

BOOCOCK. No, I have not.

BUTTERTHWAITE. That business last night at the Victoria and Albert were a well-planned put-up job organized by Sweetman, for the discredit of Labour. And if it warn't for the degenerate meanderings of Superintendent Alfred Wiper, they'd ha' succeeded and all!

BOOCOCK. It sounds highly unlikely to me. Colonel Feng's only been here for nigh on . . .

BUTTERTHWAITE. What the hell does it matter how long he's been here! All that we're concerned with now is how soon he gets out!

    The COUNCILLORS *suck their teeth and look doubtful.*

BOOCOCK. You know perfectly well, Charlie Butterthwaite, that you were all boozing after hours. If you got yourselves into trouble you've only yourselves to thank. I will not have aspersions cast upon an unproven public servant. He were doing nowt more nor demonstrating his efficiency, and . . .

BUTTERTHWAITE. Barney, he was striking directly at *me*. It was not only political, it was bloody well personal. And I want him done with!

BOOCOCK. I will not discuss it further. Will you take a look at my leg, Doctor; it's been acting up again.

    BLOMAX *kneels and examines the leg.*

BUTTERTHWAITE. Barney, I don't think you quite understand the realities at issue. In our party and our principles, upon which we stand four-square – do we or don't we?—

COUNCILLORS. We do.

BUTTERTHWAITE. – we are confronted with a crisis upon a national scale. Is Labour, or is Labour not, to find a triumphant resurgence ? I hope so. So do you.

BLOMAX. Quite a normal stiffening, I think. I'll send some more embrocation.

BUTTERTHWAITE. But no effort in Westminster is worth a damn thing by itself without a sound rammed foundation in the provincial localities. And as far as this locality is concerned if we permit the Tories to fix our police force, we're on t'first road in to mucky marsh, and your old Uncle Charlie knows it. Am I right, fellow Councillors ?

COUNCILLORS. Aye . . . I dare say . . . I wouldn't dispute it. . . etc.

BUTTERTHWAITE. Mr Mayor, am I right ?

BOOCOCK. It may well be as you say. But if we sack a Chief Constable on inadequate grounds the Home Secretary can withdraw the Government grant from the finances of our Watch Committee. And then who's going to pay for keeping the pavements safe from cosh-boys ? You ? Out of *your* winnings ? Don't make me laugh. We'd best get back to Committee. Doctor, would you mind just giving me an arm as we walk down the corridor; it's not quite eased off yet. Come on, you'll be late.

Exit BOOCOCK *with* BLOMAX. *The* COUNCILLORS *move to follow him.*

BUTTERTHWAITE. If there is a police traffic officer giving advice on that roundabout, just you treat him distant. I want them to know that I know what I know.

COUNCILLORS. Aye . . . Well . . . we'll see how it turns out . . . etc.

Exeunt COUNCILLORS.

BUTTERTHWAITE. Upon inadequate grounds. All right. Make 'em adequate . . . Lend me ten bob, will you ?

LEFTWICH. What, me? Are you mad?

BUTTERTHWAITE. Constable Leftwich, it's a generation or two since you last trod the beat, but nevertheless you are wearing the uniform. Declare yourself, Leftwich! Commit your allegiance! (*He offers* LEFTWICH *a pocket flask.*)

LEFTWICH. Commit it to what?

BUTTERTHWAITE. To the Council of this town in democracy assembled or else – and I shan't take it kindly if you choose the alternative – to the oppressive bonds and authoritarian regiment of a crypto-fascist police organization! Which?

LEFTWICH. Do I have to choose either?

BUTTERTHWAITE. You do, lad, you do. Because as from this moment a state of formal war exists. Come on, now. Commit yourself.

LEFTWICH (*drinking*). I know where my bread's buttered. It's buttered in *here* . . .

BUTTERTHWAITE *takes the bottle and drinks.*

BUTTERTHWAITE. Barney won't play, and this one's too important for fiddling it behind his back. So we can't get Feng directly. What we're going to do is to employ his own tactics. Discredit him by discrediting the behaviour of his troops.

LEFTWICH. Now just you be careful. Why not leave it settle for a little while longer?

BUTTERTHWAITE. I have been struck at! Directly! In person! Herbert, I want some secrets. Who pays the top bogeys how much for keeping quiet about what?

LEFTWICH. I couldn't really say. It used to be the tarts, but since the new Act come in I've lost all me locations in *that* corner o' wickedness.

BUTTERTHWAITE. I want summat deeper. But I think we're on t'right lines . . .

LEFTWICH. Copacabana?

BUTTERTHWAITE. Naked dancing? . . . Maybe . . . but just

how rude is it? And what evidence is there that the police are conniving at it?

LEFTWICH. As far as I know there's none. Except that big Gloria's been to bed with Alfred Wiper.

BUTTERTHWAITE. Who told you that!

LEFTWICH. My brother-in-law's a window-cleaner, and he looks at what he sees.

BUTTERTHWAITE. I suppose he didn't look far enough to find out where t'money comes from . . . I mean, that club's new builded, it must ha' cost a lot o' brickwork.

LEFTWICH. Who were t'contractors? 'Durable Construction', warn't it?

BUTTERTHWAITE. Aye . . . now they also put up a new malt-house for Harry Sweetman two year sin'. It proves bloody little, but we *are* on t'right lines . . . I think it's high time I betrayed the working classes, don't you? And patronized an entertainment that is normally above my means. (*He consults his diary.*) I've nowt on next Monday. What about Monday? All right then, write it down, the Copacabana, Monday. And we'll see what shape of others have got nowt on on that evening. Ha, ha. You watch me conquer yet again where few will follow and none will praise me till I do it, and then they'll all fall on their knees!

He sings, with LEFTWICH *joining in the refrain.*

O Boney came from Corsica, oh hi oh,
He conquered the Peninsula, John Franzwo.
He went and beat the Prooshians, oh hi oh,
And then he beat the Rooshians, John Franzwo.
Boney was a General, oh hi oh,
And then he was Imperial, John Franzwo.
Boney was a warrior, oh hi oh,
Begod he was no tarrier, John Franzwo.

And so on, dancing round in a circle, drinking their whisky, then exeunt.

SCENE EIGHT

Outside the Copacabana Club.
  Night.
  Enter BUTTERTHWAITE *and Labour Councillors.*

BUTTERTHWAITE. A preliminary reekin-ayssance. Who'll be
  the first to enter the portals of iniquity and see how the other
  half lusts?
HOPEFAST. I expect we'll have to be members.
HARDNUTT. It'll cost us at least a quid apiece, you know.
BUTTERTHWAITE. Out of the party funds, lad. It's a dele-
  gated investigation, this. And I'll answer to the secretary if
  there's any questions asked . . . Lend me five bob, will you?
  We'll have to buy a beer if we're going to look natural. Come
  on, lad, come on! Who paid for the taxi from the Victoria
  and Albert?

  HARDNUTT *gives him the money.*

Right, we'll go in.

  They approach the entrance and the DOORMAN *appears.*

DOORMAN. Evening, gentlemen. Members?
BUTTERTHWAITE. We're not, but we can be. What does it
  cost?
DOORMAN. Eighty-five shillings renewable annually. Member-
  ship, however, does not take effect till twenty-four hours
  after payment of first subscription.
BUTTERTHWAITE. You mean we can't get in here while tomorrow night! Why, we might all be blown up first thing i'
  t'morning! My lad, at this very moment the generals of the
  Western world are stooping over t'map tables, the mill-wheel
  of our lifetime is whirling under spate! . . . Now come off
  it, sonny Jack. You know damn well if we'd just arrived in

town on a one-day business conference you'd have opened
up directly.

DOORMAN. Not unless you had a sponsor, I'm afraid, sir . . .

> BUTTERTHWAITE *signals to* HARDNUTT, *who fiddles with
> his wallet.*

But it's not at all impossible that something could be
managed . . . Just one moment, if you please . . . (*He dis-
appears inside.*)

BUTTERTHWAITE. See what I mean? They're breaking the
law already. Note the time.

> *The* DOORMAN *reappears.*

DOORMAN. You're fortunate, sir. A lady inside has offered to
be your sponsor. So if you'll just sign the book . . .

> HARDNUTT *passes money to* BUTTERTHWAITE, *who
> passes over tip.*

Thank you very much, sir, indeed, sir, very much . . . Now,
eighty-five shillings multiplied by four, exactly seventeen
pounds . . . and entrance fee five shillings each makes
eighteen pounds precisely . . .

> HARDNUTT *pays him.*

Thank you, gentlemen. Straight forward if you please . . .
Thank you very much.

> *They enter the club*

SCENE NINE

Inside the Copacabana Club.
  *Not many customers at tables. Waitresses in brief versions of
Flamenco skirts. A few hostesses in evening gowns. Latin American
music. A pseudo-Spanish dance-routine taking place on the small
stage.* YOUNG SWEETMAN (*drunk*) *at a table with a hostess.*

BUTTERTHWAITE *and* COUNCILLORS *advance into the room. They are shown to a table.*

BUTTERTHWAITE. We'll have a Guinness and a double Scotch to go with it.

WAITRESS. We don't serve Guinness, I'm afraid, sir.

BUTTERTHWAITE. You don't? Then you ought to. It'd put a bit o' blood under that nice white hide o' yourn, lass. Heh heh. What *do* you serve?

WAITRESS. Certainly whisky.

BUTTERTHWAITE. That's a bit o' good tidings, any road.

WAITRESS. But I'm afraid there's no drinks allowed without something to eat.

HARDNUTT. We don't want nowt to eat. We had us suppers already.

WAITRESS. It doesn't need more than a sandwich, you know.

HOPEFAST. All right then, four sandwiches.

HICKLETON. We don't have to have a sandwich every time we refill, do we? It's too much like hard work.

WAITRESS. Not unless you want to.

BUTTERTHWAITE. All right. And look sharp, love, won't you? We're evaporating in this heat. (WAITRESS *leaves them.*) Place seems a bit empty. They can hardly make it pay at this rate of attendance, can they?

HARDNUTT. I dare say the fancy don't come in while after midnight.

BUTTERTHWAITE. Aye, very likely.

HICKLETON (*watching a hostess*). Eh, do you reckon *she's* one on 'em?

BUTTERTHWAITE. I'd not be surprised . . . Hey up, she's coming over.

HOSTESS *approaches them.*

HOPEFAST. Now then, Charlie, watch it. We're disinterested observers.

BUTTERTHWAITE. Disinterested bloody slag-ladles. We're

full members of this joint and we're going to take advantage
. . . Go on, love, have a chair. Get the weight off your thigh-
bones ?

She sits down at their table.

HOSTESS. I don't mind if I do.

BUTTERTHWAITE. What are you drinking ?

HOSTESS. I'd like a tomato juice if you please, Alderman.

BUTTERTHWAITE. Eh, she knows who I am ! There's some in
this town pay proper respect where it ought to be paid. Take
a bit o' note, you lot . . . but you're wanting summat
warmer nor tomato juice . . . surely ? Put a bit o' blood
under that nice white hide, you know ? Go on, love . . . have
a glass o' gin.

HOSTESS. Call it a Babycham. I've got work to do.

She makes a signal to the WAITRESS.

BUTTERTHWAITE. Ho ho, have you, ducky, have you ? That's
what I like to hear, the craftsmanship approach, very good,
eh ? Ho ho, work to do . . .

HICKLETON (*watching the dancers, who are varying their
routine*). Eh, Charlie, what about that ?

BUTTERTHWAITE *makes a lecherous noise.*

What do you think, is she going to get 'em all ripped off ?

YOUNG SWEETMAN (*lurching towards them*). What do *you*
think, Councillor ? Wouldn't you like to have a go at her
yourself, eh ?

YOUNG SWEETMAN'S HOSTESS (*restraining him*). Come on,
love, behave.

YOUNG SWEETMAN. Why shouldn't I behave ? I represent
the standards of civilization in this paleo-paleo-paleolithicalo-
lithealithic community. I've had an education.

He subsides into his HOSTESS's *lap.*

BUTTERTHWAITE. My God, you have an' all . . . I imagine, though, we have to wait while end of the evening for t'right spice o' t'show.

HOSTESS. Not tonight you don't.

HOPEFAST. Not? Why not?

HOSTESS. Haven't you heard? There's going to be a raid.

BUTTERTHWAITE. A raid? You don't mean the police?

HOSTESS. That's right.

HARDNUTT. Oh my Lord, no . . .

HOPEFAST. I say, Charlie, that's gone and torn it, hasn't it?

BUTTERTHWAITE. Has it? I'm not sure . . . How do you know there's going to be a raid?.

HOSTESS. I don't know exactly. The warning just came. Gloria said she was passing it round all the members who might not want their names in the paper. Just in case something was to go wrong, you know. But you see, we were told that there'd be no danger before midnight, so there's nothing really to worry about. We're having all the popular routines now, and after twelve o'clock there'll be nothing but ordinary vocal numbers and dancing to the band and all that. We'd hoped the place would be as full as usual but a bit earlier on, but it looks like they all took fright, doesn't it?

BUTTERTHWAITE. They'd take fright in this town if a centipede ran ower t'road. Get their names i' t'papers! They think it's worse nor doing murder! Ah well, we won't worry. We're getting some o' what we paid for. We can allus come again.

HARDNUTT (*who has been given the bill*). Can we, by God? Take a look at this!

BUTTERTHWAITE. And they call this a sandwich! It's not even got a top on. (*As the* WAITRESS *is going away*.) Hey up, love! We want a Babycham for t'young lady.

HOSTESS. It's all right, she's brought it.

BUTTERTHWAITE. But I never ordered it yet.

HOSTESS. Oh, just the telegraph . . .

HARDNUTT. Damned expensive telegraph . . . fifteen and six for one Babycham, Charlie!

BUTTERTHWAITE (*watching the dance*). Shut up, lad, I'm watching summat. Use a bit of aesthetic appreciation, or else get off home. I'm here to enjoy meself. (*He cuddles the* HOSTESS.) Eh, what, me little sweetheart? Every man's entitled to his own Dolce Vita, isn't that the truth?

HOSTESS. Aye, lad, it's the truth.

BUTTERTHWAITE (*becoming uproarious*). It's the buttock-naked truth! (*He shouts to the performers, who are near the end of the act.*) Go on, tear it off, I want to see the lot!

Blackout. Lights come up. The Club stage is now empty. GLORIA *is standing beside* BUTTERTHWAITE.

GLORIA. Control yourself, Alderman, this isn't the cattle market . . . Can I join you in a whisky? Cost price for the Corporation. (*She waves to the* WAITRESS, *then points to the bill.*) Don't you pay that. You're honoured guests tonight. (*To the* HOSTESS.) Marlene, you ought to ha' warned me. I warn't to expect we'd be entertaining royalty. As a matter of fact, we warn't to expect that the royalty would be likely to find this a congenial establishment. We tend to cater for what you might call the . . .

BUTTERTHWAITE. The acquisitive and the affluent. Ah, the caterpillars o' the boss class. *I* know, I've said it all. But between what we say and what we find congenial . . .

HOPEFAST. You see, we did damn well at Beverley Races this afternoon.

HICKLETON. Did we?

BUTTERTHWAITE. We did. We made a killing. And now we're out to find ourselves some carnal satisfaction.

GLORIA. So I hope we can provide it for you. Though it's forced to be a bit curtailed tonight.

BUTTERTHWAITE. Aye, aye, she's explained already. (*Four dancing girls, one pair dressed in balloons, the other pair in little bells, appear on the club stage. Nude tableau behind. After a short dance on stage they come down among the tables.*) Hello, hello, hello, what do we do wi' these?

DANCERS. Poppety pop, pop a balloon . . . ring a ding, ding, ring a little bell.

Audience participation.

BUTTERTHWAITE. Pop.

HICKLETON. Pop.

BUTTERTHWAITE. Ding-a-ding.

HICKLETON. Ding-a-ding . . . etc.

An electric bell suddenly rings loudly. The DOORMAN *comes in shouting 'Twelve o'clock Midnight'. The Dancing girls hurry off. Tableau closes.* BUTTERTHWAITE *and the* COUNCILLORS *are left in the middle of the floor. The band starts to play 'The Blue Danube'.* YOUNG SWEETMAN *is three parts insensible and his* HOSTESS *tries in vain to get him to move.*

GLORIA. Won't you dance, then, Alderman? (*She begins to waltz with him, and other couples follow suit.*)

BUTTERTHWAITE. Me dance . . . ho ho, dance. *I'll* give you a dance! (*To band.*) Quicken it up, lads; can't you see we're leaving you behind! (*Music changes to a Tango.*) That's a bit more like it! *One* two three four, *one* two three four, etc . . .

LUMBER and a PC (*in plain clothes*) *enter and sit down at a table. The dancing fades away.* BUTTERTHWAITE *points at them and leers.*

If you ever walk down our street
You will see a right pretty seet,
All the policemen four five six
A-knocking on the doors with big black sticks!

LUMBER. Do you think we could have half a pint of bitter beer apiece, please, miss?

WAITRESS. Oh no, I'm afraid not, you see it's after hours.

LUMBER. Yes, of course, it is, isn't it?

BUTTERTHWAITE. Go on, you give it to him. As a present, on the house! He's an agent provocative, but so long as it's clearly understood all round no harm need be done! Isn't that so, Sarn't Lumber?

LUMBER. I think we'll have a cup of coffee. And it wouldn't be a bad idea if certain other gentlemen present were introduced to that excellent drink.

> BUTTERTHWAITE *laughs.* YOUNG SWEETMAN *rises unsteadily, and tries to walk to the door. He staggers into* WIPER, *who has just come in, and who ignores him.*

WIPER. I'm sure we would all be glad to share the joke, Alderman.

BUTTERTHWAITE. And why not indeed? Would you call it a dirty joke? Pornographic? Indecent?

WIPER. I don't think so. Why should I?

BUTTERTHWAITE. Then what are you doing here? You tell me that.

WIPER. I am acting upon an information that the entertainment provided at these premises is of a nature liable to cause offence by reason of obscenity.

GLORIA. And is it?

WIPER. Sergeant?

LUMBER. Upon our arrival here, sir, dancing was in progress in a normal fashion. Men strictly dancing with women without undue proximity. There was no display of nakedness nor other indecent exhibition.

GLORIA. And the licensing laws, Sergeant?

LUMBER. Were being properly observed. Ḥa h'm.

> YOUNG SWEETMAN *finally effects his departure.*

WIPER. In that case it is evident that there are no grounds whatever for the bringing of charges. May I apologize, Madam, for an unfortunate error?

GLORIA. I'm sorry you've been troubled.

BUTTERTHWAITE. Wait a moment, wait a moment . . . As a magistrate and a leading citizen, *I* desire to lay an information against the conduct of this club.

GLORIA. Why, you cunning old . . .

BUTTERTHWAITE. We have just witnessed a demonstration of the passing about among the tables of four little doxies dressed in nowt but balloons – or, in the case of two of 'em, bells – which we were invited to burst or to tingle as the case may be. I am in no doubt whatever that had it not been for the approach of midnight – liberally signalled, I may say – they would have been rendered entirely naked within the handgrasp of the customer. There were other irregularities, too, which I will detail in due course. What are you going to do about it?

WIPER. You, er – heard what the Sergeant said, Alderman. He observed no sign of . . .

BUTTERTHWAITE. Indeed he did not. Because you know and I know and our Gloria knows that the management had been forewarned.

COUNCILLORS. *And* we can corroborate it.

GLORIA. It's all a pack of lies; it's an absolute frame-up.

WIPER. This is very serious indeed, and can only be gone into in the proper manner of procedure. Please attend my office in the morning. We can then discuss it in . . .

BUTTERTHWAITE. Oho no, none o' that patter, mate!

WIPER. I wouldn't advise you to try and be too rapid. I don't think it will pay off . . . Sergeant, come along.

> *Exeunt police. The dancers, etc., are now all on stage more or less dressed.*

BUTTERTHWAITE. Before you raging ladies come and scratch my eyesight out, I had better make one thing clear. I didn't come here to deprive you of your livelihoods. However, in the fell and calamitous grinding of two mighty opposites, someone has to go to t'wall. And them wi' fewest clothes on o' force gets squeezed hardest! Do all o' you girls belong to a union?

A GIRL. Most of us don't.

BUTTERTHWAITE. You don't? A pitiful state of affairs, which only goes to show how right I was to come here. Councillor Hopefast, will you make out a memo for the next meeting o' t'trades council, in re the possible affiliations for members of this industry. They're sweet and jetting little wildflies, and they deserve our firm attention.

(*He sings.*)

> When I was a young man in my prime
> Hoor ray Santy Anna
> I knocked them yeller gals two at a time
> All on the plains of Mexico!

He leads his COUNCILLORS *out, laughing grossly.*

GLORIA. All right, all out, we're closing, we're done for, clear it away, no evidence, nothing – my God that bloody old tup, but he'll get his horns curled yet!

Act Two

SCENE ONE

Sweetman's house.

Doorbell rings (off) SWEETMAN *in a dressing-gown hurries across the stage to answer it.* LADY SWEETMAN *in a dressing-gown comes in after him and stands listening.*

SWEETMAN *(off)*. Superintendent Wiper! At this time of night!

WIPER *(off)*. I'm sorry to disturb you, Sir Harold, but something very awkward . . . *(Mumble, mumble.)*

SWEETMAN *(off)*. What . . . what . . . Good God!

WIPER *(off)*. Do you think I could come in, sir? I mean it *is* rather . . .

SWEETMAN *(off)*. In? D'you mean 'in'? Just a moment, I . . . *(*SWEETMAN *re-enters.)* It's all right, my dear, it's nothing important . . . Would you mind going back to bed?

LADY SWEETMAN. Harold, I . . .

SWEETMAN. Bed, please. *If* you don't mind!

LADY SWEETMAN. Harold. Very well. *(She goes.)*

SWEETMAN *beckons in* WIPER.

SWEETMAN. How dare you come here, straight to this house!

WIPER. I had no alternative. I'm getting meself into a right pitchy mess-up looking after your interests.

SWEETMAN. My what did you say?

WIPER. We have never dealt together personally on this matter before, but the Copacabana is your private investment. And don't you try and deny it.

SWEETMAN. I most emphatically do deny . . .

WIPER. No, it won't do. You know perfectly well what goes on there, and who's been getting paid for keeping it protected. The time has now arrived for *you* to protect *me*. You're an Alderman and a magistrate, so use it to some purpose!

SWEETMAN. Yes . . . How much does Butterthwaite know?

WIPER. He knows that the police raid was established with collusion . . . Good God, he was told it straight by one o' those half-wit tarts! But I don't think he knows details and I don't think he knows about *your* concern, specific.

SWEETMAN. Was he drunk, by any chance?

WIPER. Drunk? I smelt a pong off all four of 'em like a streetful of breweries!

SWEETMAN. Breweries? Yes.

WIPER. Yes, well . . .

SWEETMAN. What was he doing? Precisely?

WIPER. Dancing the tango.

SWEETMAN. Wildly?

WIPER. Uproariously.

SWEETMAN. Then we'd better tell the Chief Constable. (*He goes towards the telephone.*) No. Wait. Have they been charged? I mean, for drunkenness, or the like?

WIPER. Not yet, no . . .

SWEETMAN. Then see that they are not. The accusations they have brought are, ha-hm, very wild indeed, and we are in considerable danger here of a first-class political row. Men of that type who have been in absolute power for over thirty years, why, they'd stick at nothing. We don't want to see a responsible public servant like Colonel Feng turned into a political shuttlecock. Do we? Get hold of all the other customers who were in the club this evening and get sworn affidavits as to the innocence of the show, and also, if you like, the hooliganism of Butterthwaite. Impress Colonel Feng with the hooliganism of Butterthwaite.

WIPER. What about the club itself?

SWEETMAN. Yes . . . I'll have to think of something. I may turn it to advantage . . . Yes. Good night, Superintendent.

As he shows him out, LADY SWEETMAN *re-enters.*
YOUNG SWEETMAN *enters and meets* WIPER.

YOUNG SWEETMAN. Oh my God, not here as well. Oh God, I'm off. (*He goes out again.*)

SWEETMAN. Maurice! You come back here, boy!

WIPER. I'm sorry about this, Sir Harold. I suppose you won't want me to take an affidavit off of *him*?

SWEETMAN. Was he there, too? . . . Good heavens . . . No, we can't risk exceptions, take his statement with the rest – in the morning. There are five steps to the front door. *Don't* miss your footing. Good night.

WIPER *goes out.* SWEETMAN *calls:*
Maurice!

Re-enter YOUNG SWEETMAN.

It's all right, he's gone. Now then: who were you there with? Blomax's girl?

YOUNG SWEETMAN. No.

SWEETMAN. Oh, weren't you? Astonishing . . . Has she not got you caught yet, then?

YOUNG SWEETMAN. Caught? Do you mean . . . ?

SWEETMAN. Yes, I damn well *do* mean it! Now I give you a fair choice, boy, leave her alone, or get out of my brewery. There's a great deal of villainy turning itself round in this town that you know nowt about. And think yourself lucky the police have done nothing more than warn me about you.

YOUNG SWEETMAN *goes in.*

Do you know what the time is?

LADY SWEETMAN. What did he want?

SWEETMAN. Who?

LADY SWEETMAN. The Superintendent.

SWEETMAN. Maurice. The boy was drunk.

LADY SWEETMAN. So I see . . . Can they send you to prison ?

SWEETMAN. What . . . !

LADY SWEETMAN. I couldn't help overhearing. How deeply
are you mixed up in it, Harold ? Have you been bribing the
police, have you been . . .

SWEETMAN. No. Emphatically! No. I have not! Now will you
please go back to bed!

LADY SWEETMAN. I wish you weren't so bad-tempered. I'm
only trying to . . .

SWEETMAN. I'm sorry. I didn't mean to be. No . . . but, er,
it's just a return of the old bother, it makes me a bit edgy . . .
(*He mimes a pain in his heart.*) I'll take a drop of medicine and
come to bed when it settles . . . Go on, now. Happy
dreams . . .

She goes, avoiding his embrace.

Happy dreams and sweet awakenings . . .
    It has been argued and by no less a voice
    Than that of the Prime Minister, that today
    Class-struggle is concluded. All can rise
    Or fall according to desire or merits
    Or (it may be) according to finance.
    I am as rich as any man in Yorkshire,
    I brew good beer and drink my own good product.
    I fabricate perfected breakfast food
    And crunch it with my family round my table.
    Both beer and breakfast food are drunk and crunched
    By simultaneous millions through the land.
    So Sweetman should have risen, so he has,
    But to what eminence ? Financial, yes.
    And social: yes indeed. My wife has mink,
    My daughters, jewels and suitors : My three tall sons
    Inhabit, or have inhabited, public schools.
    They grow to love the world I set them in,
    And, loving it, become it as they walk.

I am a prince, I am a baron, sirs!
And yet I have no sovereignty, no.
For what is power of gold when politics
At every turn deceive my high aspiring?
The election lights on Butterthwaite – not once
But three times three, or nine times nine, I fear.
No national trend, nor local, gives me hope
Of an improvement. Yet Butterthwaite must fall
And fall so low that not the whole ineptitude
And hopelessness of Tory forecasts can
Reverse his long-delayed catastrophe.
He has himself prepared his own trap-door
And greased his easy hinge. Tonight, he did it!
All it needs now, cagy play and watch
For luck to rock the lock and heave the lever:
And he's down! Prison? . . . No, I do not think so . . .
I am too expert. And in their good time
I turn to the electorate and they turn
In *my* good time, to me! And turn for ever! Yes . . .

Exit

SCENE TWO

A room in the Town Hall.

Enter BOOCOCK, BUTTERTHWAITE *and* LABOUR COUN-
CILLORS.

BOOCOCK. This is very troublesome altogether, Charlie. I hope
you haven't gone too far.

BUTTERTHWAITE. I haven't, Barney.

BOOCOCK. Just how sozzled were you at the Copacabana,
Charlie?

BUTTERTHWAITE. At the Copacabana, Barney, I was as sober
as a chief constable. Isn't that the truth?

COUNCILLORS. Aye, it's the truth.

BUTTERTHWAITE. The buttock-naked truth!

BOOCOCK. I have no desire whatever to make a statement to the Press.

BUTTERTHWAITE. If you don't, I will.

BOOCOCK. I am quite sure that you will . . .

Enter JOURNALISTS.

Gentlemen, good morning. I am sorry you have been brought here. I have remarkably little to say. Except that it does appear that all is not well with the borough police force.

1ST JOURNALIST. Is it true, Mr Mayor, that the Copacabana Club . . . ?

BOOCOCK. I am naming no names.

2ND JOURNALIST. Have you discussed it with the Chief Constable?

1ST JOURNALIST. It is arguable, is it not, that the Chief Constable has the right to conduct his *own* investigation into matters concerning the . . .

BUTTERTHWAITE. I'll answer that, Barney. Now look here, young man. The police are public servants and responsible to the public!

1ST JOURNALIST. But surely the Home Secretary . . .

BUTTERTHWAITE. The Home Secretary's nowt to do wi' it! The Home Secretary's a Tory and he lives in bloody London! The Government here is *us*, and we're not satisfied. Mister Feng's police force is putrid with corruption and if he don't take a long-handled dung fork to it pretty damn quick, I want his resignation! What's more, I'm going to get it. He has wrapped himself up, neck and navel, to an unscrupulous political minority. I am preparing a full exposure. (*He flourishes a document.*) On this piece o' paper I've got half the facts I'm seeking. When the list is complete, I shall broadcast it out before the voters o' this borough! They'll know what to do! . . . *And* he won't get his first-class travelling expenses neither, I can tell you.

BOOCOCK. I, er, I hope, gentlemen, you won't try and build this up into too much of a sensation . . . er . . . thank you very much . . .

Exeunt all save JOURNALISTS.

JOURNALISTS. Thank you, Mr Mayor.

1ST JOURNALIST. Right. Number one demonstration of prejudice and bias. Now for number two.

2ND JOURNALIST. Boots polished, trousers pressed, anybody need a haircut ? Very good. Shall we take our places ?

They move round the stage

SCENE THREE

The Police headquarters.

JOURNALISTS *still on stage. Enter* FENG, WIPER *and a* PC.

FENG. Gentlemen, I am exceedingly sorry that Alderman Butterthwaite has chosen to publish these allegations. There is, of course, *no* political influence behind the conduct of the police. What else do you expect me to say ?

2ND JOURNALIST. Would you be willing to talk matters over with His Worship the Mayor, if . . .

FENG. His Worship the Mayor has apparently taken as gospel everything Alderman Butterthwaite has seen fit to tell him! So what is there left to talk about, pray ? Personally I would welcome an inquiry. An independent inquiry, conducted by the Home Office. And none other! That is all. I thank you. Good morning.

JOURNALISTS. Good morning, Colonel. Thank you very much . . .

The PC *shows them out and then stands well aside.*

FENG. Now tell me, Superintendent. What am I to think ?

Both you and Sir Harold have given me the benefit of your no doubt independent analyses of this miserable affair, and certainly the public attitude of our Socialist friends would appear to bear you out. But supposing behind their demagogic antics there were in fact some truth? This sergeant you sent round to the club . . . what's his name? Lumber?

WIPER. Yessir. Sarnt Lumber.

FENG. What's his record?

WIPER. An exceedingly good one, sir. I would personally stand very fast indeed behind Sergeant Lumber . . . We could, of course, suspend him until the matter has been cleared up?

FENG. No. They would tell us, would they not, that there is no smoke without fire. But you will investigate, Superintendent, both deeply and confidentially, and I shall be investigating your investigation, and I shall be investigating *you*, sir.

WIPER. Oh . . . in that case, Colonel Feng, I must ask you to accept my resignation.

FENG. No. If you have done your duty, you will indeed feel your honour impugned. But it is not only *your* honour, it is the honour of the entire force, it is *my* honour, sir, *mine*, that is being dragged like a dead dog through the egalitarian garbage of these streets!

WIPER. You're quite right, sir, quite right. I withdraw my resignation.

FENG. I am glad to find your reaction so extremely correct . . . Now above all, Superintendent, let us not get rattled. Cool nerves, keen brains, no statements to the Press. We will soon defeat these unworthy attempts. They are a symptom of the age, I have met them before. It is not difficult to prevail against them. I look forward to your report.

    Exit WIPER. PC *helps* FENG *into coat and hat and umbrella and goes.*

I am a man under authority. Having soldiers under me, or at least constables, and I say to this man 'go' and he goeth, and

to another 'come' and he cometh, and to my servant 'do this'
and he doeth it . . .
Not difficult to prevail but difficult indeed
To live and hold that prevalence, yet live
A social and communicating creature.
The law by nature is civilian,
But it can only work through mode of warfare.
So, we, like soldiers through the English streets,
They fear us while they look to us for strength.
The violence of authority seems to grow
In face of growing violence of crime,
Wrying the neck of our disturbed profession.
They call me Colonel, but by courtesy,
I command and serve, and which is which? Who knows?
I tell you, I do not. We used to wear
Top hats and sober clothes like sober tradesmen
But where top hats were worn the heads were broke,
So, military helmets. And the tunics,
Once frock-coats, breed badges and bright buttons,
Confirming in their cut to use of war.
We are not armed. I fear we shall be soon.
I hope we must be. There are too many dead.
Yet then how can we say we only serve
Civilian purposes? The pay is low
So nobody will join. Then raise the pay
And bad recruits will join for money only?
I have no hope and therefore walk alone:
Only alone can I know I am right.

SCENE FOUR

A public park.

FENG, *on stage still, walks about in meditation, then sits down
wearily on a seat, which a* PARK ATTENDANT *brings him.*

WELLESLEY *comes in, depressed. She walks about, too, then sits down as well and pays the* ATTENDANT *for her seat.*

FENG. Er h'm . . . Miss Blomax, is it not?

WELLESLEY. H'm? . . . Oh yes. Good morning.

FENG. I – er – I think we have had the pleasure. Er – Feng – how do you do?

WELLESLEY. We met at the Sweetmans'.

FENG. We did. At the Sweetmans'.

WELLESLEY. Are you all by yourself, then – or—?

FENG. Oh, yes: quite as usual, all by myself. A short turn in the park during the luncheon-break. Companions, of course, invidious, to a man in my position. As it were, the ship's captain.

WELLESLEY. Ship's—?

FENG. Oh yes. Private quarters under the quarter-deck and so forth: unwise to be too general, a necessary loneliness, I am sure you will understand me, you being also known in these curious parts as an enemy alien, are you not, Miss Blomax?

WELLESLEY. A what?

FENG. I mean, from the South?

WELLESLEY. Oh no, I live in Westmorland.

FENG. Oh yes. Of course. The forests . . . Your father is a native here?

WELLESLEY. I think he was born in Twickenham.

FENG. Ah? Ah yes, the South . . .

> *They sit for a while.* FENG *acknowledges the salute of a passing* PC.

You made, I recollect, at Sir Harold's table, a few remarks about the government of the town, which struck me at the time as, er – somewhat penetrating, Miss Blomax. You will no doubt forgive me if I appeared to have dismissed them. I have now, however, reason to believe you may have spoken more shrewdly than you realized.

WELLESLEY. Oh, I realized very well. You can tell all you

want to know about the climate of the town by the arrangement and the trimming of the trees in this park.

FENG. Ah yes, the trees. I quite agree with you. Barbarous. No notion how to plant. No notions at all. Borough engineering. A tee-square and a compass and lop off every branch that refuses to conform. Barbarous!

WELLESLEY. I wouldn't have thought you'd have had that much sympathy for a nonconformist tree.

FENG. Trees are not people. They are a gentle entertainment provided by our Creator for ourselves and for Himself. It is churlish to abuse them. We must educate our society and prevent such abuse.

WELLESLEY. Educate? . . . Oh, I'm so glad I didn't go to school here. I've got my father to thank for that if for nothing else. The day that you leave school here you're expected to reach the age of forty in about three hours and that's all. If you won't do it, you know what you get? Hump of the old shoulders and the old grunt comes out at you!

> Too young, too tall, and your eyes too bright,
> You look too near and you look too hard,
> You dream too deep in the deep of the night,
> And you walk too long in my backyard.
> You stand and ask for your white bread
> And you stand and you ask for your brown,
> But what you will get is a good horse whip
> To drive you out of town.

How old are you, as a matter of interest?

FENG. Oh? Oh, sufficiently old. No longer irresponsible. Rigid, you might say. Hardened arteries, young lady, unsympathetic and crumbling. Hardness, however, is nothing if not necessary. It derives from my post and my years in the Colonial Service and the necessity therein for unwavering powers of decision. And so I *have* decided. Quite suddenly. Unexpectedly. I am, alone, not sufficient, in fact I am bewildered. Particularly now, surrounded as I am by a confusion of democracy and alien loyalties, for support I turn – where? Of necessity to another alien. I would like you to become my wife . . . Or do you not perhaps share my belief in the similarity of our predicaments? I have within me – I mean as a man, not a policeman – an extraordinary humanity, of necessity concealed. Improbable longings, attempts at self-betrayal, I think I can crush them, by this improbable method. I would be glad of your opinion.

WELLESLEY. Oh dear . . . Oh no . . . I don't think it's very likely. I mean, I don't think –

FENG. Perhaps it is not. It would have been easier for me to have forgotten my impulse and to have continued our conversation upon a more usual subject. As it might be, the trees. Perhaps it is not too late for me yet to forget it . . . or, I observe you are a pedestrian. I always prefer to talk to pedestrians, at least of our milieu . . . They are the less likely – you see – to bear a grudge against my occupation . . . but I have a car around the corner. Do you think I could possibly offer you a lift anywhere?

WELLESLEY. I was just sitting in the park. There is nowhere I want to go to, really . . .

FENG. Yes. By all means. I wish I could sit with you further. But duty, alas . . . Good day to you, Miss Blomax. I, er, I would look forward very much to meeting you again, some time? . . . Good day . . .

Exit FENG.
She sits for a while, then YOUNG SWEETMAN *enters.*

YOUNG SWEETMAN. Wellesley . . . hello . . . Wellesley.

WELLESLEY. . . . I suppose you've come to tell me that they have told you that you must never see me again?

YOUNG SWEETMAN. Well, as a matter of fact . . .

WELLESLEY. All the old grey heads are breaking one another's blood out, because of who saw what of what girl below the waist, when we all know very well they would *all* love to see it. And why shouldn't they? It's a free country. Have you seen it?

YOUNG SWEETMAN. What?

WELLESLEY. At the Copacabana, Maurice. Have you seen it?

YOUNG SWEETMAN. As a matter of fact, yes.

WELLESLEY. And who tells the truth about it? You tell me that, the Reds or the Fascists?

YOUNG SWEETMAN. Neither, of course.

WELLESLEY. So there you are. Yet those are the people who claim they can regulate your life and my life, and make our unwavering decisions. Not for what they think of us, but for what they think of each other. We have no obligation to them. Only to ourselves; we ought to fight for what we want. What do *you* want, Maurice?

YOUNG SWEETMAN. You.

WELLESLEY. Do you? – I wish I knew what *I* did . . . I have a father and he calls himself a stumbling-block. If only there was someone to show me the way to turn him into a stepping-stone . . .

She goes out. YOUNG SWEETMAN *follows after her calling* 'Wellesley . . . Wellesley . . .'
Enter BLOMAX *with a brown paper parcel.*

BLOMAX. Oh dear, oh dear . . . Beverley Races, what a performance! Ben Jonson's Delight was pulled by his jock and I lost a cool fifty. What's more, I wasn't warned. I don't know why the stewards don't enforce these things better. Something's gone very queer with my sources of advance information. And not only at Beverley. What have I come back to! Well, you've seen it more than I have. *I* don't know where it's going to conclude . . . I suppose it would be strategical to have a word with Gloria? I last left her at Doncaster, very astonished. On such a beautiful evening – now that club of hers is apparently closed – she will no doubt be found supine in her back garden, enjoying a drink of tea . . .

SCENE FIVE

The back garden of GLORIA's *house.*

BLOMAX *remains on stage.* GLORIA *and* WIPER *enter for sun-bathing in the garden with a crate of beer.* WIPER *is playing an accordion. They do not notice* BLOMAX *at first.*

BLOMAX. Oh well, more or less . . . Somebody's sense of crisis isn't very highly developed. I suppose you could call it the good old British phlegm . . .

WIPER (*singing*).

> The lady's walls are large and high
> The lady's grass is green and dry
> The lady herself is green and blooming
> And big fat Alfred, he's consuming . . .

Here, have another . . . (*He passes a bottle.*)

GLORIA (*to* WIPER). I hope you know what you're doing, sprawling here in broad daylight. I don't call it safe.

WIPER. Of course it's bloody safe. I came in the back gate, I go out the ditto, and we're not overlooked . . .

BLOMAX. Cock-a-doodle-doo . . .

They both leap up in alarm.

WIPER. Good God, how did *you* get in here?

BLOMAX. I carry a key in my little fob pocket.

WIPER. Oh you do, do you? And might I ask you why?

BLOMAX. And might I ask *you* why you've abandoned Mrs Wiper in such very hot weather with all the washing-up in a stuffy little kitchen?

WIPER. Leave my wife out of it.

BLOMAX. All right then, you leave *mine*.

WIPER. What? What's that!

He whips round on GLORIA, *who nods her head.*

GLORIA. Doncaster Registry Office. Monday morning. On his way to the races. It seemed the safest notion. But that gives you no cause to come barging in here as if you owned the bloody place . . .

BLOMAX. Now then, my dear, don't let's get edgy. A woman in your condition . . .

WIPER. But why didn't you tell me?

GLORIA. I didn't want to spoil things.

WIPER. You didn't want to spoil things . . . !

Knocking on the garden gate.

GLORIA. Oh my Lord, who's that! (*She calls out.*) No thank you, not today; I never buy at the gate!

Knocking continues.

I'd better open, I suppose. Keep out of sight. We don't know *who* it might be.

She hurriedly pulls on a housecoat over her bikini. WIPER *thrusts himself into his trousers and gathers up his shirt, tunic, etc.* BLOMAX *runs into the house.* GLORIA *opens the gate.* LADY SWEETMAN *enters.*

Lady Sweetman! How do you do?

LADY SWEETMAN. I am not very well. I have a migraine head-ache. Do you think I could come in a minute?

GLORIA *has to let her in the gate.*

Sir Harold Sweetman, Sir Harold, I may tell you, Sir Harold is extremely upset.

GLORIA. Aye, I can believe you . . .

WIPER, *who has not quite finished doing up his buttons, is caught.*

LADY SWEETMAN. Superintendent Wiper?

WIPER (*adjusting his buttons*). Good evening, Lady Sweetman.

LADY SWEETMAN. I know what you are here for, Superintendent. I know all about it.

WIPER. You do?

LADY SWEETMAN. And may I say I am appalled. You see, Sir
Harold is a sick man. He has a coronary condition. All these
cabals, these distasteful intrigues, I may tell you, are killing
him. (*She sniffs at her camphor.*)

GLORIA. A very jolly deathbed and all by the look of his com-
plexion.

LADY SWEETMAN. Coronary trouble expresses itself in an
unhealthy heightened colour.

GLORIA. Aye . . .

LADY SWEETMAN. However, we have no course but to be
practical. I came here to find out what my husband refuses
to tell me. How deeply is he involved in this unpleasant affair
at the Copacabana?

WIPER. Up to the lug-oyles.

LADY SWEETMAN. Oh . . . He is most confident, you understand, that he will be able to extricate himself, and even, I
think, use it to political advantage.

WIPER. I'm delighted to hear that, Lady Sweetman. It really
does me good.

LADY SWEETMAN. But is his confidence justified?

WIPER. It all depends on Colonel Feng and how deep he
decides to delve. He could burn our bottoms yet, could
Colonel Feng.

GLORIA. Never mind about Feng. What about Butterthwaite?

LADY SWEETMAN. Has he made a definite accusation?

GLORIA. No, but he soon will.

LADY SWEETMAN. And if so, can he prove it?

GLORIA. That chap can prove anything if he's left alone with
it long enough. It's up to us to get in first and on a field of
our own choosing. Do him down through summat else.

LADY SWEETMAN. Not politics. It mustn't be politics. Think
of my husband's heart.

GLORIA. All right then. We'll keep it personal. But what?

LADY SWEETMAN. I think we should consider Mr Butter-thwaite's character. Such outrageous vulgarity must be there for a purpose, you know. Nobody could behave like that naturally.

WIPER. Oh, I don't know, Lady Sweetman. An astonishing great deal comes very naturally to some of us. (*He offers her a beer*.) Here – have a wet. The old family firm, you know.

LADY SWEETMAN. No, thank you . . . No, it is deliberate. He is concealing a social weakness. Of course, he is bound to feel inferior in many respects.

GLORIA. I can tell you one respect where he not only *feels* but he very definitely *is*.

LADY SWEETMAN. Oh. And what is that?

GLORIA. The gee-gees.

LADY SWEETMAN. The—

WIPER. She's not wrong, you know, she's right. If he tried to fix the ballot boxes as crafty as he fixes the Tote, there'd be no Labour Party left.

LADY SWEETMAN. Tote, Superintendent? Gee-gees? I don't quite . . .

GLORIA. The races, Lady Sweetman. He loses his bets.

LADY SWEETMAN. Ah . . . Oh well, that makes it much easier. We must expose him, of course.

WIPER. How? He never bounced any cheques so far as I know . . .

GLORIA. He never *used* any cheques. But there must be a couple o' hundred quid at least queuing up in his IOU's.

LADY SWEETMAN. You see? It's all quite easy. We must find out who his creditors are and, er, assemble what my husband calls a Pressure Group. Sir Harold will be so grateful, you know. He never will believe that we women have a place in public life, but—

GLORIA. It's assembled already, the Pressure Group. It con-sists of one creditor only and his name is Wellington Blomax.

LADY SWEETMAN. Oh – Dr Blomax!

GLORIA. You know him? Well, he's just acquired a highly intelligent new wife.

LADY SWEETMAN. Oh, I'm so glad. I've always said that poor child of his needs a properly organized home, and I don't think she's been getting it.

GLORIA. No . . .

LADY SWEETMAN. Well, we must approach Mrs Blomax and make her understand – as I am sure that she will, being a woman – that her husband has a manifest duty to the community—

BLOMAX (*inside*). Wellesley, I'm warning you, you'll not be welcome out there—

GLORIA. Hey up – who's in the house!

Enter WELLESLEY.

WELLESLEY. He's just told me you're his wife!

LADY SWEETMAN. *You* are!

GLORIA. I dare say it does come as a bit of a surprise . . . Lady Sweetman, my – er – my stepdaughter, I suppose . . . It's the first time we've met.

LADY SWEETMAN. How very convenient. So we can keep it all in our own little circle and save so much unpleasantness. Now, Wellesley . . .

GLORIA. Superintendent, it's time you were off. Your recreation's over. Get back to Mrs Wiper.

WIPER. What? Why? Hey—

GLORIA. I don't want you to know too much. You'll only muck it up again if you do. But it is very unwise to fall asleep too soon in the shade of so dangerous an orchard. Keep hold on the fruit-basket – watch out for what drops.

WIPER. What drops? Where?

GLORIA. Butterthwaite. He's ripe enough . . . Go on, get off with you.

WIPER. Oh, oh, very well . . . Good evening, Lady Sweetman.

Exit.

LADY SWEETMAN. Good evening, Superintendent . . . Quite a nice man – when you get to know him better.

GLORIA. Nice? Oh aye . . .

WELLESLEY (*takes beer*). Do you mind, I feel thirsty . . . He left one of his little notes on his surgery door to say where he was for the benefit of his patients. It'd just serve you right to get six kids with measles and a couple of polio subjects interrupting the honeymoon. (*To* LADY SWEETMAN.) I suppose you've come to see my father to complain about me and Maurice and all the rest of that?

LADY SWEETMAN. Complain? Oh my dear child, I'm not going to complain. Do you *want* to marry Maurice? He wants to marry *you*, you know.

WELLESLEY. I have had other offers. I have not yet made a choice. All that I want is my right to do so, unprejudiced, when I want, do you see? I want it and I'll fight for it.

BLOMAX *enters, behind, listening.*

LADY SWEETMAN. Oh, you young people – so noisy about your *rights*. But what about your responsibilities, Wellesley? I don't know whether you will understand this, my dear, because, of course, you're not entirely English, are you? But I am afraid that you yourself must to some extent be held responsible for your father.

WELLESLEY. Responsible? Me? Are you out of your mind?

LADY SWEETMAN. I have always been told he is a very good doctor – at least for his panel patients. But as a professional man, he must know very well he is known by his friends.

WELLESLEY. His friends aren't *my* friends.

LADY SWEETMAN. Yes, my dear, I know. And *you* must make yourself responsible for seeing they are no longer *his*. I am going to be quite strict about this, Wellesley, and I'm going to apply pressure. He must be made to understand the folly of his conduct. And then we shall *all* be happy. You will, *and* Maurice. Yes . . . Good-bye, Mrs er – Blomax, I leave it all in your hands . . . Oh dear, my poor head . . . In your hands, Mrs Blomax. I do hope I can trust you . . .

> *Exit*
> BLOMAX *comes forward.*

GLORIA. So you overheard us, did you ? . . . Pressure. You'd do well to prepare yourself.

BLOMAX. I don't know what you are talking about, Wellesley, my dove. I bought two pair o' kippers. Not much, but they're protein. You see, I had a bad day.

GLORIA. The news may not have filtered through to you at the Beverley Grandstand, but Alfred Wiper and your flash companions from the Victoria and Albert have grown somewhat incompatible.

BLOMAX. Flash companions indeed! They are very old friends of mine.

GLORIA. That's the trouble. You realize what's happened to Alfred ? He is lined up with Sweetman. And your daughter, as it happens, has a taste and fancy also to line up with Sweetman . . .

WELLESLEY. Wait a minute . . .

GLORIA. You just keep quiet, love. All I want *you* to do is to stand over there and look pathetic. (*To* BLOMAX *again.*) You'd be well advised to take example and to line yourself up likewise. I mean, get rid of Butterthwaite, and join your own class of people. Don't you want her to stand in the favour of her chosen new in-laws ? And besides, your own position in regard to the police isn't all that it might be. Suppose they were to hear about what you've been prescribing for certain other of your female patients ?

BLOMAX. An issue of mercy, their condition demanded it . . .

GLORIA. Yes . . .

BLOMAX. Yes ... of course, I do acknowledge a definite duty towards my neglected little daughter .. But *I* don't know ... Charlie Butterthwaite? What do you expect me to *do* about him, Gloria?

GLORIA. Tell him where you stand and tell him who you are. Be decisive. Insult him. Press him for your debts. You'll be done with him *then*. Don't tell me you've got qualms?

WELLESLEY. How can he have qualms? He's an old rotten rascal and he's given me no good ever. I want what I want and I'm going to break his head for it. Are we to have these for supper?

She takes the kippers into the house.

BLOMAX. You'd better go and help her. She'll turn those kippers into charcoal if you give her half a chance.

GLORIA. We want an answer from you before you go to bed.

BLOMAX. Bed?

GLORIA. Aye, bed ...

> And the shape of your answer
> Will doubtless decide
> Whether that bed
> Will be narrow or wide! – hubby!

She goes into the house.

BLOMAX. Well, whether it's one or whether it's the other, I still seem to have invited into it the east wind and the west and they're scrapping like two catamounts between my skin and my pyjamas ...

He picks up the empty bottle, pours out the dregs into one bottle, and drinks it.

Fact of the matter is, I *have* been betraying my class. Wellesley *is* entitled to the natural advantages of her place in society, the snooty little bitch. I am, after all, a comfortable man: and

I don't want to be disrupted. When all is said and done, this
town is run by an ignorant overweening yobbo: and it's time
I stood up firm to him and accepted the responsibilities of
my superior education . . . Furthermore, he owes me money.

He goes into the house

SCENE SIX

A room in the Town Hall.

Enter BOOCOCK, LEFTWICH *and* HOPEFAST.

HOPEFAST.
> He came and asked for thirty quid,
> I said I hadn't got it.
> I said I wasn't made o' brass,
> He said he bloody knew it.

BOOCOCK.
> I can't imagine Charlie
> Running really short o' money.
> He hasn't said a word to me.

HOPEFAST.
> I think there's summat funny.

LEFTWICH.
> He's lost it on the horses.

Enter HARDNUTT.

HARDNUTT.
> I think there's summat funny.
> Did you hear Charlie Butterthwaite
> Wor trying to borrow money?

BOOCOCK.
> He never said a word to me.
> I've been often pleased to lend him

The odd quid here and there,
I gave it him, he gave it back,
All fair and no one wondered.

LEFTWICH.

He's lost it on the horses.

BOOCOCK.

He can't have done.

HARDNUTT.

He did.

HOPEFAST.

He did.

HARDNUTT.

It sounds to me like balaclava Bugles,
This day some clown has blundered.

BOOCOCK.

We all know Charlie Butterthwaite,
And know him without turpitude,
Nine times he's held the rank of Mayor,
And now the peoples' gratitude.
With all the battles he has fought
In all his loyal rectitude
If he should be in trouble
We should grant him our support.

Enter HICKLETON.

HICKLETON.

What's up with our old Charlie,
Asking everyone for money?
I mean to say he's often short . . .

BOOCOCK.

We all of us are often short.

HICKLETON.

He asked me for one hundred quid!
And coming at a time like this,
The day we've all but clapped the lid

On Feng and Sweetman and the Tories . . .
I think there's summat funny,
And I hear there's funny stories
Have been spread around about.

HARDNUTT.

His face wor red and white
And his eyes wor poking out.

HICKLETON.

And asking me for five score quid.

HOPEFAST.

He rang me up i' t'midst o' t'night,
First in a chuckle, then in a shout.

HICKLETON.

And then he came to my front door.
I said, o'course, I hadn't got it.

HICKLETON ⎱
HOPEFAST ⎰

I said I wasn't made o'brass.

ALL 3 COUNCILLORS.

He said he bloody knew it!

Enter BUTTERTHWAITE.

BUTTERTHWAITE. Hello! I know. I've got red ears . . . All
right, I don't come twice to a sold-out chip-oyle, t'subject's
done with. Now, Mr Mayor, there's a delegate outside from
the Forces of Reaction. Are you going to talk to him?

BOOCOCK. I am. And this time, Charlie, you keep your oar out.
I am highly concerned for our reputation abroad. Have you
seen the *Yorkshire Post* today?

BUTTERTHWAITE. Aye, it were good reading. I tell you,
they're getting frightened.

BOOCOCK. I don't call it good reading. We're in the London
Telegraph an' all, let alone that two-faced *Herald*. The time
has now come for appropriate negotiations.

BUTTERTHWAITE. Appropriate? All right, but Feng has got to go.

BOOCOCK. Eh dear . . . I don't know . . . Herbert, let him in.

LEFTWICH *ushers in* F. J.

F. J. Good evening, Mr Mayor. May I take it you are speaking for the Labour Party as I in my turn am speaking for the Conservatives?

SWEETMAN *comes in and stands at the back.*

BUTTERTHWAITE (*pointing to* SWEETMAN). I see him, over there!

BOOCOCK. Charlie, do you mind?

F. J. Bearing in mind the unsettling effect of such a dispute and particularly in regard to the criminal element of the town . . .

BOOCOCK. Granted.

F. J. I beg your pardon?

BOOCOCK. Granted.

F. J. Mr Mayor, I beg you, please moderate your attitude. The police should be above party recrimination.

BOOCOCK. Granted.

F. J. Sir Harold is thinking in terms of an independent inquiry. He has authorized me to . . .

BOOCOCK. Alderman Butterthwaite has laid a definite information. It is the duty of the Chief Constable to either prosecute the Copacabana or to give adequate reasons for refusing to prosecute. If he should finally determine to refuse, then I imagine an inquiry would be mandatory. But until then, certainly not.

F. J. But, Mr Mayor . . .

BOOCOCK. And let alone the whole question of corruption in his ranks!

F. J. If you will not agree to a Home Office inquiry, Sir Harold is fully prepared to lay the facts at his disposal in front of the electorate. And they are not entirely synonymous with those presented by Alderman Butterthwaite.

BOOCOCK. Who has presented *no* facts! Sub judice evidence cannot be publicly brought forward.

F. J. Not brought forward. Slid.

BOOCOCK. I beg your pardon?

F. J. Granted. I said 'slid'. Rumours deliberately insinuated. We may be reactionaries, Barney, but we're not complete idiots. There's plenty of personal dirt we can throw into the next election. We don't like it, we've never done it, but if we have to, we will!

BOOCOCK. I'm sure your hearts will bleed.

F. J. Oh, and by the way, the art gallery. You may not believe it, but there are certain people who regard it as important.

BOOCOCK. *I* regard it as important. What the hell are you talking about?

SWEETMAN. It has been shuffled once too often. I am now making it my personal concern.

Exeunt SWEETMAN *and* F. J.

BOOCOCK. Well, you all heard him. An independent inquiry! Now that's a very big concession. I think we ought to take it.

COUNCILLORS *murmur agreement.*

BUTTERTHWAITE. Oh, no, no, no . . . I'm not being fobbed off wi' no cocoa-and-water compromises. I want my gullet stuffed wi' the good fat roast goose to the point of a vomit, *and* I'm getting it an' all.

BOOCOCK. Ah . . . What do you think he meant about the art gallery, Charlie?

BUTTERTHWAITE. The art gallery's been attended to.

BOOCOCK. And after what manner attended to, Charlie?

BUTTERTHWAITE. It's all in the Committee Minutes if you care to look it up. A unanimous decision was taken against any further discussion of the point.

BOOCOCK. Two Conservatives on that Committee. Which way did they vote?

BUTTERTHWAITE. They were unavoidably absent.

BOOCOCK. Oh, they were, were they? By, Charlie Butterthwaite, if I wor a younger man I'd put my bloody booit into thee! Who do you think you are, going behind my back like that!

BUTTERTHWAITE. I'll tell you who I am.

> I'm the King of this Castle, Barney,
> And that by right of conquest,
> Elected for main engagement
> In each and every issue
> Our party has pursued
> Throughout perilous generations.
> I turned tramcars over
> In the turmoil of twenty-six,
> I marched in the hungry mutiny
> From the north to the metropolis,
> I carried the broken banner.
> When hungry bellies bore no bread,
> I dreamed of my dinner
> In the wasted line of dole,
> And by fundamental force of strength
> I fetched my people through it.
> Call it the Red Sea, call it
> The boundaries of Canaan,
> I carried them over,
> My care, my calculation
> Lived as a loyal Englishman
> Through long-suffering and through languishment,
> I chiefly did, and I chiefly deserved.
> Can you deny it?

BOOCOCK. No. Chiefly is true. But party is party. We cannot call it 'King'.

BUTTERTHWAITE. I spoke by way of metaphor.

BOOCOCK. We cannot call it 'King'.

BUTTERTHWAITE. Ah, Barney, Barney, Barney . . . Constable Leftwich, look at us both! Which one's the King?

LEFTWICH. Neither. I'd say Mrs Boocock.

They all laugh.

BUTTERTHWAITE. How *is* the missus, Barney?

BOOCOCK. Sarah continues robust.

BUTTERTHWAITE (*taking him aside*). And I suppose she still holds the old Boocock cheque-book, eh?

BOOCOCK. Ah . . . I wondered when you were going to pluck up face and come to me about it. How much is the total?

BUTTERTHWAITE. She'd never let you have it.

BOOCOCK. Three figures, they wor telling me . . . I'm afraid that she wouldn't. I'm afraid there's not a chance. Now a tenner or a fiver.

BUTTERTHWAITE. Nay, I'd not take it.

BOOCOCK. All right, I'll not force you . . . It's time we were off home. You can be locking up, Herbert; the office staff will all have gone.

LEFTWICH. Goodnight, Mr Mayor.

BOOCOCK (*turning back on the way out*). Now, Charlie, this inquiry, think it over very careful. I believe we should agree to it . . .

BOOCOCK AND COUNCILLORS. Night, Charlie, night Charlie . . . etc.

Exeunt all save BUTTERTHWAITE *and* LEFTWICH.

BUTTERTHWAITE. Go and lock up. I won't be half an hour. I've got some letters to attend to.

LEFTWICH. I say, Charlie, is it that bad?

BUTTERTHWAITE. There's nowt that bad, Herbert, as can't be made better with a bit o' pride of achievement in some other field. All I want to do is get rid o' Feng. If I can manage that, I don't give a bastard's egg if I spend the rest o' my life i' t'workhouse!

LEFTWICH. Well, you were born i' t'bloody place, worn't you?

Exit LEFTWICH.

BUTTERTHWAITE. Wellington! Wellington! You scarlet intestine-rummaging dun, where ha' you got to?

Enter BLOMAX.

BLOMAX. Are you alone yet?

BUTTERTHWAITE. I am.

BLOMAX. Have you got it?

BUTTERTHWAITE. I have not.

BLOMAX. I am sorry to do this, Charlie! I've got to have that money!

BUTTERTHWAITE. Five hundred bloody nicker . . .

BLOMAX. Charlie, you're a cheat. You're a chiseller. You're rotten. You are not a loyal friend.

BUTTERTHWAITE. What!

BLOMAX. I mean to quarrel with you, Charlie. I am forced to cast you off . . .

BUTTERTHWAITE. Wellington . . . if you weren't in bad trouble, you would never use such words. Come on, lad, what is it? Are you being blackmailed?

BLOMAX. Oh, Charlie, I am! You see, it's been like this. I'm going to be frank with you, Charlie. I – I er don't know how to put it . . . it's a question of – a – question of – all right, professional reputation. Yes. Now here is the truth! Over-indulgent prescriptions! Suppose I put it that way? . . . I only regarded it as an extension of a normal bedside manner. But it looks like coming up at a coroner's inquest, so I've got to pay up or hic haec hoc, I'm done!

BUTTERTHWAITE. Are you telling me the truth?

BLOMAX. The absolute and clear-starched verity! I'm always being half blackmailed, but this time it's dead serious. Oh,

Charlie, I've done you a power of services up and down this
town as a general intelligencer, and if ever you've found me
of any use at all . . .

BUTTERTHWAITE. It has never been said that Charlie Butterthwaite was the man to watch his mates fall under. Gratitude
wi' Charlie for services rendered is the king-post of his roof-
tree:

> It holds the tiles above his house-place
> The smoke-hole for his fire
> It overhangs his weighty table
> And the bed of his desire!

Wellington, you'll have your money, but out o' *my* bank-
balance? Oh dear . . . How are we going to manage?

BLOMAX. I don't know. How are we?

BUTTERTHWAITE. Burgle t'Town Hall.

BLOMAX. It's all right *laughing* . . .

BUTTERTHWAITE. Wellington, I'm not laughing . . . Did I
ever tell you I was born in the workhouse? Well I was, and
it was horrible. Oh, they've not got me back there yet, not a
carrot nor a stick can compel this bloody donkey where he
doesn't want to go! (*He sings, with a little dance.*)

> In the workhouse I was born
> On one Christmas day
> Two long ears and four short feet
> And all I ate was hay.
>
> Hay for breakfast, hay for dinner
> Lovely hay for tea,
> I thanked my benefactors thus
> Hee-haw hee-haw *hee !*

Now then, it's none so very difficult. All you need to know is
the right key to t'safe. I've got it on me watchchain. We
make a quick glance around in the interests of security, good,
they've all gone home to their teas, we open it up . . . (*He*

opens the safe.) And . . . the Borough Treasurer's petty cash!

(*He sings.*)

> When I was grown as tall as this
> I asked if I might go
> Into the world, the lovely world,
> I saw it through the window!

Aye, and they gave me permission and all:

> Get out, they said, you dirty brute,
> You've grown up quite disgusting.
> The world is welcome to your stink
> And to your horrid lusting.
> I thanked my benefactors thus . . . !

BLOMAX. Charlie, I say, Charlie, is this the real issue? I mean to say, there's no real hurry – it's not really that urgent . . .

BUTTERTHWAITE. Of course it's the real issue, you consequential fathead! There's nigh on a thousand in here. I don't know how many times I've had to tell these skiving clerks this is *not* the Barclays Bank!

BLOMAX. But surely they'll have made a note of the numbers?

BUTTERTHWAITE. Not on your life they haven't! Ho, there's some head going to roll in this office tomorrow morning. (*He is counting out packets of banknotes.*) There's your five hundred. Put it in your pocket! Go on, put it in!

(*He sings.*)

> I thanked my benefactors thus
> Hee-haw hee-haw haw.
> I could not understand, you see,
> Just how it was they thought of me
> Or what it was they saw!

What am I going to do wi' t'rest? I might keep it. But I won't. It'll only draw attention . . . I know . . .

He sings, and as he does so he scatters money about the stage.

> I travelled out into that world
> With never a backward glance,
> The street was full of folk, they said,
> He's got two ears upon his head
> He's got four feet upon his legs
> He's got . . . My God, look what he's got,
> They cried, Get back to France!

I said, what do you mean, France? I've never been to France in my life! I wor born in the workhouse. I never set foot over the doorstone while this morning!

> They cried, Get back to France!

Oh my God, it makes me tired . . .

> I could not think what I had done
> That I was so derided
> For Nature gives no donkey less
> Than what I was provided.

You see what I'm doing? We scatter it around, thereby indicating a similitude of ludicrous panic . . . as though disturbed in the act we have fled from the scene in terrified disorder.

> I said – hee-haw – you're very rude
> I do the best I can.
> You couldn't treat me worse, I said,
> If I was a human man!

(*He begins wiping fingerprints away.*) And the minute I said that they all fled away. Not a soul in sight in the whole of that long city . . . starved and hungry, there I stood, Wellington. Ooer, and a rumble-oh in my poor thin belly. All the pubs were shut, aye, and the chip-oyles an' all . . . I

walked along slowly by a pawnbroker's window, and as it
chanced, I saw my reflection in a gilt-framed ormulo mir-
ror . . .

> O what a shock, I nearly died,
> I saw my ears as small as these,
> Two feet, two hands, a pair of knees,
> My eyeballs jumped from side to side,
> I jumped right round, I bawled out loud,
> You lousy liars, I've found you out!
> I know now why you're fleeing . . .
> I am no donkey, never was,
> I'm a naked human being!

You know, after that, it was easy . . . all I had to do was to
buy a suit of clothes . . . they came back, they came back,
me boy, and there I prospered, there I grew . . . and you
look at me now!

BLOMAX. But how are we going to cover all this up?

BUTTERTHWAITE. Do you mean to tell me you haven't been
listening to a word I was singing. I have just given you my
entire and lamentable autobiography and all you can say is
'How do we cover it up!' . . . All right then, I'll tell you. It
is now eight o'clock as near as makes no difference, and by
reason of the inclemency of the weather, it is all but dark outside. I am going to proceed home at a normal pace. On entering my garden gate at approximately eight-twenty-five, I am
going to be struck on the head by a blunt instrument, wielded
by an unknown criminal, who then secures my bunch of keys,
leaps into his motor-car, and drives to the Town Hall. He
gains entry through a side door, passes through the adminis-
trative offices, and opens the safe. On his departure, he leaves
the keys i' t'lock-oyle.

BLOMAX. What about the night-watchman?

BUTTERTHWAITE. Do you mean Herbert Leftwich? We gave
him the telly in his room six months ago, and he never stirs

out of it while eleven o'clock at earliest . . . Now I'll tell you *your* part! You go straight off home, too. And you'll wait beside your blower till about a quarter-to-nine when my landlady (or concubine or whatever you call her) rings you up with an urgent call for assistance. On arrival, you examine my person, and discern a serious contusion on the top of me nut. All right, I'll have to provide one. But I don't want to kill meself. I rely on your diagnosis to make it appear sufficiently brutal. And don't you turn up with all that hot paper stuck inside your wallet. Take it out and bury it. And any rate, don't spend it all at once. But you don't want to spend it, you're being blackmailed – my God, they could trace it back to you if you hand it all over in one lump to some villain.

BLOMAX. I think I could hold out on him for a few days longer, but—

BUTTERTHWAITE. I think you'd better had. Our job's to fox the police, not to assist them . . . Fox the police. By God, it *will* fox 'em and all. Feng – we've got him diddled! Corruption they can live with, but incompetence – ho ho! Leftwich will have bolted the front door by now. You go out the side way, and see you leave it open. I'm going down by Leftwich's office to establish my time of departure. He'll let me out the main door and return straightaway to warming his old frustrations in front o' the juke-box jury . . . So there we are, get home with you! And no bloody dawdling, Wellington, or I promise you I'll twist your windpipe out!

Exeunt.

After a pause, enter LEFTWICH. *He is on his rounds, with a torch. He sees a banknote on the stage, picks it up with a 'Tut-tut', sees another, picks it up, sees another, and so on, casually, until he is led by his paper-chase up to the unlocked safe. He puts the money in, and turns away.*

LEFTWICH. I never knew a more careless lot in all my born

days. The place could have been robbed ten times over. (*Double-take. He rushes back to the safe, opens it, looks in, shuts it, and turns wildly round.*) Hey! Stop thief!

LEFTWICH *rushes to the side of the stage and presses a button. Alarm bells ring, all round the theatre.*

Police cars, gongs and engines heard. Uniformed PCs *run in, look at the safe, run out again, run in again, take up positions.*

LUMBER *and* WIPER, *in plain clothes, run in. Fingerprint man and police photographer set about their work.* LEFTWICH, *hurriedly replacing the money on the stage where he has found it, avoids being seen by the others, and succeeds in pocketing at least one banknote.* BOOCOCK *comes in, registers horror, collides with* WIPER *on the staircase: general confusion.* JOURNALISTS *come in with flash cameras. They take a series of photographs, illustrating:*

(1) WIPER *and* LUMBER *examining evidence.*

(2) BOOCOCK *ditto.*

(3) WIPER *and* LUMBER *taking statement from* LEFTWICH.

(4) BOOCOCK *taking statement from* LEFTWICH.

(5) WIPER *and* LUMBER *taking statement from* BOOCOCK.

(6) WIPER, LUMBER, BOOCOCK *and* LEFTWICH *taking statements from four* LABOUR COUNCILLORS, *who enter in disarray.*

(7) SWEETMAN *and* F. J. *examining evidence on their entry.*

(8) *The entry of* FENG.

FENG, *entered last, quickly examines the situation, while everyone else stands back.*

FENG (*to* WIPER, *confidentially*). Probably an inside job, Superintendent. But difficult to establish, I dare say. However, carry on.

Exeunt.

Act Three

SCENE ONE

A tea garden in the park.

Enter BLOMAX *carrying a folded newspaper.*

BLOMAX. I never thought it would work. I let myself be hypnotized by the magic of his personality . . . him and his contusion . . . sufficiently brutal . . . *my* diagnosis . . . It wouldn't have knocked out a three-days-old baby, what I found on his top! And they're playing cat-and-mouse with me now . . . for over a week it's been going on!

A plain-clothes PC *enters, reading a newspaper.*

That's a great big purring tom over there, with official-issue boots on, and he's looking at me through a little hole in the fold of his *Sheffield Star*. Of course, I can do the same. (*He opens his paper and makes a hole in it with his finger, through which he watches the* CONSTABLE.) But where does it get me? I think I'll have a cup o' tea. There's surely no danger in that?

A PARK ATTENDANT *arranges tables and a* WAITRESS *lays them.*

BLOMAX *sits down at a table which is laid ready, pours himself a large cup of tea and swallows it noisily. Takes aspirins. The* PC *also sits down at an opposite table and continues watching from behind his paper.*

A man who has sat at a table at the rear of the stage turns round and is seen to be FENG. *Noticing* BLOMAX, *he half gets up, indecisively.* BLOMAX *recognizes him and chokes into his tea-cup.*

Oh . . . it's got extremely stuffy sitting down all of a sudden

. . . I think I'll take a turn in the park . . . (*To the* WAIT-RESS.) Don't bother with the change, miss. You can buy yourself a . . . a knick-knack! (*He gives her a pound note and hurries out.*)

The PC *gets up to follow, but is intercepted by* FENG.

FENG. What was he doing here?

PC. Third teaplace he's visited since dinnertime, sir. A large pot o' tea and a couple of aspirins in each one. I fancy he's getting nervous.

FENG. So I observe. A change of tactics, Constable. Go after him now and take him down to the station. Tell the Superintendent to see if he can persuade him to reconsider his original statement. I think he might be ready to.

PC. Very good, sir . . . (*To the* WAITRESS.) I've left it on the table. (*Exit* PC.)

The WAITRESS *approaches* FENG.

WAITRESS. The usual, sir?

FENG. If you please. A variety of cakes. I thank you . . . Ah . . .

WELLESLEY *enters.* FENG *holds a chair back and she sits down with him.*

Miss Blomax . . . I'm so glad you could come. I have ordered the tea . . . I do not think, Miss Blomax, that you ought to have come . . . I do not think I should have asked you.

WELLESLEY. Go on, tell me why.

FENG. It is not possible.

WELLESLEY. Of course it is . . . I'm going to have one of these with the toothpaste in. (*She takes an éclair.*) Why don't you have one yourself? And drive off the black bull from the top of your tongue.

FENG.

> It is not possible that I should tell you why.
> I have not known you very long.
> For right or wrong
> Except when authorized for formal public utterance
> I must endure perpetual public silence.
> And so, for private purposes, I find
> My words are of necessity muted.
> You have not seemed to mind.
> You have drunk tea,
> Eaten cakes and toasted bread
> And jam, and you yourself have talked to me
> And I have been transported.
> Did you know it?

WELLESLEY. Oh yes, I knew it.

FENG. But did you share it? . . . No.

WELLESLEY. It's not my job to share it. It's your job to be courageous, I suppose, and nasty when you have to . . . Sometimes you can be quite gentle, and, of course, you're sentimental . . . But I don't approve of you, you know. I think I should make that clear because you seem to be working up to a renewal of your proposal.

FENG.

> No! It is not so. It cannot be.
> It is not possible. I am destroyed in you.
> Do you not see,
> By my official bond I am destroyed
> And you yourself in me.
> I cannot talk or think proposals, either way or none.
> Not now. I cannot recognize your company. Not now!
> Although in one sense, I suppose, the damage has been done.

WELLESLEY. Because of my father.

FENG. I did not say so.

WELLESLEY. You don't believe what he told you about the attack on the Alderman. If you want to marry me, you're in a

difficult position . . . I don't know what to say. I don't want
my father to go to prison. I don't want to make things any
worse for you . . . you're the only one of the old grey heads
I have any respect for. I don't want to hurt you, though I
don't care if I *have* to . . . And after a fashion I'm engaged
to Maurice Sweetman, and I don't really know whether I like
him at all. In a way I'd prefer you. You *are* some sort of *man*.

FENG. Do you mean that ?

WELLESLEY. Why not ? But I mean it, *provided* . . . I wish
you would change your job. Or at least become a bit human
at it and leave my father alone.

FENG. I can't hear what you say . . .

WELLESLEY. I said, leave him alone. He's a damned twisting
idiot, but he never did serious hurt.

FENG. No, no, I can't hear! Please leave me alone! . . . Or
rather, I'll leave you . . . We might be seen together, we
have been seen together, *heard* together, look! There is the
waitress! (*He shoves some coins on the table.*) Here you are.
See. It should include the tea, all the cakes I dare say; you
want to eat them, in *my* mouth they are sawdust . . .

  WELLESLEY *goes. He tries in vain to stop her.*

No, don't you go . . . It is *I* that should be leaving *you*. (*He
collides with the* WAITRESS.)

WAITRESS. How many cakes did you have, sir ?

FENG. Cakes ? Have ? What . . . ?

  Enter BOOCOCK.

BOOCOCK. I've been seeking you all afternoon. You may not
care for what I stand for, but I *am* Chief Magistrate and I'd
say it was up to you to show yourself available for once!

FENG. Mr Mayor, I . . .

BOOCOCK. Five hundred pound and upward burgled out o' my
Town Hall, near fifteen days gone by and who's arrested ?
No one! There are professional thieves living in this town;

they keep their wives and families by it; it's your job to know
their names. All right then, bring 'em in!

FENG. Bring in *whom*, sir?

BOOCOCK. The lot in, one by one, till you find out the man!
Instead o' which to choose to doubt the open word of an alderman and a doctor, honest and reputed, doubt their word and
watch their houses, tread upon their heels i' t'street . . .

FENG. Mr Mayor, I cannot hear you!

 Enter LABOUR COUNCILLORS.

HOPEFAST. Call your traps off Charlie Butterthwaite, Feng.

HICKLETON. Call 'em off. We want your resignation.

HARDNUTT. We want your resignation!

BOOCOCK. My mind is changed toward you, you've now gone
over t'mark.

BOOCOCK AND COUNCILLORS. We want your resignation!

WAITRESS. Order your teas or else get out. We don't have
brawling here. Do you want me to call the police!

FENG. I told you, sir, I cannot hear one word that you have
said to me!

 Exit FENG.

BOOCOCK. There is no further question of reproachment or
conciliation. This is deadlock.

HOPEFAST. Done.

HICKLETON. And capped.

HARDNUTT. And outright ended.

   Exeunt

SCENE TWO

The Police headquarters.

 PCS *in outer office, ignoring* BUTTERTHWAITE, *who is walking
about with a bandage round his head. He is unshaven and appears
to have taken few pains about the order of his clothes.*

BUTTERTHWAITE (*to the audience*). Will you all take note of what I am about to say. I have been called to this police station by Superintendent Wiper. I have been waiting here for five or six hours, and not one o' these incontinent coppers has taken a blind bit o' notice!

> WIPER *enters his inner office from within. He holds a type-script.*

WIPER. Sarnt Lumber!

LUMBER (*off*). Sir?

WIPER. Time?

LUMBER. Half-twelve, sir. All fixed.

> LUMBER *enters the outer office.* WIPER *comes through to it also.*

WIPER. Afternoon, Alderman. How's the head?

BUTTERTHWAITE. Aches.

WIPER. Oh, dear me. Now to go through your statement just once again, if you don't mind the trouble . . . just a few points . . . (*Refers to typescript.*) On passing through your garden gate, two masked figures rose from behind the privet hedge, one at either gatepost, you were stood betwixt 'em . . . so?

> *He and* LUMBER *at either side of* BUTTERTHWAITE.

Which one hit you?

BUTTERTHWAITE. You did!

WIPER. Sure? It couldn't have been the sergeant?

BUTTERTHWAITE. It could not.

WIPER. But here's the contusion.

BUTTERTHWAITE. Ow, don't touch that bandage!

WIPER. We've had ballistics research in on this. No conceivable injury could from this angle cause even the most temporary failure of the faculties.

BUTTERTHWAITE. You can't catch me. *I've* read me Sexton Blake. I was turned the other way. (*He turns round.*)

WIPER. Are you in the habit, Alderman, of entering your garden backwards?

BUTTERTHWAITE. In the moment of alarm I instinctively swung round to face the open street. What's wrong wi' that?

WIPER. Aha, we're there before you. We photographed your footprints. Quite right, you *were* turned round. Now then, which one hit you?

He and LUMBER *change places.*

BUTTERTHWAITE. You did, you!

WIPER. Me?

BUTTERTHWAITE. No, not you, you booby! *Him.*

WIPER. I see. And from the rear. Now ballistics research has conclusively established . . .

BUTTERTHWAITE. Spare me the Jack Hawkins, will you! The fact remains that I got coshed and here's the wound to prove it. Now get around that if you can.

WIPER. We've got.

BUTTERTHWAITE. You've what?

WIPER. Constable, let's be having him!

Two PCS *bring in* BLOMAX, *rather the worse for wear and holding a mug of tea.*

BUTTERTHWAITE. Wellington! Have they been roughing you up? Oh . . .

WIPER. Dr Blomax, your original statement diagnosing concussion and lesions of the brain has not been borne out by further medical opinion. Do you wish to modify that statement?

LUMBER (*taking a typescript from a* PC). He does, sir.

WIPER. Let's hear it.

BUTTERTHWAITE (*as* LUMBER *is about to read*). I want to telephone my solicitor.

WIPER. All in good time.

BLOMAX. Hey, so do I.

WIPER. If you're going Queen's evidence you don't require a solicitor.

BLOMAX. Oh, Charlie, it's not my fault – they've had me in here all night; I wasn't able to withstand them!

BUTTERTHWAITE. I don't suppose you were. As I have frequently had cause to preach, you can't by individuality hold up props against the overtippling world. By solid class defence and action of the mass alone can we hew out and line with timbered strength a gallery of self-respect beneath the faulted rock above the subsidence of water! Alfred Wiper, you watch out. I bear a name that still commands proud worship in these parts!

Enter FENG, *into the outer office.*

FENG. Has the Doctor reconsidered his testimony?

WIPER. He has, sir. Here we are.

FENG goes into the inner office and WIPER follows with BLOMAX's statement.

FENG. I see. It is unusable, I'm afraid.

WIPER. But, sir . . .

FENG. There are reasons, Superintendent, relating to my personal honour, names which might be coupled. I cannot permit this particular man to have the advantage of Queen's evidence. He must stand his trial with the other.

WIPER. We can't do that! He's submitted this voluntarily – we've no choice but to take it. It'll look very queer indeed if—

FENG. Queer?

WIPER. I mean to say, sir, your personal honour . . . Well, folk are going to wonder if it hasn't already become a bit bent.

FENG. That's quite enough of that. You must find out your

own evidence by correct detective measures. I have no more
to say.

*FENG goes out through the inner door. WIPER returns to the
outer office.*

WIPER. Sarnt Lumber, a change of tactic. There is more hard
work entailed than we in our innocence had imagined. So
send the gentlemen home.

He goes back through the inner office and exits that way.

LUMBER. All right. You heard him. Go home.

BLOMAX. Oh, my dearie me, what an amazing metamorphosis
. . . (*He scurries out.*)

BUTTERTHWAITE. Well, well, well, Sergeant. Are you sure it's
worth the effort?

LUMBER. The results of human striving are very rarely worth
the effort. For instance, did you hear that after all your
worthy struggle the Copacabana Club has closed its doors
for the last time, only to re-open on the first day of May as
the 'Sweetman Memorial Art Gallery'? What about that for
the artistic interests of the town?

BUTTERTHWAITE. Why warn't I informed!

LUMBER. You *have* been informed.

BUTTERTHWAITE. In a very irregular manner . . . So he did
own that joint all the bloody while, did he?

LUMBER. I wouldn't know. According to the story, he acquired
it last week. *I* wouldn't care to come up with a contradiction.
And I don't suppose *you* would . . . under the circumstances.

BUTTERTHWAITE. Get out o' my road!

Exit BUTTERTHWAITE.

LUMBER (*calls after him*). Alderman, be careful, we're not done
wi' you yet!

Exeunt

SCENE THREE

The Victoria and Albert.

> *Enter* LABOUR COUNCILLORS, *a few* DRINKERS, LAND-
> LORD *behind bar.*

The COUNCILLORS *sit down at a table.*

HICKLETON. Why hasn't Feng resigned? There's been a
formal council vote of no confidence and yet he's still here!

HOPEFAST. The last I heard o' Charlie, they pulled him in this
morning afore he'd even had his breakfast.

A DRINKER (*sings.*)
O where are the people for to give their voice to glory?
They stand before the altar on the elbow of the Tory . . . !

Other DRINKERS *join in the song and repeat it.*

HARDNUTT. If we can't be private we can take our money elsewhere!

LANDLORD (*hurrying over to them*). I'll sort it out . . . (*To the*
DRINKERS.) Now come on, gents, have some decency while
a funeral's in progress!

> *He puts a screen round their table which conceals them from
> the rest of the room.*

But they're not wrong, you know, they're right. There's been
a definite trend in the general talk. (*He goes back to the bar.*)

HOPEFAST. When all is said and done, the image of our party
must not be distorted.

> MRS BOOCOCK *comes in and joins them behind the screen.*

MRS BOOCOCK. Have any o' you seen Barney?

COUNCILLORS. Why, Sarah, sit down, have a chair, love, it's a
surprise to see you here. What are you drinking, etc . . .

MRS BOOCOCK. That doctor's gone Queen's evidence. Start

with the Ways and Means Committee. Have we a quorum ?

HARDNUTT. We have.

MRS BOOCOCK. We've not got time to waste. Come on . . . Councillor Hopefast i' t'chair, Councillor Hardnutt and Hickleton present in Committee, Mayoress Mrs Boocock as deputy secretary.

HOPEFAST. I declare the Committee in session.

HARDNUTT. Minutes of the previous meeting regarded as read . . . Come on . . . Come on . . .

HICKLETON. Seconded.

HOPEFAST. Passed. Motion before the Committee, temporary absence of Alderman Butterthwaite necessitates reconstruction of Committee. Who's to replace him ?

HICKLETON. I move that Councillor Hathersage be deputed to do so.

HARDNUTT. Seconded.

HOPEFAST. Passed . . . Now then, Borough Education. I declare the Committee in session, have we a quorum ?

MRS BOOCOCK. I'm in on this one.

HOPEFAST. Councillor Hickleton deputy secretary, change about places . . . Councillor Hardnutt i' t'chair . . .

HARDNUTT. Minutes of previous meeting . . .

ALL. Etcetera etcetera . . .

HARDNUTT. Motion before . . . etcetera etcetera . . . Who's to replace him ?

MRS BOOCOCK. I move that Councillor Hartwright be deputed to do so.

HARDNUTT. Seconded. Passed . . . Parks Playgrounds and Public Baths Committee.

HICKLETON. Councillor Hickleton i' t'chair, Mayoress Mrs Boocock again deputy secretary.

ALL. Etcetera etcetera . . .

HARDNUTT. Who's to replace him ?

HOPEFAST. I move that Councillor Hampole . . .

ALL. Seconded, passed!

HOPEFAST. Any more for any more, we've got no time to waste!

BOOCOCK comes in and joins them. He carries a letter.

MRS BOOCOCK. Barney, where have you been?

BOOCOCK. What are you doing here?

MRS BOOCOCK. I'm having a drink.

BOOCOCK. That's most unwonted, ent it? . . . The Home Secretary in person has sent us a letter. He does not like the name our township is achieving. Indeed, he is so disturbed by it that he has threatened to go so far as to withdraw the government subsidy for our local police. Well, all I say is – this!

He tears the letter and crumples it and grinds it underfoot.

We are a self-governing Socialist community with Dearne and Don and Calder for our inviolate boundaries, and we will continue to press for the resignation of Feng!

HOPEFAST. Barney, did you hear that they've arrested Charlie?

BOOCOCK. Indeed, I did hear it. Why else have I done this?

(He points to the remains of the letter.)

MRS BOOCOCK. Our party cannot afford to be associated with thieves.

BOOCOCK. Sarah!

MRS BOOCOCK. Action has been taken, Barney. Tell him.

HOPEFAST. The natural suspicion attaching to a criminal charge has rendered inexpedient the retention of Alderman Butterthwaite on various committees. Of course, we don't rule out the eventual possibility of rehabilitation.

BOOCOCK. You . . . you can't just vote him out! There aren't sufficient present.

HOPEFAST. Provisionally we can do. The rest can be arranged.

MRS BOOCOCK. It will be arranged. I'm off to see to it now.

Barney, my dear, as usual, you have arrived a bit too tardy.
(*She goes out.*)

HARDNUTT. This is a party issue, Barney. You can't stand
independent. (*He goes out.*)

HICKLETON. None of us wanted it. None of us like it. (*He
goes out.*)

HOPEFAST. Bear in mind, Barney, he *was* short of money. (*He
goes out.*)

BOOCOCK (*stamping with frustration*). His Worship the Mayor.
His Honour and His Worship. His Grace and His Majesty
and His Worship the Mayor . . . Oh, oh, my leg . . .

> He staggers and falls, knocking the screen over. BUTTER-
> THWAITE *is standing at the bar. He is much as in the police
> station, but wearing a ragged old muffler, and a woollen tam
> o'shanter over his bandage.*

BUTTERTHWAITE. Aye aye, me old Barney. I heard what was
said.

BOOCOCK. Charlie! You're out of jail! They couldn't pin nowt
on you! Thank God for that! I believe in you, Charlie. I'm
going to combat this sordid betrayal. I will not permit . . .

BUTTERTHWAITE. You can't prevent. The wheel of years is
now rotating. I'm voted out. This afternoon, I'm drinking.

BOOCOCK. *I'll* show you my loyalty.

> BUTTERTHWAITE *laughs and* BOOCOCK *goes out.*

BUTTERTHWAITE. Who's drinking with me? Why, is there
nobody?

A DRINKER. You gave us the appearance of wanting to be on
your own.

BUTTERTHWAITE. Appearances are deceptive. Frank, here
you are! You can serve us i' t'back. (*He throws a handful of
money on the bar.*) I don't want to see anybody bahn off to
their dinners until this is drunk up. But afore you make your

choices, which gentlemen present take an interest in fine arts?

General giggles.

A DRINKER. If you mean dirty postcards . . .

BUTTERTHWAITE. Not precisely dirty postcards . . . This good brass I am expending here is the last of all my petty savings – the dregs of a lifetime of service to the community. Look, here's me Post Office book – 'Account Closed', do you see it? . . . Community? What's community? *You?* 'Oh no,' you said, 'not me,' you said – and rightly said, by Judas – 'leave it to the mugs,' you said, *'we're* lousy.' Well, Charlie's lousy too: and Charlie bears in mind that the first day of May is not only a day of Socialist congratulation but also a day of traditional debauchment in the base of a blossoming hedge-row . . . *I* pay for the drink, *you* sup it up, and in return you're going to do what I request – least-roads, I *hope* you are, for any lad as tries to finkle *me*, by gor, I'll finkle *him* till his eyes are looking out through the cleft of his armpit . . . Come on into t'back bar; I'm not calling you twice . . . (*He leads them all into the inner room.*)

SCENE FOUR

Inside the Copacabana Club . . . now an art gallery.

Artistic screens hung with paintings occupy the upper part of the stage. The front stage area is a sort of foyer laid out for a reception. One table covered with green baize holds catalogues, etc. Another table set out as a buffet with champagne and sandwiches. Paperchains from the roof. A white ribbon tied across the back of the foyer, as a formal barrier preventing access to the pictures.

GLORIA (*in a very demure dress*) *superintending buffet and catalogues,* LADY SWEETMAN *and* YOUNG SWEETMAN *hurrying about making last-minute alterations.*

Enter BLOMAX (*he is not noticed by the others on the stage*).

BLOMAX (*to the audience*).

And so we lead on, to the final cruel conclusion
Compounded of corruption and unresolved confusion.
I think the time has come to resolve it, if I can.
Here I stand alone, an embrangled English man
Nerving myself up in the torment of my duty.
The first day of May is the day of Art and Beauty,
The dust of Sweetman thrust into the eye-balls of you all
For to wash you white and whiter than the whitewash on the
   wall.
But out in the dark back lane
The great grey cat still waits by the mouse's hole.
You'll observe the general sense of bygones being bygones
. . . (*He points to* GLORIA.) Who'd recognize her now, stood
ready to draw out the corks for the nobility and gentry? Who
indeed would recognize the premises themselves, where the
only indication of what's under the underwear is on a canvas
by Titian . . . or at least William Etty? Titillation, if you
like, but in a form that even Lady Sweetman regards as
desirable.

> *The room begins to fill.*
>
> SWEETMAN *with wife and son.* FENG, WELLESLEY,
> CONSERVATIVE LADIES, F. J., BOOCOCK, COUNCIL-
> LORS *are present.*
>
> BOOCOCK *wears his chain, but no robes.*

SWEETMAN. Ha-h'm. The opening of a new art gallery is, or
should be, a pleasurable labour, for the benefit of thousands.
Therefore, I will not remind you that works of art – no less
magnificent than those from my collection which already
hang here – are lying at this moment in the cellars of the
Municipal Hospital, unthought-of and unenjoyed . . . but
not, may I hope, for ever? It gives me enormous pleasure to

detect one sign of reconciliation – His Worship the Mayor is with us today, and also many of his . . .

BOOCOCK. Not to be construed as an official occasion but purely as a social courtesy in recognition of cultural attainment.

MRS BOOCOCK. Sir Harold Sweetman, Lady Sweetman, ladies and gentlemen, we feel in the Labour Party that the provision of an art gallery, albeit a worthy objective, does not warrant the expenditure of public money upon what is, after all, a luxury amenity. So all the more do we of the Labour Party welcome the initiative of private enterprise upon this issue. I would like to say . . . 'thank you', Sir Harold. And thank you also, Lady Sweetman; you have done us all a proud and worthy service.

Applause.

SWEETMAN. Yes. Madam Mayoress, thank *you*. Now it only remains that I request my dear wife to formally inaugurate the Gallery.

LADY SWEETMAN. Let me tell you first about the dedication of this Gallery. It is called the 'Sweetman Memorial Gallery', not in memory of Sir Harold, who is still very much with us . . .

BLOMAX *picks up a glass of champagne.*

GLORIA. Hey . . .

BLOMAX. Morituro te salutant!

GLORIA. You get out of here at once!

BLOMAX. No. Dulce et decorum est pro filia pulcherrima incarceri in vinculis. Wellesley, let go of me; you'll undermine me resolution.

LADY SWEETMAN (*trying to ignore his interruption*). . . . but in memory of his father, the late Mr. Fortunatus Sweetman, whose enterprise and industry brought wealth and fortune to us all . . .

BLOMAX. I want to talk to Colonel Feng!

FENG (*to* SWEETMAN). Had you invited Mr Blomax here, sir?

SWEETMAN. Indeed I had not. Are you aware, Doctor, that this is a private function?

BLOMAX. Colonel Feng, observe my daughter. She requires a new father, and behold, here he is! I am washing myself in public with the detergent of self-sacrifice. Five hundred pounds. Take it, Mr Mayor. You know where it comes from.

(*He hands the money to* BOOCOCK.)

BOOCOCK. We all thought you'd been exonerated.

BLOMAX. No, no. I am confessing. And the extraordinary thing is, I had already confessed. I offered Queen's evidence! Why was it refused?

SWEETMAN. Was it, Colonel? Why?

FENG. Queen's evidence, albeit dramatic, is not necessarily sufficient. Or even true. You surely know that, sir.

LADY SWEETMAN (*in desperation*). So it gives me great pleasure to declare the 'Sweetman Memorial Art Gallery' open for all time to the people of this town.

She takes a little pair of scissors and cuts the tape.
Applause.

Now I hope you will all enjoy yourselves and don't go home till you've seen everything.

She and her husband contrive to move the guests up among the pictures. BLOMAX, BOOCOCK *and* FENG *remain in the foyer.* SWEETMAN *returns to them.*

BLOMAX. In any case, I can tell you, my Queen's evidence was highly sufficient – and every word of it was true. I am very sorely afraid I have been deliberately victimized. So I am making my appeal to the high society of the town.

BOOCOCK. This is very very shocking indeed, Wellington. But, Colonel Feng, Dr Blomax has been my medical adviser for a great many years. I think it would show a more humane spirit if you accepted his plea. After all, he *has* returned the money.

SWEETMAN. Yes, Colonel, surely we don't need to press this matter now in regard to Dr Blomax? That is, if he *can* give us all the full details of everything that happened . . .

YOUNG SWEETMAN. That's the voice of two magistrates, Colonel. You can't entirely neglect it.

SWEETMAN. Speak when you're spoken to.

FENG. The decision is *mine*. It is nobody else's. This man is an accomplice, but the thief himself is still at large: and until he is apprehended you must permit me to handle it as best I know how.

WELLESLEY. And handle it inevitably so that my father goes to jail? And he going to jail will leave your conscience clear enough for you to marry me.

BLOMAX. Marry? Him? You? . . . But what about Maurice? I confessed because of *him!*

WELLESLEY. And Colonel Feng confessed. He confessed he was in love with me. So I naturally asked him to destroy his integrity and make it easier for you.

FENG. Naturally.

WELLESLEY. And equally naturally he has been unable to do it. I have often dreamed I would be the beautiful destruction of the strength of a good man. It has turned out to be more comfortable to deal only with feeble ones. What about you, Maurice, how are you for integrity?

YOUNG SWEETMAN. *Me?*

WELLESLEY. Don't worry, I will marry you: because I don't have to respect you and I don't have to continually involve myself in the curls and contortions of an extraordinary code of ethics. Have you even seen a boa-constrictor that strangled itself with itself? . . . Oh dear, I feel so miserable.

The GUESTS *have drifted away from the pictures and the last few speeches have been heard by everyone.*

SWEETMAN. Colonel Feng, is this true? I mean, *have* you proposed to her?

FENG. Yes, sir, it is true, as a matter of observable fact. I will not humiliate myself, Sir Harold, by explaining my motives. But I take it that as a gentleman you will not dispute my word when I inform you most solemnly that my professional integrity has in no whit been compromised by whatever misconstruction this young woman puts upon it, *deliberately* puts upon it. She has *not* destroyed me, no . . . She does not influence me, sir, in one way or the other; my private life is private . . . It appears I am confounded, sir, by endeavouring to preserve it so, but . . .

SWEETMAN. But in fact you're telling me that if it wasn't for this little half-dago doxy that bloody robber Butterthwaite would have been behind bars a week since!

F. J. Precisely what side do you imagine you're on!

FENG. Side, do you say, sir, side! I am not, sir, aware of it. I am aware that my *own* side, my private side, Sir Harold, may well indeed be for derision, humiliated and confounded, but, sir, I am not destroyed, sir . . . I am not yet aware of *side !*

BLOMAX. In that case, Colonel Feng, you're the only man present that isn't!

FENG. You! You are not to speak further. I cannot bear it further!

BLOMAX. *I've* had to bear more than *you've* had to bear! I've had to commit myself, and as a result without intention I have dropped my poor friend Charlie where I cannot believe he will ever get out of. I thought when I determined to return the five hundred we could call it a closed book . . . but I see that we can't. Alas, the British police, with their well-known impartiality and their zeal for adamantine truth and justice, are clearly going to triumph yet again. So I now have no choice but to deliver my second preparation – all typed out in quadruplicate. (*He produces some sheets of typescript.*) Oh, Gloria, I beg your pardon, for you this is catastrophe, I have stripped us all fair frozen, with not one obligation left honoured.

He distributes his papers.

Mr Mayor, here's your copy – Chief Constable, yours! Sir Harold, here's yours! The unexpurgated history, gentlemen, of the Copacabana Club that was and Superintendent Wiper that still is, with all his little relationships that even Charlie didn't find out. And by and large the entire question of the bracing and the strutting of your backbone, Colonel Feng!

SWEETMAN (*throwing his paper on the floor*). You will not of course, Colonel, attach any credence to . . .

BOOCOCK Colonel Feng, you are holding that piece of paper upside down. Permit me to . . .

FENG *turns his back and walks away among the pictures.*
Enter WIPER *in a hurry.*

WIPER. Where's the Chief Constable? . . . Hello, what's going on?

BLOMAX *gives* WIPER *the fourth copy.*

BLOMAX. Mr Mayor, do *you* believe what I've written down on these?

BOOCOCK. I must say I am afraid it is only too plausible . . . Go on, read it, Superintendent. We would like to hear your comments!

WIPER. You jerked-up Jack-in-office, do you not realize what's happening! My comments can wait. I've got a job to do! Sir Harold, I must ask you to close down your gallery.

SWEETMAN. What . . . whatever for?

WIPER. A matter of public order. A quarter of an hour ago Alderman Butterthwaite removed himself from the Victoria and Albert with the entire mid-morning congregation of that celebrated resort, and at this present moment he is on his way out here . . . with half a hundred others, of the lowest type in town, layabouts, tearaways, every man of 'em half-seas over!

LADY SWEETMAN. But what does he want!

WIPER. I think he wants to wreck your gallery. We've only just found out, but it appears he's been working this up for over a week.

SWEETMAN. Why haven't you stopped him?

WIPER. In the middle of the town? How much open scandal do you really want to have? Up here we can contain them – I've given orders for a cordon, but . . .

SWEETMAN. Chief Constable!

F. J. Where is he?

FENG *comes back into the main stage.*

SWEETMAN. Chief Constable, come here. I am holding you responsible if there is violence or damage, entirely responsible!

FENG.

> Violence, damage . . . done already, done,
> All violence perpetrated, broken down
> In violence, brickwork cracked and fallen, damage,
> Responsibility . . . whose? Not long ago
> In this elected Council there was in violence
> Raised a violent demand I should resign.
> I did not notice it. I said that I
> Derived authority for my high office not
> From the jerk and whirl of irrelevant faction –
> You, sir, and you, your democratic Punch and Judy –
> But from the Law, being abstract, extant, placed,
> Proclaimed 'I am'! But, as you say, sir, now,
> Violence and damage, I *do* resign, sir, now.
> Good day to you, Superintendent. Law and Order?

Here is your confidence, your credence, *here*
Is your impartial service. *I* resign,
Continue, Mr Wiper . . . Preserve the peace.

*While he is speaking there is a growing clamour outside which
resolves itself into shouts of 'three times three for Charlie B',
etc. . . . and a ragged singing of 'Ilkley Moor'.
Enter* LUMBER *in a hurry, and several* PCs.

LUMBER. Colonel Feng, sir . . .
FENG (*waves him towards* WIPER). No, no, to *him* . . .

FENG *goes upstairs.*

LUMBER (*looking from one to the other*). Er . . . sir ?
WIPER. Well ?
LUMBER. It's not going too well; we were took by surprise
across the lunch hour; you see, they've all piled on the buses
. . . I'm afraid they'll be in here before I can get a full
cordon. I've three radio cars up already, but one of the lorries
has developed magneto trouble . . . I've ordered out the
mounted squad . . . what about the dogs ?

The noise grows.

They're forcing the cordon now! It's sheer weight of numbers! I've got all the PCs lined up on the steps but . . .
WIPER. Get these men to the doors! You, you, you, you –
there, there, there, there!

*The PCs rush off, at his direction, down the aisles to hold the
auditorium doors, which are being forced. Sounds of struggle
from the foyers. Some demonstrators break in. They are
carrying bottles, and placards with such slogans as 'All fine
art is a hearty fart', 'Paint me, paint my dog', 'You can't gild
a mucky lily', 'If the people scrawl, put glazed tiles on the
wall', and so on. Some placards have drawings on them of
women's bodies, etc.*

The PCs *pursue them and succeed, after fighting in the aisles
or on the stage, in chasing or dragging them out. The doors are
finally held, but only by the utmost efforts of the police.
During the commotion* BUTTERTHWAITE *has come in at the
rear of the stage. He sweeps some plates off the buffet and sits
on the table cross-legged. He helps himself to champagne and
a hunk of iced cake.*

BUTTERTHWAITE. If you've got in mind to rax me off this
table, you can have another think. There's more uses nor one
to a bottle o' bubbly, and I'm proficient in 'em all.

He sings.

As it fell out upon a day, rich Dives he made a feast,
And he invited all his friends and gentry of the best,
But Lazarus he sat down and down and down at Dives' door,
Some meat, some drink, brother Dives, he said, bestow unto
the poor!

FENG. Now, Mr Wiper, what's your next move?
WIPER. *I'm* handling this.
FENG. I know. I am highly entertained, sir.
WIPER. Sergeant . . .

LUMBER *makes a move towards* BUTTERTHWAITE, *who
poises his bottle menacingly. A little* DEMONSTRATOR
breaks through one of the doors, slips past the PCs *trying to
prevent him, and scuttles on to the stage as though for sanctuary. He squats down at* BUTTERTHWAITE's *feet, and the*
PC *pursuing him gives up indecisively.*
FENG *turns his back and affects interest in the pictures.*

BUTTERTHWAITE. Now then, Brother Boocock, are you holding up all right, are you? With all them prime Sheffield
knifeblades I've inserted in your shoulder bones.
BOOCOCK. I am still in great part vertical. Which is more than
can be said for you, Charlie. I don't know why you've done

this, but your last remaining friends can do nowt for you now. You have pulled your own self down.

BUTTERTHWAITE. Aye. But there's others aside from me have had their hands on t'ropes, though . . . haven't they, me old Wellington ?

BLOMAX. Charlie, I've been pulling on all the ropes round here. Not only on yours.

BUTTERTHWAITE. Go on ? Who else is done for ?

BLOMAX *makes a gesture towards* FENG.

Oh no, not Colonel Feng ! You've not got rid of Feng ! Not *you* . . . Oh God, *you* ! The subsidence of water . . . After all my subtle skirmishes, my cannonadings, my outflankings . . .

BLOMAX. You yourself were outflanked, Charlie. Although you didn't know it, at the crux of the campaign I was fighting for the Prussians. This unhappy Chief Constable was never at war at all.

BUTTERTHWAITE. Oh, but he was, though . . . he was in treaty with Sweetman.

BLOMAX. You've always enjoyed my little bits o' patter, Charlie. But you should never ha' believed 'em.

BUTTERTHWAITE. So that's how it was . . . the beloved physician . . . Colonel, I say Colonel, I'm talking to *you* ! I give you no apology. You're a strong-backboned man and you chose of your own free will to do our dirty work. And if it's turned out a sight dirtier than might have been foretold, I am sure that you will find yourself an occupational philosophy, and remain like Barney Boocock in great part still vertical. Oh, oh, oh, I have lived. I have controlled, I have redistributed. The Commonwealth has gained. The tables have been spread. Not with bread and marge, you know, like they used to in the workhouse, but with a summation of largesse demanding for its attendance soup-spoons in their rank, fish-knives and forks, flesh-knives and forks, spoons

for the pudding, gravy and cruet, caper sauce and mayon-
naise . . . and I by my virtue stood the President of the
feast! . . . All right, you've got the belly-ache, and so I've
got to go. But I don't take it kindly. Philosophy be damned.
There's a foul wind blows over t'moor-top on this cold Mayday morning. The peoples of the world are marching and
rejoicing alongside the saluting-bases, but here I've called to
action a detachment of forces that have never heard a bugle!
My army today is a terrible shambles. Look at 'em, fellow
Councillors; you ruled 'em, *I* ruled 'em, and we never knew
who they were! I'll tell you who they were; they drank and
slept and skived and never punched a bloody clock when
clocks was for the asking. We piped to them and they did not
dance, we sang them our songs and they spat into t'gutter.
(*He pats the little* DEMONSTRATOR's *head.*) I was the grand
commander of the whole of my universe. Now all that's left
me is the generalship of these. I need to assume a different
order o' raiment. (*He pulls the baize tablecloth to him and
arranges it like a shawl.*) Three times three, but all that's left
is paper.

He pulls down a paper chain and hangs it round his neck.

Three times three is nine, but the old cocked hat's bashed in.
So here's a replacement.

*He picks up a ring of flowers that has been garnishing the
buffet and puts it on his head.*

. . . In my rejection I have spoken to this people. I will
rejoice despite them. I will divide Dewsbury and mete out
the valley of Bradford; Pudsey is mine, Huddersfield is mine,
Rotherham also is the strength of my head, Osset is my law-
giver, Black Barnsley is my washpot, over Wakefield will I
cast out my shoe, over Halifax will I triumph. Who will bring
me into the strong city, who will lead me into the boundaries

of Leeds? Wilt not thou, oh my deceitful people, who hast cast me off? And wilt not thou go forth with Charlie?

LITTLE DEMONSTRATOR. Hey ey, we're going, we're all going forth together!

BUTTERTHWAITE. No. Oh no. Oh no, you aren't. The only place you're going is into t'black maria.

Police car noises from offstage and voices giving orders.

LUMBER (*to* WIPER). Sir, it's the reinforcements . . .

WIPER. Right, Mr Butterthwaite, we'd like a word with you outside.

The PCs *drag out the* DEMONSTRATOR, *and then come for* BUTTERTHWAITE, *who lets himself go limp. As* BUTTER-THWAITE *is removed up the aisle, he sings:*

BUTTERTHWAITE.

> Out he goes the poor old donkey
> Out he goes in rain and snow,
> For to make the house place whiter
> Who will be the next to go?

> Clean the kitchen and the parlour,
> Scrub the wall and scrub the floor,
> Clean the hoofmarks off the lino
> And the smears from off the door.

> Climb a ladder and wipe the windows,
> Swill the roof with water clear,
> Pour your soap suds down the chimney
> Till none can tell what beast was here.

> When all is washed and all is scoured
> And all is garnished bright as paint,
> Who will come with his six companions
> And a stink to make you faint?

*The song is taken up by those outside the theatre, and con-
cludes (if time allows) with a fortissimo reprise of the first
stanza.*

SWEETMAN. Thank you, Superintendent. Most commendably
accomplished, sir.

BOOCOCK. There is still a very great deal to be gone into and
sorted out. Nothing of what has happened redounds to anyone's credit. So who's going to make a start and establish a
fair inquiry?

BLOMAX. Oh it's not so bad as all that. The start has already
been made. Our accumulated garbage has all been carted out
and there's nothing more to do now but to polish the sides of
the dustbin a bit and keep away the horse-flies. The Conservative Party, on balance, will find the whole business . . .

SWEETMAN. The whole business should, on balance, weigh
slightly to our advantage.

F. J. I think it should.

SWEETMAN. Yes.

BLOMAX. While the Labour Party, on the other hand . . .

HARDNUTT AND HICKLETON. We prefer to defer comment
upon this unsavoury episode.

HOPEFAST AND MRS BOOCOCK. But we wish nevertheless to
publicly dissociate ourselves from it.

ALL THE COUNCILLORS AND MRS BOOCOCK. We lay the
matter with confidence before the good sense of the electorate.

BLOMAX. The Superintendent will resign . . .

WIPER. Of my own free will, please note, no questions asked,
and I get a pension.

BLOMAX. My darling daughter Wellesley will marry her
fiancé . . . Go on, go on, give him a kiss.

   WELLESLEY *does so.*

And in consideration of my future tact and silence on all

public occasions, I, her useless father, shall be liberally accepted into the bosom of his family. (*He shakes* SWEETMAN *by the hand.*) How d'you do, sir?

SWEETMAN. How d'you do?

BLOMAX. Lady Sweetman . . . ?

LADY SWEETMAN. My dear Doctor . . .

BLOMAX. May I present my dear wife?

LADY SWEETMAN. I would be delighted, Doctor. My dear Mrs Blomax . . .

BLOMAX. It's really so much tidier and altogether less awkward. I have made arrangements for a private maternity ward in Leeds . . .

WIPER. To be, of course, defrayed from the aforementioned pension.

BLOMAX. Wellesley, my darling, why don't you kiss him again? No one's going to interfere.

She does so.

ALL AS CHORUS (*except* FENG).

No one's going to *dare* to interfere.

FENG. I am very sorry, Miss Blomax, to have exposed you to the imperfections of your person at so unseasonable a time. I trust that it will not be long before you regain your equilibrium. Gentlemen, I am going to London. I shall inform the Home Secretary how much I have appreciated the efficiency and speed with which the Superintendent dealt with this . . . Gangway, if you please, I'm coming through . . . (*He leaves.*)

ALL.

We stand all alone to the north of the Trent
You leave us alone and we'll leave you alone
We take no offence where none has been meant
But you hit us with your fist, we'll bash *you* with a stone!
Withdraw those quivering nostrils

We smell as we think decent
If we tell you we've cleaned our armpits
You'd best believe we've cleaned 'em recent
We have washed them white and whiter
Than the whitewash on the wall
And if for THE WORKHOUSE DONKEY
We should let one tear down fall
Don't think by that he's coming back . . .
The old sod's gone for good and all!

THE END

ALTERNATIVE SPEECHES FOR PROLOGUE AND EPILOGUE

(1) BLOMAX' *opening speech* (*Act One*):
Ladies and gentlemen, I am a native
Of the Greater London conurbation.
I found at first your northern parts not very conducive
To what was perhaps my more courtly mode of deportment:
But having arrived here I soon made the adjustment,
Involving geographically an appreciable mutation,
(I mean, in landscape, climate, odours, voices, food):
I put it to you that such a journey needs
In the realm of morality an equal alteration.
I mean, is there anything you really believe to be bad?
If you lived in the south you might well think it good.
You might well think, as I do,
That you should change the shape of your faces,
Or even double their number
When you travel between two places.
The values of other people
Are not quite as you understand them.
I would not overpraise them,

I would not recommend them,
I am certainly not here in order to condemn them.
From the beginning to the end
Each man is bound to act
According to his nature
And the nature of his land.
Your land is different from theirs.
Why, (county by county*) it has its own music.

*   *   *

(2) *Concluding* CHORUS (*Act Three*):
We stand all alone to the north of the Trent
Let them leave us alone and we'll leave them alone
We take no offence where none has been meant
But they hit us with their fist, we'll bash 'em back with a stone!
They can pull up their damn nostrils,
We smell as we think decent.
If we tell them we've cleaned our armpits
They'd best believe we've cleaned them recent.
We have washed them white and whiter
Than the whitewash on the wall
And if for the WORKHOUSE DONKEY
We should let one tear down fall . . .
Nobody need think that he's going to come back:
The old black leech is gone for good and all!

*   *   *

* Words in parenthesis to be omitted in the West Riding of
Yorkshire.

Armstrong's Last Goodnight

AN EXERCISE IN DIPLOMACY

TO CONOR CRUISE O'BRIEN

who (to quote John Skelton) wrote

'. . . of Sovereignty a noble pamphlet;
And of Magnificence a notable matter,
How Counterfeit Countenance of the new jet
With Crafty Conveyance doth smatter and
    flatter,
And Cloaked Collusion is brought in to clatter
With Courtly Abusion; who printeth it well in
    mind
Much doubleness of the worlde therein he may
    find.'

And not only did he write it but he was also not
ashamed to act upon his observations.

General Notes

This play is founded upon history: but it is not to be read as an accurate chronicle. The biggest liberty I have taken with the known historical facts is in connecting Sir David Lindsay with the events leading up to the execution of Johnny Armstrong in 1530. But these events must have involved considerable political and diplomatic manœuvring, and it is known that Lindsay was not only the author of *The Three Estates* and Lord Lyon King of Arms but also regularly employed upon diplomatic missions for the Scottish Crown. His own views upon the Armstrong business may be partly deduced from the lines in *The Three Estates*, where he makes his crooked Pardoner offer for sale as a blessed relic –

> . . . *ane cord, baith gret and lang,*
> *Quhilk hangit Johne the Armistrang*
> *Of gude hemp, soft and sound;*
> *Gude, halie pepill I stand for'd*
> *Quha ever beis hangit with this cord*
> *Neidis never to be dround.*

Also, in *Complaint of the Common-weal of Scotland* he says, of the state of the Border counties:

> *In to the South, allace! I was neir slane;*
> *Ouer all the land I culd fynd no relief:*
> *Almost betuix the Mers and Lowmabane*
> *I culd nocht knaw ane leill man be ane theif.*
> *To schaw thair reif, thift, murthour, and mischief,*
> *And vicious workis, it wald infect the air:*
> *And as langsum to me, for tyll declair.*

From which we may guess that (*a*) he was able some years later to regard the celebrated hanging with sardonic and perhaps complacent detachment, and that (*b*) he by no means approved of the violent activities of the Border freebooters, who have in succeeding centuries found their own romantic advocates.

It is only fair to state, however, that there is – as far as I can discover – no evidence at all that Lindsay had anything whatever to do with James the Fifth's punitive expedition of 1530.

I have also made rather free with the date of the Reformation. English heresy was not likely to have been worrying the Church in Scotland at this date, and it is still less likely that any forerunners of John Knox were wandering the Ettrick Forest. But Lindsay himself took what might perhaps be called a Radical-Conservative view upon religious questions: and certain modern parallels prompted me to introduce these views into the play and to present a more extreme philosophy in the person of the Evangelist.

I have no idea whether or not Lindsay had a mistress.

In writing this play I have been somewhat influenced by Conor Cruise O'Brien's book *To Katanga and Back:* but I would not have it thought that I have in any way composed a 'Roman à clef'. The characters and episodes in the play are not based upon originals from the Congo conflict; all I have done is to suggest here and there a basic similarity of moral, rather than political, economic or racial problems.

The language of the play offered certain difficulties. It would clearly be silly to reconstruct the exact Scots speech of the period – as quoted in the two passages from Lindsay's work given above. But on the other hand, Scots was at this time a quite distinct dialect, if not a different language, and to write the play in 'English' would be to lose the flavour of the age. The Scots employed by modern poets such as MacDiarmid and Goodsir Smith owes a great deal to Lindsay, Dunbar, Henryson and the other writers of the late Middle Ages and early Renaissance: but it is also a language for the expression of twentieth-century concepts. In the end I have put together a sort of Babylonish dialect that will, I hope, prove practical on the stage and will yet suggest the sixteenth century. My model in this was Arthur Miller's adaptation of early American speech in *The Crucible.*

Note on Sets and Costumes

The play is intended to be played within the medieval convention of 'simultaneous mansions'. These are three in number and represent the Castle (for the Armstrongs), the Palace (for the Court) and the Forest (for the wild land of the Borders). The Castle and the Palace are practicable buildings, one on either side of the stage, each with a roof from which actors may speak. They need not be more than porches or tabernacles: but their style should be definite and suggestive. The Castle is a rough stone building, with battlements and a defended gate or doorway: the Palace is a more elaborate structure in the

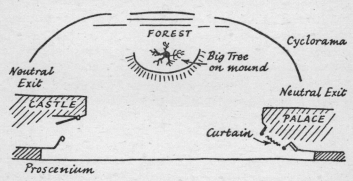

SKETCH PLAN OF SUGGESTED STAGE ARRANGEMENT

The Forest may be painted all round the Cyclorama: or else only in the centre, and the sides of the stage surround painted a neutral colour. Wherever in the course of the play a character enters or leaves the stage without it being specified that he does so via one of the three 'mansions', the Neutral Exits shewn on the sketch are intended to be employed. If there is room, space may be left between the Castle and the Palace, and the inner side of the Proscenium Arch, and this space used for entrances and exits via these two 'mansions' when several characters are involved and there is risk of overcrowding the doors of the 'buildings'. As the 'simultaneous' staging is a medieval device, and extremely formal in its conception, a formality of style should be adopted in the painting and design of the 'mansions'. If they are too naturalistic, the production will appear incongruous and peculiar.

fanciful Scots manner of Linlithgow Palace or Roslyn Chapel, painted and gilded, and topped with pretty finials. The entry is closed with a curtain, which should be painted to resemble tapestry. The Forest, which occupies the central upstage area, is basically a clump of trees. These should be dense enough to afford at least two concealed entrances for the actors: and one large tree (which should be practicable) stands in front, to the centre, and can be raised on a small mound.

The costumes should be 'working dress' – that is to say, each of the characters should be immediately recognizable as a member of his respective social class, rather than as a picturesque element in a colourful historical pageant. The borderers will wear mostly leather and hodden grey: the Politicians (Clerks, Commissioners, Secretaries, etc.) will be in subfusc gowns, with perhaps some use of small heraldic badges to indicate their local alignments. Lindsay wears a non-committal black suit, and adds to this at different times his herald's tabard, his scarlet robe of office, and a leather coat like Armstrong's. The King is first seen in full regalia like an old MS. illumination. Later he appears in Highland dress for hunting. This Highland dress (and that of the Soldiers in the same scene) belongs to a period prior to the introduction of clan tartans, and its basis is the long saffron shirt – sometimes worn with a short waistcoat. The Soldiers should have bare legs and bare heads, and are armed with claymores and targets: the King could be more 'civilized' and wear hose, embroidery upon his waistcoat, and a plain bonnet. When Gilnockie dresses up in the last act he puts on an assortment of clothes obtained in raids, and they do not necessarily agree very well with each other. But his general appearance must be extremely gaudy and peacock-like. The Evangelist should wear a very plain suit of cheap material, becoming threadbare. The Cardinal's Secretary has the Dominican habit of black and white.

The bagpipes are, of course, lowland pipes, which were not a specifically Scots instrument at this time, but played fairly generally throughout Western Europe – c.f. the paintings of Dürer and Breughel.

Notes on the Characters

THE KING   He is only seventeen, and small. He appears young for his age, and when dressed in his regalia looks like a sacred doll.

LINDSAY   In his late forties, but quick and athletic in his movements, and sprightly in his speech.

MCGLASS   Young, ardent, and handsome.

THE LADY   Aged about thirty-five: strong, sensual, and humorous.

THE MAID   Like her mistress, but slighter in body and fifteen years younger.

GILNOCKIE   A great bull, or lion, of a man: he has difficulty in talking coherently, a congenital defect like an exaggerated stammer that he is only able to overcome when extremely excited or when he sings. Full of a certain innocence of spirit. Aged about forty.

GILNOCKIE'S WIFE   A nervous, chaste lady, in great fear both of and for her husband.

THE ARMSTRONGS   Tough loyal clansmen, devoted to their Laird. The GIRLS are their younger relatives and do the work in the house and fields. (Gentry, not peasants.)

STOBS   A bitter, hard, rigid, cruel man.

YOUNG STOBS   As harsh as his father, but more impulsive.

MEG   Throughout the play she is shocked with grief; but before the death of her lover she has been warm, gentle, and quiet.

WAMPHRAY   A foolish handsome man, middle-aged, tough and rude-mannered.

THE EVANGELIST   Aged about thirty, prematurely grey hair: a converted sensualist, his rigidity derives as much from inward doubt as from strength of character.

THE COMMISSIONERS   Experienced political gentlemen, whose emotional public remarks bear little relation to their real feelings.

THE CLERKS   They appear to be both older and wiser than their Commissioners: but, in fact, the two types are designed to work together as a team.

THE SECRETARIES   These men are really responsible for the political decisions and policies of their masters, and know it.

THE PORTER   A pompous mouthpiece, and that is all we know of him.

THE HIGHLAND CAPTAIN   Speaks with the unexpected politeness and gentleness of the Gaelic soldier. He and his men look, and no doubt fight, like wild animals.

Notes on the Casting

There are thirty parts in this play, but it may be played by a company of sixteen, if seven of the actors take more than one part, as follows:

I   FIRST SCOTS COMMISSIONER
    SECOND ARMSTRONG
    CARDINAL'S SECRETARY
II FIRST HIGHLAND SOLDIER
    SECOND SCOTS COMMISSIONER
    STOBS
    LORD JOHNSTONE'S SECRETARY

III   FIRST ENGLISH COMMISSIONER
      FIRST ARMSTRONG
IV   SECOND ENGLISH COMMISSIONER
      THIRD ARMSTRONG
      LORD MAXWELL'S SECRETARY
V   SCOTS CLERK
      YOUNG STOBS
      PORTER
      HIGHLAND CAPTAIN
VI   ENGLISH CLERK
      KING
VII   WAMPHRAY
      EVANGELIST
      SECOND HIGHLAND SOLDIER

The remaining roles (including all the female parts) cannot conveniently be doubled. At a pinch, the GIRLS could be omitted entirely. The parts of the KING and the THIRD ARMSTRONG perhaps present problems if the respective actors have other parts to play: because it may be thought that the KING should, in order to produce a better effect in the last act, be as it were isolated: and I have suggested that the THIRD ARMSTRONG should be the Piper: in which case he may be a specialist and not necessarily a versatile actor. But this is a matter for local circumstances and taste to determine.

PS.   Also at a pinch, but may I hope only a very sharp one, two of the COMMISSIONERS may also be omitted – one from each country.

Note on Production

For the production of this play by the National Theatre at the Old Vic (1965) it was found useful to begin Act One with Scenes Three and Four, followed by Scenes One, Two and

Five. This was done in order to make an English audience familiar with the language before the more complex exposition of the plot had to be embarked upon. (Wamphray's death is an episode which more or less explains itself in visual terms, whereas the conference scene has to be *verbally* understood or it makes no sense.) I think this readjustment of scenes justified itself, and producers who wish to use it may do so: but from the point of view of the overall shape of the play, I prefer my original arrangement, which is accordingly printed here.

John Arden

Armstrong's Last Goodnight was first performed at the Glasgow Citizens' Theatre on 5 May 1964, with the following cast:

JAMES THE FIFTH OF SCOTLAND	Hamish Wilson
SIR DAVID LINDSAY OF THE MOUNT	Leonard Maguire
ALEXANDER MCGLASS, his Secretary	John Cairney
A LADY, Lindsay's Mistress	Lisa Daniely
HER MAID	Hannah Gordon
FIRST SCOTS COMMISSIONER	Phil McCall
SECOND SCOTS COMMISSIONER	Ian McNaughton
FIRST ENGLISH COMMISSIONER	Brian Ellis
SECOND ENGLISH COMMISSIONER	Glen Williams
CLERK TO THE SCOTS COMMISSIONERS	Alec Monteath
CLERK TO THE ENGLISH COMMISSIONERS	Stephen MacDonald
THE POLITICAL SECRETARY TO LORD JOHNSTONE	Phil McCall
THE POLITICAL SECRETARY TO LORD MAXWELL	Brown Derby
THE POLITICAL SECRETARY TO THE CARDINAL OF ST ANDREWS	Glenn Williams
PORTER TO THE ROYAL HOUSEHOLD	Alec Monteath

CAPTAIN OF THE HIGHLAND INFANTRY

Stephen MacDonald

SOLDIERS

Bill Henderson

Peter Gordon Smith

Brian Ellis

James McCreadie, Jnr.

David Gloag

Ian Sharp

Thomas McNamara

JOHN ARMSTRONG OF GILNOCKIE   Iain Cuthbertson

HIS WIFE   Janet Michael

WILLIE ARMSTRONG   William McAllister

TAM ARMSTRONG   Alex McCrindle

ARCHIE ARMSTRONG   Alistair Colledge

FIRST GIRL OF GILNOCKIE'S HOUSEHOLD   Bonita Beach

SECOND GIRL OF GILNOCKIE'S HOUSEHOLD

Aileen Salmon

THIRD GIRL OF GILNOCKIE'S HOUSEHOLD

Wieslawa Kwasniewska

PIPER   Jimmy Wilson

GILBERT ELIOT OF STOBS   Harry Walker

MARTIN ELIOT, his son   Bill Henderson

MEG ELIOT, Stobs's Daughter   Anne Kristen

JAMES JOHNSTONE OF WAMPHRAY   Brown Derby

A PROTESTANT EVANGELIST   Ian McNaughton

Directed by Denis Carey

Designed by Juanita Waterson

The action of the play takes place in Scotland, early in the second quarter of the sixteenth century.

Act One

SCENE ONE

[LINDSAY, ENGLISH *and* SCOTS COMMISSIONERS, *their* CLERKS.]

A trestle table in the middle of the stage, arranged with papers and ink etc., and stools placed for a conference.
LINDSAY (*in his herald's tabard*) *enters.*

LINDSAY. There was held, at Berwick-upon-Tweed, in the fifteenth year of the reign of James the Fift, by the Grace of God King of Scotland, and in the nineteenth year of Henry the Eight, by the Grace of God King of England, ane grave conference and consultation betwixt Lords Commissioner frae baith the realms, anent the lang peril of warfare that trublit they twa sovereigns and the leige peoples thereunto appertainen. The intent bean, to conclude this said peril and to secure ane certain time of peace, prosperity, and bliss on ilk side of the Border. I am Lord Lyon King of Arms, Chief Herald of the Kingdom of Scotland. It is my function in this place to attend upon the deliberations of the Scots Commissioners and to fulfil their sage purposes with obedience and dispatch. As ye will observe: when peace is under consideration, there is but little equability of discourse. The conference this day bean in the third week of its proceeden.

> LINDSAY *retires into the Palace, and immediately appears upon the roof, from which he watches the rest of the scene.*
> *The two* SCOTS COMMISSIONERS *enter from the Palace* (LINDSAY *stands aside and bows to let them pass*) *and take their seats. With them is their* CLERK.
> *There is a pause.*

Then the ENGLISH CLERK *comes in, bows to the* SCOTS, *and takes his seat. He is followed by the* FIRST ENGLISH COMMISSIONER, *who bows and takes his seat.*
Another pause.
Enter SECOND ENGLISH COMMISSIONER; *he bows, sits, and then stands.*

SECOND ENGLISH COMMISSIONER. My lords: many weighty questions have been brought these weeks beneath discussion, and I think I may say that at least a partial agreement has been arrived at. The line of succession to the Scottish royal house; excise due upon merchandise imported or exported; claims arising from damages inflicted during previous hostilities – all these are satisfactorily settled.

FIRST ENGLISH COMMISSIONER. Heresy—

SECOND ENGLISH COMMISSIONER. Yes. The prevention and deterrence of subversive transportation of professors of alleged heresy between the realms. In the present disturbed state of Christendom, clearly we must—

FIRST SCOTS COMMISSIONER. The religious intentions of King Henry are as yet some whit ambiguous. Can he offer ane precise definition of what he means by heresy? The Court of Consistory at Sanct Andrews will desire—

FIRST ENGLISH COMMISSIONER. We have an annotation in the margin to that effect, sir. In God's Name let us not confound our business in the quagmires of theological dialectic.

SECOND SCOTS COMMISSIONER. We'll be here while neist year's harvest else. Gang forwarts, gif ye please, sir.

SECOND ENGLISH COMMISSIONER. Very well, we now come to a crucial and exceedingly delicate matter, which both parties have, I believe, agreed to leave until the last. I mean, the Security of the Borders. Or rather, their present insecurity. Indeed, lords, their present state of bleeding anarchy and murderous rapine – to use no stronger words. I do not wish to revive bitter memories of past destruction. But I must remind you, lords, that the very accession to the throne of His Grace King James was consequent upon—

SECOND SCOTS COMMISSIONER. It was consequent upon the death of his father at the Field of Flodden, sir: and we're all very weel acquent with it.

SECOND ENGLISH COMMISSIONER. And how terrible was that battle. It appears to me that Scotland is not yet recovered from it. And no man here can desire its repetition.

SECOND SCOTS COMMISSIONER. Were it repeatit, it could weel find ane different conclusion. Scotland was ane dis-unitit kingdom that unlucky tide.

FIRST SCOTS COMMISSIONER. I think we have little need of historical recapitulation here. Sir, I will anticipate your argument. Ye are about to denounce the raiden and ridens of our bold Scots borderers, are ye nocht? Ye hae lost upon the English side ower mony cattle, horses, sheep, pigs, roof-trees, byres, kirk-ornaments, tableware, personal jewellery, and the maidenheids of women. Very good. We will acknowledge these circumstances as regrettable. But you are here for peace – ye have tellt us so yourself.

SECOND ENGLISH COMMISSIONER. It is imperative for peace that there be no more masterless raids from Scotland into England in search of booty. Or if there be, the offenders must be punished, at the hand of Scotland's Grace, and he be seen to punish them. This has not happened, has it? There is more than a suspicion that outrages of recent years have been openly encouraged, indeed in origin set on, by great men in your kingdom—

SECOND SCOTS COMMISSIONER. Sir—

SECOND ENGLISH COMMISSIONER. And great men, sir, who stand too close to Scotland's throne.

SECOND SCOTS COMMISSIONER. I want to hear their names!

SECOND ENGLISH COMMISSIONER. It were better not, I think.

SECOND SCOTS COMMISSIONER. Aha, why nocht?

SECOND ENGLISH COMMISSIONER. I do not care to rub it deeper, sir, but—

SECOND SCOTS COMMISSIONER. There's been nae riden without good reason. For every heid of cattle the Scots hae grippit, your English carls took twelve. I have a paper here—

SECOND ENGLISH COMMISSIONER. We too are furnished, sir, with papers—

FIRST ENGLISH COMMISSIONER. Permit me for one moment.

He reads from a paper:

December the 21st, last; John Armstrong of Gilnockie and his brother Armstrong of Mangerton harried twenty miles within the English ground and burned and killed their way from Bewcastle to Haltwhistle.

January the 15th: the men of Liddesdale and Eskdale rode further yet, to Hexham, and there obtained by force five score horned beasts and drove them home under moonlight, led on this occasion by John Armstrong of Gilnockie and Gilbert Eliot of Stobs. The same John Armstrong and another Eliot – I think a Martin Eliot—

FIRST SCOTS COMMISSIONER. Aye, he's the son of Gilbert – ye seem to be correct thus far.

FIRST ENGLISH COMMISSIONER. I thank you. Martin Eliot. They set their ambush on the road between Carlisle and Brampton and held to ransom no less a traveller than the Lord Abbot of Monkwearmouth and two brethren of his cloister, threatening these holy men with abominable indignities if payment were delayed.

SECOND SCOTS COMMISSIONER. And was it?

FIRST ENGLISH COMMISSIONER. Foolishly, perhaps, it was not. Two months after that the same Armstrong of Gilnockie in confederation with – with a man called James Johnstone of Wamphray—

FIRST SCOTS COMMISSIONER. Na na, ye are in error there,

sirs: Wamphray and Gilnockie are at feud. Confederation betwixt 'em's inconceivable. Look for ane other name.

SECOND ENGLISH COMMISSIONER. The name may well be mistaken. The offence took place. Has there been offered compensation? Indeed no, there has not. Why not? I reiterate: there are great men who wink at this, and England's Grace has said it is intolerable.

FIRST ENGLISH COMMISSIONER. His very word. Be warned by it. He is an angry King.

SECOND SCOTS COMMISSIONER. God: what ane turbulence of lyen janglers is this same warld we dwell in! Ye have held this business till the end, lords, gullen us and lullen us three weeks ane front of peace, of friendship, amiable words, nae threats, nae rage, nae conflict. And now it comes! I have speirt of myself ilk day, is England turnen Christian at last? Ha, ha, we have our answer! Forbye, it craves ane starker man than you are to put this Commission in dreid. We tell you, lords – in maist severe and potent voice: nae Scottish borderer receives his chastisement until sic time as we observe ane good reciprocation. Ye nourish your ain limmer thieves in Redesdale and in Tynedale – see them hangit first, and then we'll deal with ours! There is nae mair to say. Ye are deliberately provocative, and ye intend to break this Council!

FIRST ENGLISH COMMISSIONER. Indeed sir, we do not.

SECOND SCOTS COMMISSIONER. Intend it or no, then it has had that effect. Negotiation is concludit. Be reason of your intransigence. You can tell that to England's Grace, when ye gang back barren to Windsor or to Westminster. Be sure we'll tell it plain eneuch in the Palace of Halyrood.

> SECOND SCOTS COMMISSIONER *goes out, into the Palace.*

SECOND ENGLISH COMMISSIONER. I warn you, this is most unwise.

FIRST ENGLISH COMMISSIONER. England's Grace has set
his heart upon this treaty. Should he find himself balked
therein, we cannot answer for the consequence.

FIRST SCOTS COMMISSIONER. Aye, ye won Flodden. But ye
didna win the kingdom. Nor will ye win it, by ane second
cast, nor third, nor fourth, against it. We are forwarnit of
your malice, lords, and we ken but owerweel whaur the
blame of further war will lodge.

> FIRST SCOTS COMMISSIONER *goes out into Palace.*
> The ENGLISH COMMISSIONERS *go out.*
> LINDSAY *retires from the roof of the Palace.*

SCENE TWO

[LINDSAY, ENGLISH *and* SCOTS CLERKS.]

The CLERKS *are left behind, assembling their papers and
clearing away the tables and stools.*

SCOTS CLERK. Permit me, sir, ane short and private word with
you.

ENGLISH CLERK. With pleasure, sir.

SCOTS CLERK. We have heard, sir, the necessair defiances
deliverit in public and publicly receivit. Now sir, for the
inwart verity of the business, the whilk is writ upon nae
record, but I trust will rin to England's ear directly. Are ye
with me, sir?

ENGLISH CLERK. I am.

SCOTS CLERK. The matter of the unruly borderers is in nae
guise easy to conclude. Their depredations in truth are as
muckle towards Scotland as they are towart England, and
the Liddesdale and Eskdale men are sae well entrenchit in
their hills, in their strang towers of defence, that they are
nocht to be howkit therefrom without grave danger to the

State and expense upon the Treasury. There are, indeed, as has been said, great men in Court at Halyrood that will assume the borderers' part against all injury, and yet upon their power King James is forcit to lean, whatever be his ain opinion of their lealty. He is ane young, but prudent King, and kens his peril. Therefore, the binden and controllen of these Armstrangs, Eliots, Maxwells, and the lave, maun find itself by sure and slow advancement; and gif God will, through policy, nocht force. Are ye with me?

ENGLISH CLERK. Can it be done? And if it can, how long will it take? King Henry is impatient.

SCOTS CLERK. King Henry maun contain his patience Christ-like, sir, and virtuous, as is his wont. But the matter is in hand. The maist ferocious of these thieves, and — I will admit to ye — the hardest to suppress, is John Armstrang of Gilnockie. King James has in his grace and wisdom ordainit ane confidential emmissair to treat furthwith with Armstrang, seek some fair means of agreement, and in the end secure baith the lealty and obedience of this dangerous free-booter.

ENGLISH CLERK. Do you think that it is possible?

SCOTS CLERK. Here is the emmissair.

LINDSAY *enters from the Palace*.

Sir David Lindsay of the Mount. If he canna dae it, there is nae man that can. Sir David, d'ye see, is ane very subtle practiser, he has been tutor to the King, is now his herald, ane very pleasurable contriver, too, of farces, ballads, allegories, and the like delights of poetry. He has wit, ye ken, music, ane man of rhetoric and discreet humanity. Do I flatter ye, Sir David, or are ye indeed serpent eneuch to entwine the Armstrangs in your coil?

LINDSAY (*to* ENGLISH CLERK). Come here, sir, here . . . Whilk man of us twae is the better dressit, d'ye think?

ENGLISH CLERK. Dressed?

LINDSAY. Aye, dressit.

ENGLISH CLERK. I scarcely understand you, sir. But if you
intend a sense of correctness and decency of apparel, I do
not think myself in any way at fault. My clothes express my
function: unassuming, cleanly, subfusc. You, of necessity,
wear your official livery, which is, of necessity, both splendid
and delightful, and suited to the pageantry of state. Is that
what you would have me say?

LINDSAY. Aye, it'll serve. Splendid and delightful. As it were,
ane ornament for a Mayday foolery or ane heathenish idol
dedicate to blood-sacrifice. I will remove it, d'you mark?
There is ane man under it, and remove what's left upon
him, and there's naething for ye but nakedness. What can
we dae wi' that in the service of diplomacy?

> The rags and robes that we do wear
> Express the function of our life
> But the bawdy body that we bear
> Beneath them carries nocht
> But shame and greed and strife.
> It is pleisand to naebody
> Of its hairy sweat and nudity;
> Save belike to ane cruel tormentor
> Whaur his whip will leave the better bloody mark,
> Or save belike to our ain rejoict Creator,
> Whaur he walks through the green glade
> Of his fair garden and his fencit park,
> Or save belike to ane infatuate tender woman:
> And then best in the dark.
> Yet here I stand and maun contrive
> With this sole body and the brain within him
> To set myself upon ane man alive
> And turn his purposes and utterly win him.
> That coat is irrelevant:
> I will wear it nae further
> Till Armstrang be brocht

Intil the King's peace and order.
I will gang towart his house
As ane man against ane man,
And through my craft and my humanity
I will save the realm frae butchery
Gif I can, good sir, but gif I can.

ENGLISH CLERK. Is there not, however, a more certain way than that ? Your Commissioner mentioned a feud between the Armstrongs of Gilnockie and, er, and—

SCOTS CLERK. Wamphray. James Johnstone of Wamphray. Aye, they are at feud.

ENGLISH CLERK. Then why not offer Wamphray, from the hand of the King, some sort of emolument – I mean, in short, give a bribe to one ruffian to do away with the other ?

SCOTS CLERK. M'm, we did consider it. And Johnstone was agreeable. But the man is a greit-heidit fool: he's no killt Armstrang yet, and I canna believe he ever will. It was sheer waste of hard-gathert taxes.

LINDSAY. Mair than taxes, man – humanity. To murder ane murderer is a'thegither waste, and bad waste at that. Like silly wee childer that pick up a caterpillar – they crush it in their fingers, and then ye find them greeten ower the dearth of butterflies in summer. Besides, it's no sae simple. This caterpillar is protectit. He is the vassal of Lord Maxwell.

SCOTS CLERK (to ENGLISH CLERK). Ane tyrannous and malignant peer at the Court and ane constant threatener of rebellion. Nae Armstrang rides against England outwith his implicit permission.

LINDSAY. Or indeed occult command. The nobility of this land, sir, are mair treacherous and insensate than ony gang of thieves in Christendom . . . I wad never condemn ane proposition to murder Lord Maxwell. There are mony good poison mushrumps grow in the Ettrick forest – on my road to Gilnockie I could gather ye a wee bag, eh ? Will I dae it ? Wad ye like it ?

SCOTS CLERK (*gives an embarrassed giggle*). Just so, Sir David, just so . . . When do you intend to ride?

LINDSAY. To Gilnockie? Directly.

SCOTS CLERK. And what people will ye bring?

LINDSAY. Aye well, there will be the lady—

SCOTS CLERK. The lady? Your wife.

LINDSAY. Did I say that? She is ane paramour, sir – aha, ye do mislike it?

SCOTS CLERK. Ah na na . . . But when all is said and done, sir, do you find her presence ane absolute necessity?

LINDSAY. Absolute. At unpredictable intervals: but absolute. (*To* ENGLISH CLERK.) Do ye remember the story of the Gordian knot?

ENGLISH CLERK. I think that I may recollect—

LINDSAY. Aye well, there was ane emperour, and he went with ane sword and cut it. He thocht he was ane god, walken. Why in God's Name could he no be a human man instead and sit down and unravel it?

SCOTS CLERK. You yourself, Sir David, are to show him the way there, I take it.

He takes him out of earshot of the ENGLISH CLERK.

And shew him it with speed, as ye hope for your salvation! Scotland can nocht sustain ane other war with England. The conference is broke, the urgency is merciless—

LINDSAY. Aye, aye, we ken . . . (*To* ENGLISH CLERK.) He says it is ane urgency. Well, Lindsay's urgent, too. Observe him: he's awa'. (*Exit into Palace.*)

ENGLISH CLERK. I will report to the Grace of England what I have been told: and I will pray for your success. Good day, sir, fare you well. (*Exit.*)

The SCOTS CLERK *stands hesitating for an instant and then goes into the Palace.*

SCENE THREE

[GILNOCKIE, WAMPHRAY, ARMSTRONGS.]

Hunting horns, sounds of hounds and horses.
    Enter, through the Forest, GILNOCKIE *and his men, dressed*
    for the chase.
    WAMPHRAY *comes with them, arm in arm with* GILNOCKIE.

WAMPHRAY (*to audience*).
    To the hunten ho, cried Johnny Armstrang
    And to the hunten he has gaen
    And the man that seeks his life, James Johnstone,
    Alang with him he has him taen.
FIRST ARMSTRONG.
    To the hunten ho, cried Johnny Armstrang,
    The morning sun is on the dew,
    The cauler breeze frae aff the fells
    Will lead the dogs to the quarry true.
SECOND ARMSTRONG.
    They huntit hie, they hunted law,
    They huntit up, they huntit down,
    Until the day was past the prime
    And it grew late in the afternoon.
    They huntit hie by the Millstane Edge
    Whenas the sun was sinken law—
GILNOCKIE. Ca aff the dogs!

    This cry is taken up offstage and horns blow again.

SECOND ARMSTRONG.
    Says Johnny then, ca aff the dogs
    We'll bait our steeds and hamewart go.

    They sit down to rest.

THIRD ARMSTRONG.
    They lightit hie at the Ewes Water Heid

Between the brown and benty ground
They rested them but a little wee while:
Tak tent then lest ye sleep too sound.

FIRST ARMSTRONG. We hae gien ye but poor hunten, Wamphray. The dun deer of Eskdale had word ye were comen, I think. They're awa beyond into Teviotdale to bide on their lane there until we show them our backs.

GILNOCKIE (*passing a flask*). Tak a drink while we rest. Let the huntsmen earn their meat. Sit ye down for God's sake.

WAMPHRAY. It was ane gentlemanlike and honourable action for ye, Gilnockie, to celebrate the reconciliation betwixt our houses with this day's sport, howsoever frustratit, and a bottle of good usquebaugh. Gie ye lang life and fruitful riden.

FIRST ARMSTRONG. And the Grace of God betide us all intil ane time of peace and friendship.

GILNOCKIE. We have but few years left us, James.

FIRST ARMSTRONG. And then we maun gang to our graves. The Laird of Gilnockie wad tell ye, forbye, this reconciliation requires some formal handfast and ane apparent declaren before witnesses.

GILNOCKIE. You men, are ye with me, hear it, all you men! Your hand!

He clasps hands with WAMPHRAY *in a ceremonious fashion.*

FIRST ARMSTRONG. Neither Armstrang nor Johnstone frae this day furth shall pursue their ancient enmity. All plots, devices, ambuscades or manslauchters, either to t'ither, conceivit, intendit, or made in time past are hereby void, forgotten, and entirely outwith the consideration of our lives. In their stead stands friendship, britherhood, and ane certain protection and assistance against all heinous attempts. Is that weel spoken? Gilnockie wad be glad of your agreement.

WAMPHRAY. Under witness of God, Jesus His hangit Son, and the Haly Ghaist in Trinity, I call it weel spoken.

Johnny, God help me, I could desire ane equal word frae
Gilbert Eliot of Stobs. You are yet close confederate with
him; could ye no mak his people turn towart me in peace in
like manner with your ain?

GILNOCKIE. Gilbert Eliot? The man has ane dochter.

FIRST ARMSTRONG. It wad be nae matter of difficulty,
Wamphray, gif there were little mair than driven kye or
broken byres in dispute betwixt the Eliots and yourself. But
Gilbert believes ye hae lain wi his dochter.

GILNOCKIE. Against her will, he tells me.

WAMPHRAY. Ah na, na, na, against her will is ridiculous.

GILNOCKIE. But ye did swyve the lassie?

WAMPHRAY. Aye, that I did.

FIRST ARMSTRONG. Ye are ane free widower, however.
Gilnockie wad speir what prevents ye frae marriage.

THIRD ARMSTRONG. Ye will mind that Gilnockie's ain wife
is the sister of Stobs: ane alliance betwixt the three houses
wad be gey convenient, Wamphray.

GILNOCKIE. Convenient. Wad be honourable. Tak ye ane
other drink!

WAMPHRAY. Alliance, marriage, are ye out of your senses?
Gif I called Meg Eliot my kirkfast marriet wife, within less
than a year my ain greeten wean'd call the pigman of
Wamphray by the name of bloody uncle! Ach God, she is
ane gat-leggit strumpet, Johnny, and I tell you I kent it the
first half-hour after!

GILNOCKIE. After? What after?

WAMPHRAY. Heh heh, what d'ye think?

FIRST ARMSTRONG. Ye'll no tell that to Stobs.

WAMPHRAY. I seek nae opportunity to tell anything to Stobs.
He can find it for himself.

FIRST ARMSTRONG. Gif he finds *you*, sir, you will be finishit.
His castle is nae mair than ten miles awa frae here. Suppose
that *he* should hae chosen to hunt these fells the day? What
wad ye do?

WAMPHRAY. I wad call upon my host for assistance and protection in accordance with his word.

FIRST ARMSTRONG. Aye. Gilbert nor his sons wad never do you violence gif you were standen with the Armstrangs: there's nae question o' that. Forbye he is ane sudden man with his weapon, Gilbert; he has three and twenty notches cut in his hilt for the lives he has taen of men that were in search of his. I mind that he said to the Laird: I ha never yet heard of the laddie that wad kill me, he said, but what I was forewarnit of it and dealt him ane quick vengeance before he could sae mickle as graith up his brand.

GILNOCKIE. Speir at him what wad he do—

FIRST ARMSTRONG. He says what wad ye do, what action wad ye set afoot, gif ye heard there was ane complot made by your enemies to brenn your house aboon your heid and you in your nakit bed with your wife and your bairn, sleepen?

WAMPHRAY. Gif I heard that, I wad – I wad first demand matter of proof of it, Gilnockie.

GILNOCKIE. Aye, aha, aye?

FIRST ARMSTRONG. There was ane trustless word abroad that sic ane black design was in process upon Gilnockie, upon the safety of our castle, upon Janet the Laird's wife, upon his bairn within the cradle, upon the good men in his hall – is this the truth?

WAMPHRAY. Gilnockie, he said trustless. Trustless is true. Nae circumstance else.

GILNOCKIE. Wad ye tak aith upon that?

WAMPHRAY. What?

FIRST ARMSTRONG (*producing a book from his pouch*). Wad ye swear upon the Gospel? Ye are aware of nae plot by fire or by steel to destroy John o'Gilnockie while he sleeps?

GILNOCKIE. There's the Book, there.

FIRST ARMSTRONG. Are ye preparit to swear it, sir?

WAMPHRAY. I hae gien ye already ane handfast of friendship.

GILNOCKIE. Aye: mak it sicker. Tak aith upon the Book.

WAMPHRAY. Gilnockie. Ye do wrang. Indeed, ye do me wrang to insist upon this thing.

GILNOCKIE. Insist? Jamie, I wad never.

FIRST ARMSTRONG. Your word, sir, is your honour, and it's no to be disputit. Sit ye down with the Laird, you are his good friend. But ye ken very weel, upon this Border, a man maun look keen to his ain proper safety.

GILNOCKIE (*sings*).
There's nane may lean on a rotten staff
But him that risks to get a fall:
There's nane that may in a traitor trust
Yet trustit men may be traitors all.

FIRST ARMSTRONG. I assure ye, sir, they may.

GILNOCKIE. Toom the bottle, Jamie, we're nane of us fou yet.

WAMPHRAY. Nor like to be neither, on the edge-hills of Teviot. Good luck then and good horsemanship to auld Gibby of Stobs, and the reeken breeks of his dochter! He-hech—

(*He sings.*)

And when he came to the hie castle yett
He beat upon that door
Oh where are you, my lily-white love,
Where are you, you dirty whoor!

He gives a drunken laugh and lies back. The others do likewise, and all appear to fall asleep. When WAMPHRAY *is clearly snoring heavily, the* ARMSTRONGS *sit cautiously up.*
GILNOCKIE *signs to the* FIRST ARMSTRONG, *who slips off into the Forest.*

GILNOCKIE. Brand. Get his brand. Tangle it up.

The SECOND ARMSTRONG *takes* WAMPHRAY'S *sword and wraps twine about the hilt, tying it to the scabbard.*

Let's hae his gully-knife.

The SECOND ARMSTRONG *passes over to him* WAM-PHRAY'S *knife.*

You the gun.

The THIRD ARMSTRONG *picks up* WAMPHRAY'S *hand-gun.*

THIRD ARMSTRONG. Loadit.

GILNOCKIE. Aye. Water.

THIRD ARMSTRONG. We've nae water here. Do ye want me to—

GILNOCKIE. Then pour in bloody usquebaugh and ask nae mair fool questions.

THIRD ARMSTRONG (*pouring whisky down the barrel*). This is no a very provident method, Gilnockie. I doubt—

GILNOCKIE. Do it.

THIRD ARMSTRONG. Aye.

GILNOCKIE (*looking at the sword*). He'll yet pull that out. See. Mak it sicker.

He improves the knots at the sword-hilt. The FIRST ARMSTRONG *returns, holding a bridle.*

FIRST ARMSTRONG. Here's his bridle.

GILNOCKIE. What hae ye done wi' the horse?

FIRST ARMSTRONG. I've whippit him hame to bloody mither.

GILNOCKIE. Good. He's still asleep.

He puts back the sword.

SECOND ARMSTRONG. Gilnockie. Are you entirely clear that this affair is in consonance with your—

GILNOCKIE. With my what?

SECOND ARMSTRONG. With your – with your honour, Gilnockie?

GILNOCKIE. What's your name?

SECOND ARMSTRONG. My name is Armstrong.

GILNOCKIE. Aye, I thocht it wad be. Then you see that you keep it.

They stand around waiting, and looking into the distance.

FIRST ARMSTRONG. A quarter hour frae now and the red sun's drappit under. Whaur to hell are the Eliots?

A horn in the distance.

Ah: here they are. It should be Gilbert the Laird and his eldest son, aye riden like a pair of wildwood bogles! (*He speaks to the sleeping* WAMPHRAY.) James Johnstone of Wamphray, ye are ane sackless murderit man.

GILNOCKIE. Wake him up: wi' that.

The THIRD ARMSTRONG *blows a horn in* WAMPHRAY'S *ear.*

WAMPHRAY (*starts up*). Eh, who, what—

FIRST ARMSTRONG. Wamphray, we're trappit. There's fifteen of the Eliots riden ower the north rigg. Mount your steed, man, and gang!

WAMPHRAY. Eh, what, gang whaur?

FIRST ARMSTRONG. Back to Gilnockie's castle; they are riden at feud!

GILNOCKIE. Get to your horses!

His men run out into the Forest.

Come on, man, awa—

WAMPHRAY. Johnny, whaur's my horse?

GILNOCKIE runs out after his men.

FIRST ARMSTRONG (*off*). Awa hame to bloody mither!

THIRD ARMSTRONG (*off*). Wamphray, ye are ane forsworn traitor, and ye maun bide there for what comes after ye!

Their laughter is heard receding, off.

SCENE FOUR

[WAMPHRAY, STOBS, YOUNG STOBS, MEG.]

WAMPHRAY *looks around him in despair.*

WAMPHRAY. Bide here for what – fifteen men, fifteen Eliots, on their horses, at feud— (*He tries to draw his sword.*) The kindless bastard! (*He looks around and picks up his gun.*) And what's he done to the gun? Sodden, sodden weet and cloggit wi' usquebaugh – why, the gun's fou! Jamie's fou, too . . . Gully, gully, he's not even left me my gully-knife, gin he'd left me but that I could cut free my brand—

He sits down helplessly, tugging at the knots on his hilt.

STOBS (*off*). Johnstone?

YOUNG STOBS (*off*). Johnstone of Wamphray.

STOBS (*off*). Are ye there, my mannie, are ye there?

YOUNG STOBS (*off*). We're here.

STOBS (*off*). We want ye.

> STOBS *and* YOUNG STOBS *enter from the Forest. They carry hunting spears.*

Wamphray. Ye ken our names and ye ken our quarrel. There is auld feud betwixt us lang syne, Wamphray, and this month it is augmentit. Ye hae lain leg across my dochter and we're here to kill ye for it. Will ye stand to your death like a man, or will ye squat upon your hurdies like a wee doggie wi' the worms?

> *He pricks him with his spear and* WAMPHRAY *jumps up and back. He holds his scabbarded sword on guard in front of him.*

YOUNG STOBS. That brand's little good to ye, gif Gilnockie kent his business.

> WAMPHRAY *fights them hopelessly, using his sword as though it were a cudgel, but they force him back to the big tree, and pin him to it with their spears.*

WAMPHRAY. When ye neist gratify your wame at Johnny Armstrang's table, speir at him frae me, what betidit with his honour?

He dies.

STOBS. I do nocht regard this as a relevant question. Gilnockie has certain proof that this thing we hae pit down, here, was collaborate with ane undiscoverit enemy to oerthrow Gilnockie's people. And, with his people, ours. He will remain here on this fellside for the better nourishment of the corbies. Ride.

The two ELIOTS *go out through the Forest, leaving the spears in the body.*
MEG *enters at another side of the Forest. After a pause:*

MEG. Jamie? . . . Jamie? . . . Ah, they hae finisht their wark with ye, Jamie, they hae finisht it gey complete. There are nae better butchers in the land.

She pulls out the spears. The body slumps down and she kneels beside it.

In twa minutes they hae turnit ye intil ane auld man; ye werena that last week.
    These lips that were sae red and fat
    Will snarl across your chaps for ever
    Like the grin of a dirty rat:
    The yellow hair sae sleek and fine,
    That did illuminate your hard hasty skull
    And the deep secret dale here of your chine,
    In twa minutes has revertit
    To the draff-black bristles of a wild-wood swine.
    James, ye cruel drunken lecher James,
    Whaur is now departit
    Your thrust and tender carelessness of lust?
    And in what unkent bed do ye scatter

Your barren seed this nicht ? Aye, totter,
Stagger, stumble intil sleep :
Nae Matthew, Mark, nor Luke, nor John, will keep
Their watch oer you—
To baith your woman and your godly faith
Ye were untrue.
Are ye comen, my wearie dearie,
Are ye comen, my lovely hinnie,
I will find ye a wee bracken bush
To keep the north wind frae aff your ancient body.

She drags the corpse out into the Forest.

SCENE FIVE

[LINDSAY, MCGLASS.]

LINDSAY *enters from the Palace.*

LINDSAY (*to audience*). The grief of this woman is the grief of
the Common-weal of Scotland. Naebody to hear it, and but
few to comprehend it, gif they did. And of those few, how
mony could comprehend the means of consolation ? Where
is my secretair ? Alexander ? Mr McGlass !

Enter MCGLASS *from the Palace.*

MCGLASS. Are ye ready for the road, Sir David ? We had best
lose nae time setten furth. God kens what could happen
upon the South-West Border before we get there. They tell
me there is ane manslauchter within ten mile of Carlisle
every third day.

LINDSAY. I wait, Mr Alexander, for my wanton and un-
punctual lady. Whaur is she, d'ye ken ?

MCGLASS She was to hae left Linlithgow in good time to hae
met with us on the road, but this day I have ane letter frae

Jedburgh to say that she is held there by the ill condition of the weather and that she will proceed to Gilnockie's castle on her ain when there is better chance of travel.

LINDSAY. I am of opinion, Mr Alexander, that the lady's love and inclination towart me is somewhat fainter than it did use to be. Do you imagine she will hae fand ane better man for her pastime?

MCGLASS. Better man than Lindsay? Better for what? The poetry of love or the wicked deed itself? Either gate, I think it were scarce possible.

LINDSAY. Ye have ane gey feeble notion then of the bounds of possibility. Will ye no sing ane sang as we travel?

MCGLASS. Gaelic or Scots?

LINDSAY. Scots, man: we're in the Lawlands. And mak it ane sang of the unkindness of womankind.

MCGLASS (*sings as they march with* LINDSAY *joining in the refrains.*)

> When I cam hame frae riden out
> I fand my love in bed.
> A minstrel harp hung on the rail
> And a coat of the scarlet red.
> 'What man was here?' I speirt at her
> And this is what she said –
>   'Oh a dree dree dradie drumtie dree.'
>
> 'My brither cam at mirk midnicht
> He was sae cauld and weet
> That I maun fetch him intil bed
> And warm his frozen feet.
> Indeed his feet are warm eneuch
> And his instrument sae sweet
>   Plays a dree dree dradie drumtie dree.'

LINDSAY. Aye, and it's now time to hear a bit out o' *your* instrument. Here is the castle of Gilnockie: we stand before his yetts: gie him ane blaw of the wee trump.

MCGLASS, *who carries a bugle horn, blows a blast.*

Blood and wounds, are they all deaf in there ? Blaw again.

MCGLASS *blows a second call.*

SCENE SIX

[LINDSAY, MCGLASS, GILNOCKIE, *his* WIFE, ARM-
STRONGS.]

GILNOCKIE'S WIFE *appears on top of the Castle.*

GILNOCKIE'S WIFE. Who are ye ? What's your business ?
Frae what place d'ye come here ? This is John o'Gilnockie's
castle and the Laird has nae desire for strangers. Declare
yourselves directly.

LINDSAY. Madam: I am sent here by the King.

FIRST ARMSTRONG *appears at the Castle gate.*

FIRST ARMSTRONG. And whatten King wad that be ?

MCGLASS. King James of Scotland: what King d'ye think
else ?

FIRST ARMSTRONG. King of Scotland ? King of bloody
Lothian. That's the best name he carries here.

GILNOCKIE'S WIFE. Willie, Tam, Archie – here are men frae
the King—

Two more ARMSTRONGS *emerge from the Castle, with
weapons.*

Fasten their hands. They hae come here to wark us ane
treason.

The men seize LINDSAY *and* MCGLASS *and tie their hands
behind their backs, and take away their swords.*

FIRST ARMSTRONG. Blawen your damn trumpets before the
yetts of Gilnockie. The Laird'll hae ye hangit.

MCGLASS. Hangit!

LINDSAY. Hangit? For what indeed?

MCGLASS. We are servants of the King—

FIRST ARMSTRONG. There's but ae King in Eskdale, my mannie, and he's King John the Armstrang. We hae them fast bandit, mistress.

> GILNOCKIE'S WIFE *has left the top of the Castle and now comes out of the gate, below.*

Will we pit them in the black hole?

GILNOCKIE'S WIFE. Na, na, no yet. The Laird'll want to see them when he is risen frae his meat.

THIRD ARMSTRONG. He'll no want to see them stood like ornament statues within the width of his yard, mistress. They maun gang beneath the trap-hatches, quick.

> *The* FIRST ARMSTRONG *begins to hustle them.*

GILNOCKIE'S WIFE. Willie, let them be. I'll speak a word wi' them first.

FIRST ARMSTRONG. The Laird'll no be pleast at it.

GILNOCKIE'S WIFE. Willie.

FIRST ARMSTRONG. Whatever ye say, mistress: ye are the Laird's lady.

GILNOCKIE'S WIFE (*to the* ARMSTRONGS). Stand a bit back, sirs; remember your places.

> *They withdraw, rather sulkily.*

Tam, will ye fetch me my chair? Tam, my chair, gif ye please!

> *The* SECOND ARMSTRONG *goes into the Castle and brings out a chair.*

FIRST ARMSTRONG (*aside*). I had best to tell Gilnockie what has chancit within his house.

THIRD ARMSTRONG (*aside*). Tak tent, he will be angry.

FIRST ARMSTRONG. I had best tell him.

The FIRST ARMSTRONG *goes into the Castle.*

GILNOCKIE'S WIFE (*sitting down on the chair*). The Laird will be angry. Ye are aware, are ye no? that the King has had him proclaimit outlaw and rebel at Edinboro Cross and that he in return has proclaimit the King nae King ower Eskdale but ane traitor to his people. Frae what cause do ye come to this border but to bring tyranny and coercion to the inhabitours thereof? I tell ye, Gilnockie will be angry, and when he is angry he is ane man to consider with. In God's Name, he is ane devil, sirs – and you yourselves are ane pair of equal devils, ye are Mephistophilis and Beelzebub, to stir up mair warfare when there is but peace and truce here and community in Christ.

LINDSAY. In Christ, madam? Is that the verity? Community with the English? The English are Christian men.

GILNOCKIE'S WIFE. The Laird and his people have sufferit mickle wrang frae the English. Ower generation and generation the English hae warkit destruction frae Carlisle to the Ettrick Forest and frae the forest to the sea-coast, and alang the sea-coast intil Forth. The Laird has his purposes – they are strang purposes for defence. He has aye been courageous in their difficult fulfilment, and what hae ye to tell him that will serve him ony advantage, but rather cruel hurt to his peace, and disadvantage to his people, sirs; for the Laird *is* his people, and his people were ance the King's, but now they are naebody's. Gilnockie is their ae protection. They maun starf outwith his hand. What are your names?

LINDSAY. I am David Lindsay of the Mount. Ye will hae heard of me, I guess?

GILNOCKIE'S WIFE. Fore God, ye are the King's Herald?

LINDSAY. I am. And this gentleman is Mr Alexander McGlass, my servant and my writer.

MCGLASS. Madam, I am maist honourit to offer ye ane salutation.

GILNOCKIE'S WIFE. What? What? What honour to mock at me in the very house of my good man, ane puir terrifyit woman, haven ane bitter weird of violence aye thrawn within my spirit, sir? Gilnockie will be angry. What soldiers have ye brocht here?

LINDSAY. Nae soldiers at a', madam.

SCENE SEVEN

[LINDSAY, MCGLASS, GILNOCKIE, *his* WIFE, ARMSTRONGS *and* GIRLS.]

GILNOCKIE *enters with* FIRST ARMSTRONG *from the Castle. His* WIFE *gets up from the chair and he takes her place. He looks keenly at the two prisoners.*

GILNOCKIE. Their names.

SECOND ARMSTRONG. Lindsay, McGlass.

GILNOCKIE. Mac – Mac – Mac – Glass? Ane Hielandman? He wears breeks.

SECOND ARMSTRONG. He spak to us in good Scots.

GILNOCKIE. Better than that – me – the Gaelic, me. Ha ha, how's this? Hechna, hochna, hochna, hoo! Ha ha ha—

FIRST ARMSTRONG. There is an exposition of versatility for ye, mister; what d'ye think o' that for ane good Lawland mou full of dirty Erse?

GILNOCKIE. Lindsay. That is ane name: I heard it. Delamont: Lindsay of the Mount. David Lindsay Delamont. Sir.

GILNOCKIE'S WIFE. Aye, that is correct, Gilnockie, ane kent man: Sir David Lindsay of the Mount, he is the Herald of the King.

GILNOCKIE. Herald, King? Herald, Herod, King, the wee childer. Ilk ane o' them murderit. Cut oot their throats.

Jesus Christ escapit. King Herod was ane King: and he doubtless had ane Herald.

FIRST ARMSTRONG. The Laird intends to tell ye, sir, that him that ye serve is but ane prodigious tyrant, like—

GILNOCKIE. Will be. God he is ane bloody wean yet.

FIRST ARMSTRONG. The Laird tells ye furthermair—

LINDSAY. The Laird can tell me himself. He has ane tongue of his ain, has he no? What for does he talk to me through varlets?

GILNOCKIE roars.

GILNOCKIE'S WIFE. Sir, ye had best apprehend—

FIRST ARMSTRONG. Ye had best apprehend, sir, that the Laird has had ane impediment in his speech syne the day of his nativity. He receives his interpretation through the words of his leal gentlemen.

GILNOCKIE'S WIFE. You are discourteous to remark upon it, Sir David.

GILNOCKIE. Gentlemen. That's no the women. Haud your damn't whist.

GILNOCKIE'S WIFE. I crave pardon, indeed, John, for the interruption of your discourse—

He glares at her and she is silent.

GILNOCKIE (*fingering* LINDSAY's *clothes*). Silk. Satin. Velvet. Gowd – is it gowd?

GILNOCKIE'S WIFE. It's gilt-siller, Gilnockie. I'm no yet ane Marquess.

GILNOCKIE. Aye? No yet's Johnny.

MCGLASS. Ye could be, could ye no?

GILNOCKIE (*showing his own clothes*). See. Linsey-woolsey. Buft leather. Steel. Hackit steel. Hackit flesh. Here is ane brand. (*He draws his sword.*) She gies ye answer to her name. Tell him.

FIRST ARMSTRONG. He calls his brand Kings' Dread,

Delamont. Because that is her manner of life. Compare them.

He measures GILNOCKIE'S *sword against* LINDSAY'S.

GILNOCKIE. Langer, braider, heavier. Nae King whatever—

FIRST ARMSTRONG. Nae King whatever has had the might to put down Armstrang. Jamie Stuart the Fourth sent against us ane officer, and horsemen forbye. And hear ye what sang was made by his people – the Laird wi' his ain hand slew—

GILNOCKIE (*sings*).

> I slew the King's Lieutenant
> And garr'd his troopers flee
> My name is Johnny the Armstrang
> And wha daur meddle wi' me?

The ARMSTRONGS *pick up the refrain and repeat it.*

LINDSAY. Wha daur? David Lindsay daur. King Johnny of Eskdale indeed! King Curlew of the barren fell. King Paddock of the wowsie mosses. Ye squat on your blood-sodden molehill and ye hoot, Johnny: and naebody in Scotland considers ye mair than a wet leaf blawn against the eyeball on a day of September wind. So ye slew the King's Lieutenant, hey? And whatten reck d'ye imagine the King made of that? What hour or what wee minute was reft out of the Royal sleep, what disturbit instant was thrust in for you betwixt James Stuart and his concubine when he heard word of the peril of Gilnockie in the corner of his border? Fore God, ye have ane precellent conceit of your power, Mr Armstrang!

GILNOCKIE *growls*.

Ye are ane inconvenience, I will grant ye. Ye are ane tedious nuisance to the realm. Ye are indeed cause for ane itchy paragraph or twae in some paper of state. But were ye the great man of danger and subversion that ye fain, sir, wad

think yourself, can ye credit then the King's Herald wad
hae come to your house wi' nae footmen nor horse, nae
pikemen nor archers, nae bombardiers nor pioneers – wi'
nocht in God's Name but ane demi-priestling writer and
sax inches of bent brass bugle! I crave your pardon, Sandy,
I had nae intent to disparage ye, but the noise that ye mak
on your instrument can scarcely be callit the clangour of
warfare.

GILNOCKIE. Armstrang. Mr Armstrang. *Mister*—

FIRST ARMSTRONG. The Laird has his proper entitlement of
style. He's no ashamit to use it, nor yet to hear it usit.
Gilnockie, gif ye please, when ye open your mou to the
Laird!

LINDSAY. Gilnockie, gif ye will. He draws his rent frae the
local middens, by all means let us concede him the flattery
of their name.

> GILNOCKIE *leaps forward and grips* LINDSAY *by the
> throat, shaking him in rage.*

FIRST ARMSTRONG. Will we hang him, Gilnockie?

SECOND ARMSTRONG. Cut his heid off?

THIRD ARMSTRONG. I'll dae it – this minute!

GILNOCKIE (*throwing* LINDSAY *down*). Na . . . Ane precellent conceit. Nocht, in God's Name, but ane writer and ane
bugle. To stand against me. Johnny. For what?

FIRST ARMSTRONG. Aye, tell him; for what?

GILNOCKIE. Willie, search his purpose.

FIRST ARMSTRONG (*hauling* LINDSAY *upright again*). You
are ane courageous man, Delamont, to heave up your
undefendit face intil the face of Gilnockie. Gif you're no here
for coercion, ye maun hae brocht with ye ane offer of terms.
Do I pursue the passage of your mind correctly, Gilnockie?

GILNOCKIE. Aye.

FIRST ARMSTRONG. Declare to the Laird, then, first, what
does the King want?

LINDSAY. He wants to prevent ane English conquest of the kingdom. For what else is he King?

GILNOCKIE (*laughs*). And is the riden – Gilnockie, Stobs, or paddock of the mosses – ride intil England, and prick them, prick them – can we – hey?

FIRST ARMSTRONG. The Laird means, Delamont, that when he and his good-brither Eliot mak ane raid intil England, the whilk ye hae just tellt us is ane insignificant provocation at the hands of unregardit men, then what way can this insignificance gar the great King of England set abroach ane formal war? Can we prick King Henry's quarters indeed thus sharply – when our lances are sae blunt, and short, and pitiable?

LINDSAY. I had nae sort of intent towart sic ane implication. Your raidens and ridens are naething of import whatever. But English policy *is*: and English policy, continual sin the time of heroic Wallace, is the domination of Scotland and the destruction of her rulers. True, or untrue?

GILNOCKIE. True.

LINDSAY. Aha, we progress. Now let us bear our minds back, a wee space intil history. I could bear mine the mair freely gif my hands were to be loosit – gesticulation, whiles, is ane useful stimulant to the deftness of the tongue—

GILNOCKIE. Na.

LINDSAY. Ah . . . Intil history. Bannockburn. Ane victory. Wha won it?

GILNOCKIE. We did.

LINDSAY. You. And the Bruce?

GILNOCKIE. The Bruce? He was nocht, was nae place, was but deid but for gentlemen. Armstrang. In that battle. There was he. Aye and Eliot. Otterburn alsweel. It was Armstrang did mak prisoner Hotspur Percy. Of this aye house the bonny gentlemen.

LINDSAY. Precise. Ane veritable conception of history indeed. It was upon sic perilous occasions that the Lawland gentlemen

alane did create the defence of this realm: when baith
monarchy and nobility were shook with internecine faction
like the bell-ropes in the tower of Giles's Kirk!

MCGLASS. At Bannockburn— The Bruce—?

LINDSAY. Sandy: I am in ane spate of words – be silent. Gif
Henry of England, as he plans, as I ken weel he plans, should
turn his calculation, sir, towart ane second Flodden – King
James bean young and oer-tormentit by a wheen sorry
intriguers at his Court – whaur will then reside the protection
for our people?

GILNOCKIE. Here.

LINDSAY (*walking round each of the* ARMSTRONGS). Here ...
here: here: here. And the King is conscious of it, sir, and for
that reason he doth pray you pardon his prior intransigence
against the valour of your clan. He has sent me to tell you
that gif you will render him ane true and leal obedience
hencefurth, he will put his Royal trust in you, and look to
you and yours to keep his historic Crown for ever integrate,
and Scots! There is ane specific offer—

GILNOCKIE. Specific: aye.

LINDSAY. Ane specific offer of Royal privilege I am commandit to present to ye. I will ask Mr Alexander to expound
it now – he is weel versit indeed in the legalities and practi-
calities. Sandy?

MCGLASS. The King's offer is maist bountiful, ane preclair,
majestical, and unprecedentit offer – I hope ye will agree.
Upon receipt of ane true assurance frae John, Laird of
Gilnockie, that he will follow the course of war ahint nae
other banner than that of King James of Scotland, King
James has determinit to create and dispone for him ane
office of mickle dignity and honour: to wit, Warden of
Eskdale and Free Lieutenant of the King; permitten the said
John, upon occasion of fray, the sole right and privilege
within Eskdale, Liddesdale, and Teviotdale, of defence,
command, and levy. I wad add to that, forbye, that ony

passage of theft across the borders of England in time of peace or truce is maist strictly to be renouncit. Renunciation receivit, King James will then rescind the decrees of outlawry and rebellion heretofore postit against John of Gilnockie, and will issue free pardon for all offences committit by the said John or any of his people in time past . . . There ye are!

GILNOCKIE. Nae theft; nae feeden. Then whaur?

FIRST ARMSTRONG. Then whaur, says the Laird, will we obtain our sustenance?

LINDSAY. Ane land unburdenit with the fear of war contains within its ain acres mickle sustenance, and growth of sustenance, Gilnockie: sheep, nolt, swine, fish, fowl of the air, corn upon your hillside fields – and merchants in your towns – ye'll prosper, sir: ye maun attempt it – do ye daur?

GILNOCKIE. Daur? Gilnockie daur a'thing . . . Whaur's auctority?

MCGLASS. Auctority? Aye, sir, we have that. But it's here in my pouch. I canna get at it wi' my hands bandit.

GILNOCKIE. Tam.

The SECOND ARMSTRONG *takes a letter out of* MCGLASS'S *satchel. He gives it to* GILNOCKIE, *who looks at it wisely.*

Seal of the King. Good.

LINDSAY. Will ye no read the letter?

FIRST ARMSTRONG. Do ye think the Laird is ane shave-pate eunuch bible-clerk? Read it yersel.

LINDSAY. Is there naebody here can read? It is writ in good English. Gif I were to read it ye, or Sandy here, ye wad hae but little reason to credit us, I think. Bear in mind we are politicians.

GILNOCKIE'S WIFE. I can read the letter.

LINDSAY. Will ye no let the lady read it to ye, sir? It were best ye should hear it.

GILNOCKIE (*giving the letter to his wife*). Read.

GILNOCKIE'S WIFE. It is ane extraordinair brief letter, Gilnockie.

GILNOCKIE. Read.

GILNOCKIE'S WIFE. It says but these words: 'Sir David Lindsay of the Mount is the King's tongue and the King's ear. Hear him and speak, and the King will baith speak and listen.'

LINDSAY. Precise and laconical. The King has had good tutors in the disposition of his rhetoric. Weel, sir, his ear is herewith presentit you.

GILNOCKIE. Loose.

The men release their wrists.

Warden of Eskdale. Lieutenant. Ane Officer of the King!

LINDSAY. It suits ye exceeden fitly, Gilnockie. Ye seem a larger man for it already.

GILNOCKIE. Maxwell.

LINDSAY. Ah! the Lord Maxwell. Belike ye do suspect that ye wad do wrang to cleave to the King outwith Lord Maxwell's permission – he bean your suzerain, and you in your turn—

GILNOCKIE. Pay him his rents.

LINDSAY. And divide with him your booty?

GILNOCKIE *laughs.*

SECOND ARMSTRONG. When he hears of it.

THIRD ARMSTRONG. Grip the sark frae aff your back, wad Maxwell.

MCGLASS. Do ye hauld him then ungenerous?

GILNOCKIE. Ane mansion-house in Linlithgae. Sups his broo wi' creish Kirk-Prelates. On his chaumer flair is ane carpet. Ane carpet. They did sell it him out of – out of—

THIRD ARMSTRONG. Persia. Wad ye credit that? Ane carpet out of Persia.

FIRST ARMSTRONG. But notwithstanding this: towart Lord
Maxwell the Laird has sworn ane ancient lealty.

GILNOCKIE'S WIFE. Aye, aye, lealty. It has to be considerit.

LINDSAY. Gilnockie: for mony years I had care of the King's
education. And I did instruct him in a' that was necessair in
the government of his realm. Gif he be unable at his present
age to compel to his obedience ane lord that lives as saft as
do the votaries of Mahomet: God help the kingdom!

GILNOCKIE. Aye, ha ha, God help it . . . Your wame, I
heard it nicker.

LINDSAY. Wame? Nicker?

FIRST ARMSTRONG. The Laird wad speir, Sir David, whether
or no ye've eaten the day?

LINDSAY. It is maist courteous of the Laird. We havena.

GILNOCKIE'S WIFE. Archie.

The THIRD ARMSTRONG *goes into the Castle.*

The Laird has just come frae his dinner. But meat and drink
will be providit ye, Sir David.

GILNOCKIE. Break it with ye. Bread: salt. Ye are the King's
Herald: ye bring the offer of the King. Acceptit! I am his
Officer. Ye are ane good man. Gilnockie's roof-tree renders
welcome. Welcome, sir.

He shakes LINDSAY'S *hand with ceremony.*

Mr Hieland Pen-and-Ink, your hand. Ye are ane good man.

He shakes MCGLASS'S *hand.*

SECOND ARMSTRONG. When ye shake Gilnockie's hand, ye
shake the hand of honour, sir.

LINDSAY. Indeed, I am full sensible of it.

The THIRD ARMSTRONG *comes out of the Castle, followed
by* GIRLS *carrying trays of food – brown bread and red
wine. This is handed to* LINDSAY *and* MCGLASS.

GILNOCKIE *shares it with them in a token but solemn fashion.*

(*To* GILNOCKIE'S WIFE, *who seems disapproving.*) There is ever ane sair question, madam, when a man sees his ancient life upon the brink of complete reversal. Reversal belike of lealty, aye: but of enmity alsweel. (*To* GILNOCKIE.) Maxwell will be your friend yet: and what about Johnstone?

GILNOCKIE (*choking over his refreshment*). What – whilk?

LINDSAY. Whilk? Whilk Johnstone? The Lord or the Laird? I had in mind the baith of them. Ye are at feud with the Laird of Wamphray, and Lord Maxwell is at feud with Lord Johnstone, who is Wamphray's kinsman and suzerain. There is here ane opportunity to put ane end to this sad quarrel; for the Johnstones lang syne hae been the King's servants, while you are now his Officer. Ane meritable wark, the conclusion of truce. Will ye dae it?

GILNOCKIE *laughs.*

FIRST ARMSTRONG (*aside*). What will we tell him, Gilnockie?

SECOND ARMSTRONG (*aside*). Tell him it's made, what else?

FIRST ARMSTRONG. The Laird says it's made. Wamphray is now in condition of peace, with ilk ane of the Armstrangs, and with a' men other. The Laird and himsel hae ridden in amity thegither in pursuit of the wild deer. They were accordit good sport thereat, and they drank as companions upon the side of the fell.

THIRD ARMSTRONG. They claspit their hands forbye as ane true earnest for evermair.

MCGLASS. Is this indeed the truth?

GILNOCKIE. For why nocht? I am ane Christian.

LINDSAY. I'll tell ye nae lie, Gilnockie: this was indeed unlookit for. Howbeit, it is maist pleisand and agreeable to hear, and God be thankit for it.

GILNOCKIE. Paps o' the Virgin, how delightsome it is to be at peace with auld enemies! Peace! Whaur's my piper? Whaur's music?

FIRST ARMSTRONG. Whaur's reid wine for the gentlemen? The bottle is toom, begod!

SECOND ARMSTRONG. Gilnockie cries for his music.

The THIRD ARMSTRONG *goes and fetches bagpipe.*

GILNOCKIE. Let's hae the bloody piper. Delamont, ye will dance with her. (*Indicates his wife.*) All the maids and men of Armstrang, let them set their feet to it, let them sing and gaily dance!

They dance and sing:

Oh merry blooms the hawthorne tree
And merry blooms the brier
And merry blooms the bracken bush
Whaur my true-love doth appear:
He maks his bed and waits therein
And when I walk beside
He will rise up like a laverock
And his arms will open wide—

Oh start up and leap, man:
And never fall and weep, man:
Quick quick and rin, man:
The game will just begin, man—

SCENE EIGHT

[LINDSAY, MCGLASS, GILNOCKIE, *his* WIFE, ARM-STRONGS, GIRLS, EVANGELIST.]

The EVANGELIST *enters from the Forest, carrying a pack on his back. He walks into the middle of the dancers, who fall apart from him and the music stops.*

EVANGELIST. Good people. Scotland is my native realm: but I am ane traveller, I am ane pedlar out of distant lands. In specific, the lands of Germany.

He opens his pack which contains a number of household articles, pots, napkins, wooden trenchers, etc.

And here in my kist I hae brocht hame for your advantage wark of craft and beauty, Almayne wark in wood, clay, claith – paintit and weel-corven, delightsome to your een, ane ornament for humanity, ane gaud for the material body of man. Wha'll buy it, wha'll buy it?

The WOMEN *gather round and look at his goods.*

GILNOCKIE'S WIFE (*taking a Bible out of the bottom of the pack*). What's this?

EVANGELIST. Aye, madam, d'ye look deeper? Why, what is it but ane book?

LINDSAY. Ye'll dae little good wi' books here, master. We live by blood and booty here – it'd serve ye far better to gang to Sanct Andrews.

EVANGELIST. Sanct Andrews, do ye tell me – Sanct Andrews of the Cardinal, the Doctors, the Prelates – this book to Sanct Andrews? Why, they wad cast me incontinent intil the fire of the Inquisitours for this. Brethren, this book is the undisputit Word of God. It is the Haly Scripture, sirs—

LINDSAY. In English?

EVANGELIST. Aye.

LINDSAY. Aha.

GILNOCKIE. English.

SECOND ARMSTRONG. Show it to the Laird.

EVANGELIST. The Laird. You are John Armstrang.

GILNOCKIE. English. Is ane heresy?

LINDSAY. Precise.

GILNOCKIE. Name? The name: Luther? Why?

FIRST ARMSTRONG. He says, for why d'ye bring ane German

heresy here intil Scotland? We ken little about it here, though
we hae heard of the man Luther. Expound it. To the Laird.

EVANGELIST. Here, in this forest, they tell me, there are
gentlemen that are dividit against their Princes, and brook
nocht their commandments. The Prelates of the Kirk are in
like manner this day with the Princes of the State. They are
forgotten by God because God is forgotten of them. They
are outwith His benevolence, for they wadna feed their sheep
when their sheep were an-hungerit. John Armstrang – ye
are ane mickle hornit ram – are ye weel-fed by your shepherds
– spiritual, temporal? I trow nocht. I trow nocht.

LINDSAY. And I trow somewhat different, master. The wame
of this Laird nickers nae langer. Why, he is—

GILNOCKIE. I am the King's Officer! God's tripes, I am
distendit!

EVANGELIST. Your flesh is distendit. And what of your
conscience, sir?

LINDSAY. Aye, what of it? I never yet heard that Martin
Luther did enjoin disobedience to the King.

EVANGELIST. Obedience, he doth enjoin, to the commandments of God: and the commandments of God are ane voice
that is in ilk ear present. In my puir mortal ear, or in yours,
or in—

GILNOCKIE. Here. Set him, here. You are ane heretic. For
your conscience, ye wad brenn, in the het fire indeed,
courageous?

He smacks the EVANGELIST *in the face.*

EVANGELIST. Struck with the blaws of martyrdom, I yet
maintain to you the other cheek, as is commandit me by
Jesus Christ. And notwithstanding, bear I furth my testimony.

MCGLASS. There's nae Inquisitour whatever upon these
borders here. Ye maun send him awa north to the correct
process of the Kirk – will ye do that for him, Gilnockie, and

manifest in public your true responsibility to this Christian Kingdom?

GILNOCKIE'S WIFE. To see him brennt in agony for nocht but his conscience; it wad be ane unco cruelty.

GILNOCKIE. Aye, cruelty. Delamont: *his* conscience: *mine:* what about *yours*?

LINDSAY. Wad ye speir my opinion, Mr Lieutenant? I'm nae ecclesiast. But see, this good man, he is but, as he saith, ane pedlar, his merchandise is tawdry, the wark of some Almayne boor, it's naething at a' – we mak pots as good as this in Scotland. The book alane is notable. Master, I will purchase this, I think. (*He takes the Bible and hands over a coin.*) Here ye are – tak it! Now then, Gilnockie, what will ye dae with him?

MCGLASS. Without his book there's nae evidence. Sure ye wad never brenn a man without evidence.

GILNOCKIE. No gien the Lieutenantship to roast mens' flesh for Cardinals. Fidelity, he hath. Fidelity, maist admirable. Godsake, let the carl gang!

The men who have been holding the EVANGELIST *release him, and he gathers up his goods.*

LINDSAY. And hear ye this, Evangelist, as ye tak your good leave of us. Consider what is writ in this book I hae obtainit of ye. I will gie ye ane text to mind – Sanct Paul to the Ephesians, chapter sax, verse five: 'Servants, be obedient to them that are your masters.' For treason, ye will hang. Tak tent on't – ye will.

EVANGELIST. Aye, Ephesians: same chapter, verse twelve. 'For we wrastle against the rulers of the darkness of this warld, against spiritual wickedness in hie places.' I think ye are ane man that kens weel that wickedness, but by reason of the comfort of your slothful existence, ye wad prefer to oerlook it and thereby to condone it. Within the House of Rimmon is your habitation, and very weel ye may hang me

there: but you yoursel will taste damnation. The Lord our
God is never moderate.

Exit into the Forest.

LINDSAY. I will now to the King, sir, and inform him furthwith of what has passed betwixt us. I will return in good
season and bring you the confirmation of your office.
Lieutenant and Warden, John Armstrang, for this time, I
bid you fare-weel.

GILNOCKIE'S WIFE. Sir, fare ye weel and may God's grace
gang with you. You are ane mild and virtuous envoy.

LINDSAY *gives her the Bible.*

GILNOCKIE. Salutation – wi' your bonnets aff, stand!

The MEN *line up bareheaded.*
The WOMEN *curtsey. The* PIPER *plays and leads them all*
back into the Castle.

SCENE NINE

[LINDSAY, MCGLASS.]

They walk about the stage.

LINDSAY. Aye, Sandy, salutation. Tak your bonnet aff, stand!

MCGLASS. Did he kill Wamphray with his ain hands?

LINDSAY. Him or ane other. Of course, there is nae proof of it
yet.

MCGLASS. Aye, but he will hae done it. And he receives his
reward. 'Howbeit', I heard ye say, 'It is ane pleisand and
agreeable thing to hear ye are at peace with Wamphray.'
Man, what like of peace is ane treacherous murder, for I'll
wager it was little else?

LINDSAY. Sandy, ye are gey direct. But it's no the path of
wisdom. Now, consider it this fashion: The King set

Wamphray on to kill Armstrang, gif he could. But he couldna, you see, and frae the day it became clear that he couldna, he was nae langer the King's man. Armstrang taks his place, because Armstrang has murderit Wamphray. *Because*, no in spite of!

MCGLASS. And what way do you intend to ensure that this belovit murderer will keep his promises?

LINDSAY. His promises will be broke, Sandy, for Lord Maxwell will encourage it. I believe indeed Lord Maxwell is paid to encourage it by the English Ambassador.

MCGLASS. Unproven.

LINDSAY. Unproven, but gey probable. Though Gilnockie couldna conceivably credit it. The man's ancestors won Bannockburn for God's sake! Single-handit. Did ye never read it in the Chronicles? . . . Now: because our Lord Maxwell is paid by the English to prepare provocation for ane English invasion – *because*, no in spite of – he maun receive ane better bribe than even Armstrang.

MCGLASS. He has a taste for luxury, it seems. What like of bribe wad suit him?

LINDSAY. The destruction of his enemy? Lord Johnstone intil prison: what about that?

MCGLASS. Johnstone is ane leal subject. He is innocent of treason, Sir David.

LINDSAY. It is ane axiom of state that nae Baron is ever innocent. When Lord Johnstone hears of the death of his man Wamphray—

MCGLASS. Unproven.

LINDSAY. Aye, aye, unproven— When he hears of the death he will mak ane feud of vengeance: therefore for the better preservation of the safety of the King and the realm and the—

MCGLASS. Sir: I do nocht like this policy. It is the exaltation of blind flattery and dishonour—

LINDSAY. Blind. We *are* blind: we grope on a rocky road wi' sticks too short to reach our feet. What was it I said:

To set myself upon ane man alive
And turn his purposes and utterly win him?
I've no turnit them at all, Sandy. Johnny Armstrang's purposes remain precisely the samen as ever they had been – violent, proud, and abominable selfish.

MCGLASS. He is ane terrible Gogmagog, he is ane wild Cyclops of the mountain: begod he has baith his een – but hauf a tongue in the man's heid . . . Did ye listen to his Gaelic? I think we need to cut his throat.

LINDSAY. Ye ranten feuden Hieland Gallowglass – cut his throat! Cut Armstrang's, cut Eliot's, cut Maxwell's, cut Johnstone's – whaur do we stop? Na, na, but gang ane circuit – indirect, undermine the nobility; and we begin with the furthest distant, Johnstone. Set them a' to wonder what in the de'il's name we're playen at. I think our wee King will enjoy this business, Sandy. He was aye ane devious clever knave in the schoolroom. But no courageous. That's pity. We're at his palace. Blaw your horn.

MCGLASS *blows his bugle at the Palace.*

SCENE TEN

[LINDSAY, MCGLASS, PORTER.]

The PORTER *appears on the roof of the Palace.*

PORTER. Wha is it blaws his trump before King James's yett? Stand whaur ye are and show furth your business.

MCGLASS. Sir David Lindsay of the Mount, Lord Lyon King of Arms, craves ane audience with His Royal Grace upon matter of state and policy.

PORTER. His Grace is at all times attentive to the good services of Lord Lyon. Ye will be admittit upon the instant, sirs.

He descends from the roof.

LINDSAY. We maun dress oursel correctly, Sandy. A robe and a collar of gowd upon us to furnish counsel to the King.

The PORTER *comes out to them carrying* LINDSAY'S *robes of office.*

Aha, here we are: weel attirit for ane work of politic discretion.

He dresses himself.

MCGLASS. Sir David, ye hae forgot.

LINDSAY. Forgot what?

MCGLASS. Forgot the lady.

LINDSAY. Ah na, na. She is in Jeddart, ye tellt me.

MCGLASS. Aye, but she was to proceed to Gilnockie – she will be—

LINDSAY. She will be snug in ane house in Jeddart till we're done here and can send her word. Is the King at his leisure?

PORTER. He is, sir.

LINDSAY. Then we'll enter the presence, Mr McGlass.

MCGLASS. Sir David, at your hand.

They go off into the Palace.

Act Two

SCENE ONE

[EVANGELIST, MEG, LADY.]

The LADY *comes out of the Forest and walks about a little as though waiting for someone. She wears a travelling-cloak with a hood over her low-cut gown.*

MEG *comes running out of the Forest. She does not see the* LADY, *who withdraws behind a tree.* MEG'S *clothes are all ragged and stained and her feet are bare.*

MEG. Whaur is he? Whaur are ye gaen, master? Come here, here. Aye, aye, we're alane here. It is ane richt solitaire place, here. And I will tell you ane secret.

The EVANGELIST *comes out of the Forest after her.*

EVANGELIST. What are ye, woman? Are ye ane gipsy? There are godless gipsies in Scotland in sair need of Jesu Christ, and I mysel am Christ's ain gipsy sent to exalt the sauls of the outcast folk and rebellious men of this forest. What gars ye look at me like that?

MEG. I am in dreid that ye will ravish me.

EVANGELIST. Ravish? Aye, I could. But no the fleshy body. Na, na, the immortal ghaist within it. I carry upon my worthless tongue twa words or three that will maist suddenly arrest and clarify the misconstruction of your life. Now hear this, woman. God did mak man in the image of His glory: therefore ilk ane of us is as it were ane God: but no yet manifest – our flame is as yet hid aneath the warldly bushel of expediency. Ye need nae wealth nor gifts of Princes for to cast it aff. Stand furth upon your ain, and brenn! The gipsies are God's people nae less than are the gentlemen –

let us begin with the gipsies and by the mercy of their conversion gar fire of glory rin thraeout the land—

MEG.

> Glory ? Whatten glory ? I think I will be sick.
> Master, ye carry ane muckle strang stick.
> It was ane stranger than that
> They did drive it far in
> For to harry the life
> Of the black corbie's nest.
> The puir corbie had ane wife.
> For to lig on her bare breist
> Was it her glory or his sin ?
> She kens weel, she kens weel,
> He'll ne'er tread her again.

EVANGELIST. Why, certain you are nae gipsy. I think you maun be gentry. But distractit – forsaken ? And what's this about the corbie ? About bare breists, and – and – glory ? I trow that you did yield yoursel up to ane unchaste lust and now ye feel the torment for it. Is that the truth, ye were concupiscent! Before we can expound the reformit faith here, we maun pray, woman, pray, for ane deep and grave repentance. Glory – nae glory of foul flesh. Cleanse it first, cleanse it; there will be nae atonement else—

LADY (*coming forward*). By what ordination of the Kirk are you appointit to be her confessor ?

EVANGELIST (*whirling round*). By nae ordination but by common humanity. I am in dreid for this woman of the conflagrations of Satan.

> *The* LADY's *cloak has fallen open, revealing her décolletage.*

Aye, and for you, too. Ye bear the appearance of ane frantic courtly vanity. Belike you are yet chaste and Christian: but in these wild woods, madam, the exposition of your secret parts is neither congruent nor godly. Are ye Rahab or Delilah that ye stand thus flamboyant in your lust ?

LADY. Forgie me, sir, indeed. I had nae thocht to provoke you. Though ye seem gey provokable for ane man I had ne'er met till this aye minute. I am upon a journey that went astray in the bad weather, and I seek for the castle of the Armstrangs in Eskdale.

> MEG *gives a sudden cry and backs away, rolling and groaning* 'Armstrang, John Armstrang'. *The* LADY *goes to her and makes some effort to comfort her.*

What ails the lassie?

EVANGELIST. She suffers appropriate pain for her sin, that is all. I wad prefer ye no to speak to her. You are contaminate, like ane filthy honeypot.

MEG.

> John the Armstrang is to the hunten gaen
> Wi' his braid sword at his side
> And there he did meet with a nakit man
> Alane on the green hillside.
> And John John John he killt neither hart nor hind
> At the end of the day he hameward rade
> And never a drap of blood did fall
> Frae the tip of his nakit blade.

They had stroken it instead aboon the lintel of the house of Stobs. And that's whaur I did dwell – ance. But now it is whaurever I can find— Aye, gang ye to the Armstrangs, honeypot, and tell them that ye met me, whaurever. That's the word, is the word, whaurever . . .

> *She runs into the Forest.*

EVANGELIST. I will follow her.

LADY. Aye, I doubt ye will.

EVANGELIST. It is not meet she be without companion.

LADY. I think you are ane lecher.

EVANGELIST. Na, madam, na—

LADY. But ane lecher without carnality. Can ye no see the

improvement of her saul maun wait upon the strength of her body? What do ye carry in your bottle?

EVANGELIST. Sma' beer.

LADY. Then administer it, with charity. Bring her intil shelter and look that I hear ye do her nae scaith. I am of import in this kingdom, master, and I wadna care to see ye brocht before the Inquisitours. Awa' wi' ye, catch the lassie.

The EVANGELIST *runs off into the Forest after* MEG.

SCENE TWO

[LADY, MAID, FIRST ARMSTRONG.]

The LADY *walks about impatiently.*

LADY. Am I to haver in this forest until the dark comes over me? Whaur are ye, burd – here!

Enter MAID, *breathless.*

MAID. Your pardon, madam, I had a' but lost my way. The lave of your people have gane forwart to the castle.

LADY. And nae message left in Jeddart – Sir David, in Jeddart, he left me nae message?

MAID. Nae word at a', madam. He has travellit direct to the King, they tell me.

LADY. Then we hae little alternative but to seek Gilnockie's hospitality. For what it is worth. I doubt it will be barbarous.

They approach the Castle. The FIRST ARMSTRONG *appears at the gate.*

You are John o' Gilnockie's man?

FIRST ARMSTRONG. Aye.

MAID. We hae come to his castle after Sir David Lindsay.

FIRST ARMSTRONG. He's nae here, but ye may enter. We're expecten him back within the month. Ye can bide till he comes. The Laird is hospitable, to the friends of his good friend.

LADY. I thank ye, sir, you are richt courteous.

She goes into the Castle.

FIRST ARMSTRONG. And what's *her* business wi' the King's Herald, hey?

MAID. She wad like fine to dance wi' him.

FIRST ARMSTRONG. Dance?

MAID. D'ye no jig to that like o' music here on the Border?

FIRST ARMSTRONG (*sings*). Och aye—

>   She met wi' him in the kitchen
>   Wi' the strae strewn on the flair,
>   Beside the fire he laid her down
>   His fingers in her hair.

MAID (*sings*).

>   And first he pu'd the emerauds aff
>   And then the diamonds bricht
>   That hing upon her lovely halse:
>   He didna need their licht!

They both laugh.

FIRST ARMSTRONG. That'll be an action to be seen in Gilnockie's kitchen, I can tell ye – come awa ben, my wee chanten burdie, there's good meat turns on the spit.

They enter the Castle, familiarly.

SCENE THREE

[LORD JOHNSTONE'S SECRETARY, LORD MAXWELL'S SECRETARY.]

LORD JOHNSTONE'S SECRETARY *enters from the Palace.*

LORD JOHNSTONE'S SECRETARY (*to audience*). I am the privy secretair to the Lord Johnstone of Johnstone. Here is ane evil time for all good men of nobility and lineage. My master has been wardit intil the Tolbooth prison at the order of the King: and nae good reason given.

LORD MAXWELL'S SECRETARY *enters from the Palace and stands by the door.*

That man there – I see him, he sees me – that man there, sirs, is the secretair of Lord Maxwell. Betwixt the houses of Maxwell and of Johnstone there has lang time been feud, but here today is true enormity. Sir!

LORD MAXWELL'S SECRETARY. Good day, sir. Ye are of Johnstone, are ye nocht?

LORD JOHNSTONE'S SECRETARY. As ye weel ken, sir. And you're of Maxwell.

LORD MAXWELL'S SECRETARY. My master commands me to tell ye, sir, that he has great grief at his heart for what has befell the Lord Johnstone this day; it is maist terrible to hear of.

LORD JONSTONE'S SECRETARY. God's Haly Cross, but are ye nocht ane hypocrite? It was at the device of your Lord Maxwell that my master has been wardit; it is bootless to pretend other. Can ye deny, sir, but that there is news frae the Border that Lord Johnstone's vassal and kinsman, Johnstone of Wamphray, rade to the hunten and nocht but his horse cam hame? And what man was it killt him?

LORD MAXWELL'S SECRETARY. Belike ane Armstrang or ane Eliot. He was at feud with baith of them, it matters little whilk.

LORD JOHNSTONE'S SECRETARY. Ye do admit it?

LORD MAXWELL'S SECRETARY. Why nocht? It is apparent. But ye do Lord Maxwell wrang, to credit that he condones sic murder at the hands of his vassals.

LORD JOHNSTONE'S SECRETARY. Then why is my Lord in the Tolbooth? Because the King has determinit, by the advice of David Lindsay, to concede to Johnny Armstrang

a'thing that he demands: and that includes protection frae
the just vengeancy of the Johnstones anent his wicked
murder. Armstrang is Maxwell's man: and there is occult
collusion here betwixt Lindsay and Maxwell. Maxwell
craves ane absolute auctority ower every laird upon the
South-West Border—

LORD MAXWELL'S SECRETARY. And what does Lindsay
  crave?

LORD JOHNSTONE'S SECRETARY. Aye, ane good question. I
  have nae clearness whatever about the motivations of
  Lindsay.

LORD MAXWELL'S SECRETARY. And neither has Lord
  Maxwell. Lindsay has persuadit His Royal Grace that your
  master is a danger to the kingdom.

LORD JOHNSTONE'S SECRETARY. I had rather say a danger
  to the Armstrangs.

LORD MAXWELL'S SECRETARY. Ah. Ye havena heard?

LORD JOHNSTONE'S SECRETARY. Heard what?

LORD MAXWELL'S SECRETARY. Why, man, the Armstrangs
  are the kingdom! Lindsay has had Gilnockie made Lieutenant of the Border and sole Warden of Eskdale!

LORD JOHNSTONE'S SECRETARY. He has had him made—

LORD MAXWELL'S SECRETARY. Aye! He is an Officer, ane
  Officer of sae strang ane title that it rins directly counter,
  sir, to the hereditary privileges of Maxwell his Lord.

LORD JOHNSTONE'S SECRETARY. But – but what is
  Lindsay's purpose, sir, what d'ye think can be his—

SCENE FOUR

[LORD JOHNSTONE'S SECRETARY, LORD MAXWELL'S
SECRETARY, *the* CARDINAL'S SECRETARY.]

The CARDINAL'S SECRETARY *enters from the Palace. He
is a Dominican Friar.*

CARDINAL'S SECRETARY. I will expound to ye his purpose, gentlemen. The Blessen of God be upon ye baith, and the Haly Sancts of Heaven assist your deliberations. I represent the Cardinal Archbishop of Sanct Andrews. I will declare to ye for your recollection some portion of that severe and solemn curse late set by His Grace the Archbishop of Glasgow upon the common traitors and thieves that wad break the peace of the Border. The Lord Archbishop said: 'I curse their heid and all the hairs of their heid: I curse their face, their een, their mouth, their neise, their tongue, their teeth, their crag, their shoulders, their breist, their heart, their wame, before and behind, within and without. I curse them gangen, I curse them riden, I curse them standen, I curse them sitten, and finally I condemn them perpetually to the deep pit of hell, there to remain, with Lucifeir and all his fellows.' For of necessity, gentlemen, peace between Christian realms is mair than mere expedience: it is commandit by the Kirk on peril of your salvation. And how, sirs, do we obtain that peace? Assuredly, by maken strang the kingdom, by placen trust in the hereditary Lords that administer the lands upon the marches – your master, sir, and yours: trust that they will refuse all temptation to ride in quest of private booty, trust that they will refrain frae murderous feud baith among themselves and their vassals: and last, but dearest to the hearts of all religious men, trust that they will stand ever ane firm and constant bastion against the spread of devilish heresy.

LORD MAXWELL'S SECRETARY. Heresy, sir?

LORD JOHNSTONE'S SECRETARY. Heresy? Ach, this is plain irrelevance – the man is ane fanatic meddler; let us leave him for God's sake—

CARDINAL'S SECRETARY. Gentlemen, gif ye please! I represent the Cardinal. And I was about to speak of Lindsay.

LORD MAXWELL'S SECRETARY. Aye, sir, what of Lindsay?

CARDINAL'S SECRETARY. First, he is ane adulterer. He hath

ane open paramour. I believe he even sent for her to accompany him on his embassage to the Armstrangs.

LORD JOHNSTONE'S SECRETARY. There is nae man in the Court that hasna had a paramour ae time or anither – why, the King himsel—

CARDINAL'S SECRETARY. Wait. Sir David Lindsay is alsweel ane man of maist remarkable intellect. He is ane clever makar of libidinous poetry, he has writ baith plays and pungent satires: and they are, in great part, contrair the excellence and supremacy of the Kirk. Ye were aware of this?

LORD MAXWELL'S SECRETARY. Of course.

CARDINAL'S SECRETARY. And this is the man the King has sent to safeguard the English Border? What wark does King Henry Tudor pursue within that Border at this present? I will tell ye, sirs: he does defy our Haly Father the Pape – and upon ane matter of adultery forbye.

LORD JOHNSTONE'S SECRETARY. Do ye mean to imply then that Lindsay is ane heretic? Do ye put the name of Luther on him, sir?

CARDINAL'S SECRETARY. Na, na, I wadna speak sae strang as that. Were he indeed ane Luther, the Cardinal wad barely have sufferit his extent the length he has. Na, na, we think he is but moderate. He is nae Luther yet. Likewise we think the King of England is, as yet, nae Luther: but ane sair misguidit bairn of Christ, whose cruel procedures in his realm can some day lead to Luther unless they be preventit.

LORD MAXWELL'S SECRETARY. What ye wad say, I think, sir, is in effect this: ane English aspect of religion and ane Scots aspect of policy are scarce compatible, even in a man of sae subtle a mind as Lindsay.

CARDINAL'S SECRETARY. Scarce compatible. Ane just word for it. Scarce. I wadna put it nearer than that, but—

LORD JOHNSTONE'S SECRETARY. Ye wadna? Then *I* wad. Gif Lindsay is ane heretic, by God he is ane traitor. His intentions are manifest – to mak feeble the defences of the

Border by the irruption of feud and disharmony amangst the noblemen that protect it. Hence Lord Johnstone in the Tolbooth, and after him, Lord Maxwell – whaur? The gallows? There sticks in my mind ane thing alsweel. Flodden. That dolorous field wad ne'er hae been lost had our last King James fand mair support amang his ministers. He had ane flock of faint-heart croakers at his back when he set furth to battle, and Lindsay was their principal.

LORD MAXWELL'S SECRETARY. And James the Fift, his son is but ane schoolboy still and still in dreid his umwhile tutor will command him bend his hurdies for the tawse.

LORD JOHNSTONE'S SECRETARY. He maun stand like a man, and stand like a King, with his hinder parts decently coverit, and defer his policy to naebody.

CARDINAL'S SECRETARY. Excepten ever to the Haly Kirk of Christ. Sir David Lindsay, they tell us, is maist zealous in his quality as Lyon King of Arms. Weel, sae that's his function. Let him keep to it.

A trumpet off and cries of 'Long live the King!'

The King gaes to the Abbey Kirk to hear Mass. We had best attend our masters.

LORD JOHNSTONE'S SECRETARY. Attend our masters. For me, I find but small security of employment while this new abundant tyranny of the King obtains towart his barons. Howbeit, sirs, we are agreed upon our policy. Maxwell and Johnstone are nae longer at ane enmity.

He shakes hands with LORD MAXWELL'S SECRETARY.

LORD MAXWELL'S SECRETARY. Ane blessit and Christlike conclusion. What do you say to it, sir?

CARDINAL'S SECRETARY. What should I say? I represent the Cardinal. Amen, therefore, and Benedicite.

LORD MAXWELL'S SECRETARY *and* CARDINAL'S SECRETARY *go off.*

SCENE FIVE

[LORD JOHNSTONE'S SECRETARY, LINDSAY, MCGLASS, *the* KING *and* ATTENDANTS.]

LINDSAY *and* MCGLASS *come out of the Palace.*

LORD JOHNSTONE'S SECRETARY. Sir David: Lord Maxwell and my master are nae langer at enmity.

LINDSAY. Hoho? . . . The cause of it nae doubt is the great grief Lord Maxwell feels for the misfortune of Lord Johnstone.

LORD JOHNSTONE'S SECRETARY. They tell me he is maist easily moved to tears for his fellow men in tribulation.

LORD JOHNSTONE'S SECRETARY *goes into Palace.*

LINDSAY. And nae news yet frae Jeddart? God, gif I had her here, I wad set her to lie with Maxwell. For how else can we bribe him now? This means he doth oppose Gilnockie's Lieutenantship. The King is in dreid of him and will undertake what he demands. Gilnockie will repudiate the agreement he has made with us. I think we had best advise the King to put Maxwell intil prison, on the ground of his suspectit intercourse with the English Ambassador, and thereby discredit his honour as a Scot. Sure, after that, Gilnockie wad consider him a'thegither unworthy his continuit obedience.

MCGLASS. Maxwell has ower-mony strang confederates – Bothwell, Buccleuch, the Douglases – the King wad never daur to ward him, Sir David.

LINDSAY. Wad he no? Belike. But we will yet find ane answer. Gif we canna destroy the mickle lords, we maun build up the lesser. As for example, the victor of Bannockburn . . . God, gif I had her here, I wad lie with her this minute. Sandy, we will be late for Mass.

The KING *is carried across the stage in a palanquin. He wears his full regalia and is followed by the* SECRETARIES *from the previous scene (and any other extras available).* LINDSAY *and* MCGLASS *join the procession and exeunt. Cries of* 'Long live the King!'

SCENE SIX

[LADY, MAID.]

LADY *and* MAID *enter from the Castle.*

LADY. And nae word yet frae Lindsay?

MAID. Nane at a', madam.

LADY. And for how long does he expect me to wait his leisure here? It seems that he regards me as his luggage, ane marriet burgess-wife, nae less: and yet he puts upon himself the style of poet.

MAID. He is alsweel ane politician, madam. The King's business is gey exigent and nae doubt requires great courage.

LADY. Impertinent. Ye are forbid to mak mock of his courage, burd. He has that in good measure – it's no his courage, it's his love. I'm nae jimp and rose-wand lassie ony langer – I'm hauf-gate on to be ane auld wrunkled carline, laithsome to the sicht of his een and the caress of his fingers – aye, and the snuff of his nostrils alsweel, I wadna wonder.

MAID. The snuff of his nostrils?

LADY. What else wad ye expect? I hae been dwellen all these weeks in the castle of Gilnockie. I canna describe it as the maist salubrious hall in Scotland. We're a' fair stinkards now, burd: me, you, and every servant I've got left. We're as nasty as the Armstrangs.

MAID. What for will ye no gang back to Edinburgh, madam?

LADY. What for? For David Lindsay, that's what for. Meet me, says he, upon the door-stane of John Armstrang. And

that's whaur I am – and by God I will abide here. Ach, he'll
come back, he'll mind whaur he's left me – he canna dae
without me. When all's told, the chief purpose of the man's
life is naething less than me. Lindsay is ane poet. His lady is
his existence. He has sworn it to me, burd, ane unremittit
aith, wi' the tears upon his cheek-bane.

GILNOCKIE'S WIFE *comes out of the Castle.*

Here's our good hostess. Slender she is, pale, discontentit:
why? She has ane man in her bed like a lion, and eneuch
English beer and beef in her storehouse to fill her as fat as
Potiphar's wife. Good day to ye, lady.

SCENE SEVEN

[LADY, MAID, GILNOCKIE'S WIFE.]

GILNOCKIE'S WIFE. Good day to ye, madam. Hae ye heard
    word yet frae Sir David Lindsay? Is he to come again
    presently to Eskdale?
LADY. Is he indeed? The King's business is gey exigent.
GILNOCKIE'S WIFE. Aye, but the confirmation of Gilnockie's
    title? Gilnockie wad speir gif the title of Lieutenant be truly
    his or no. Sir David gave his promise.
LADY. Then the King will surely keep it for him.
GILNOCKIE'S WIFE. Aye, but ye see, Gilnockie doesna
    entirely trust the King. For why should he? He was five
    times postit rebel: and officers sent against him: he has had
    embargo made upon his land and goods – are you yoursel
    acquent with the King, madam?
LADY. I was weel acquent with his father.
GILNOCKIE'S WIFE. His father?
LADY. Begod I slept in his bed.

GILNOCKIE'S WIFE. His bed? You did that?

LADY. I was but fifteen years auld at the time: but it was a kind of glory for me.

GILNOCKIE'S WIFE. How lang hae ye been the paramour of Lindsay?

LADY. Lang eneuch, madam, for what I've gotten out of it.

GILNOCKIE'S WIFE. He hath ane wife.

LADY. He hath.

GILNOCKIE'S WIFE. And what like of woman is she?

LADY. She did aspire in the warld at the same time that he did. She was ane seamstress of the Court, and obscure – as he too was obscure, bean but ane schoolmaster to the bairns of the nobility. They havena dwelt thegither for ane lang lang time. Sir David had a taste for mair wantonness in a wife than she could provide, and less stateliness of social port. She wad walk like ane Archdeacon up the length of the Canongate frae the palace to the kirk, and she was as dour and rectilinear as the stanes she set her feet on.

MAID. Mickle feet forbye.

LADY. Hauld yer whist, burd: I tellt ye, ye are impertinent.

GILNOCKIE'S WIFE. Madam, amang the ladies of Edinboro and Linlithgow, are there mony like yoursel?

LADY. And how d'ye mean, *like*?

GILNOCKIE'S WIFE. I mean, with nae reck of the vows of marriage – nae shame to be keepit mistress by a man that was weddit in kirk till ane other. I crave your pardon, madam, I intend nae offence. It is indeed strange for us here in the rural places to be told of these things. Gif I were to be fause to Gilnockie, I think that he wad kill me.

LADY. And gif he were fause to you?

GILNOCKIE'S WIFE. Aye, gif he were . . . Whiles, madam, he *is*. But wi' the lasses frae the tenant farms, or the tinker women upon the moss, or when he brenns ane house of the English. He wad never swyve a lady. Haly Peter, it is inconceivable. But you yoursel, madam, you are ane manifest lady, ye've had ane good education – I doubt you are capable of baith the Latin and the French—

MAID. Aye – and Greek and Gaelic.

GILNOCKIE'S WIFE. There was a strange man cam hither thrae the forest, he spak to us of Jesus Christ and the Testament, and of the New Religions in Germany: how the priests of our ain Kirk are the foretold Anti-Christ and how by penitence and martyrdom we can yet again recapture that liberty of God and of virtue that has lang syne departit frae the warld. Gilnockie said he was ane heretic: but Sir David gave him counsel it were better he should loose him and let him gang.

LADY. I ken the man ye mean.

GILNOCKIE'S WIFE. Madam, it was my opinion that he is ane godly pastor and he has indeed been grantit ane vision of divinity.

LADY. Aye – belike, belike, but—

GILNOCKIE'S WIFE. And I trow he would look gey unkindly upon the adultery you keep with Lindsay Delamont. I will tell ye this, madam, there was a lassie upon this border, she lay with a man outwith the bond of wedlock – and what befell her then?

LADY. What did befall her, madam?

GILNOCKIE'S WIFE. She was casten out by her folk: they did sparr up their yetts aginst her: and the strength of her body was broke by the cruel blaws of her father's whip. It was ane just chastisement: she had brocht shame upon his house. Forebye the shame was mine alsweel: Her father was my ain brither, madam.

LADY. What was her name?

GILNOCKIE'S WIFE. She was the dochter of the Laird of Stobs. And whaur is now the man that had her? I said whaur is he now? He sprawls beneath a bracken bush and there will be ane sair vengeance for him yet upon the heid of Gilnockie because of this murder. Here is Gilnockie.

SCENE EIGHT

[GILNOCKIE, *his* WIFE, LADY, MAID, *the* FIRST ARM-
STRONG.]

Enter GILNOCKIE *from the Castle. He is wearing a new
collar of gold links.*

GILNOCKIE. Murder.

GILNOCKIE'S WIFE. Gilnockie, I didna tell her. I wadna hae
said to her, I wad never hae—

GILNOCKIE. What murder?

LADY. Your good wife, sir, was maintainen her discourse upon
the great respect ye hauld in these parts for the virginity of
your young women. And upon the bitter punition accordit
to the seducers thereof. Is there ocht wrang in that, sir?

GILNOCKIE. Punition no wrang. Aye: bitter. Ye are ane
courteous whoor. Extradinair. Lindsay's. When does he
come?

LADY. That, sir, I canna tell ye.

GILNOCKIE. I should be Officer. Lieutenant! I hae pit up the
title. Had made to me the chain. Whaur's confirmation?

GILNOCKIE'S WIFE. Surely, John, it will be sent soon.
Lindsay is ane trustable man.

GILNOCKIE. Lindsay? To trust him? Ach, he did trust
Johnny. Because that I said I had made peace with Wamphray. Murder. What murder?

LADY. It was but in general talk, sir.

GILNOCKIE (*indicating his wife*). Na. I heard her greet.

He jerks his thumb towards the Castle.

Ben.

GILNOCKIE'S WIFE. Gilnockie.

GILNOCKIE. Ben. Or I'll spin your blood.

GILNOCKIE'S WIFE *goes into the Castle.*

LADY. Sir, you're no wise to be sae ungentle to your wife. She
doth love ye, sir, and gif she be timorous it is for your ain
safety.

GILNOCKIE. Wha's ungentle? (*To the* MAID.) You. You're
wantit within. Willie wants ye.

MAID. I fail to understand ye, sir.

GILNOCKIE. Understand me damn weel. Willie.

The FIRST ARMSTRONG *appears at the Castle gate.*

Tak her ben and steer her. Gif that's what she wants. She
has, I guess, sufferit it at your hands hereto – heretofore.

MAID. Gilnockie, I am in attendance here upon my lady. I'm
no to be matit at your will to ony man in your service.

GILNOCKIE. Then ye needna be bloody matit. But get out of
this place. Willie: I'm on my lane!

FIRST ARMSTRONG. I hear ye, Gilnockie. Come awa, lassie.
Sharp. The Laird wad be private.

He takes the MAID *into the Castle.*

SCENE NINE

[GILNOCKIE, LADY.]

GILNOCKIE. Gey private. Tak your claithes aff.

LADY. What?

GILNOCKIE. Here. I want to see your flesh. Aye, and maintain
it with infusion of mine. Johnny's the man. They never
refuse to Johnny. Tak 'em aff.

*She draws a little penknife and points it at him as he tries to
embrace her. She is laughing, and he laughs, too, as he
disengages himself.*

Aha, ha. But you *are* ane whoor?

LADY. I'm no *your* whoor.

GILNOCKIE. But whoor, it is common. Is for a' men. Is for me.

He advances upon her again, more menacingly.

I could. I could violate.

LADY. In your ain castle, Johnny? I belang to the King's
Herald: why, man, it wad be treason. And d'ye imagine he
wad bring ye the Officership after that?

GILNOCKIE. He wad kill for ye? Lindsay? Mak ane murder?
Wad he?

LADY. I canna tell ye that. I've never kent he had cause for it.

GILNOCKIE. For, gif he wad. He is maist honourable. For
honour of ane whoor to kill ane gentleman. Honour of ane
poet's whoor. Ane Herald-of-the-King's whoor. As ye micht
say it, he wad comprehend his obligation. Obligation of
honour is the thrust of ane pike, herein, here— (*He touches
his heart.*) David Lindsay is ane Herald. He wad therefore
comprehend.

LADY. Ah, Johnny, Johnny, my strang and beautiful Johnny,
you are observit. And with great disappointment, sir. I
trowit that ye had conceivit ane instant desire of love towart
me, or lust if nae better, and even lust wad flatter me. You
are ane lovely lion to roar and leap, and sure wad rarely
gratify all submissive ladies beneath the rampancy of your
posture. You are indeed heraldic, sir. Emblazonit braid in
flesh and blood, whereas David Lindsay can but do it with
pen and pencil upon his slender parchment. I did deny ye
your demand this minute because ye were baith rude and
rapid: but had ye thereupon attemptit ane mair gradual
kindlen of my body, ye micht damn weel hae had me, sir,
beneath this very tree.

GILNOCKIE. Aha . . .

LADY. But, Gilnockie. Ye hae been observit. Rude and rapid,
aye, but devious alsweel. What ye desirit was never in
principle me, it was the proof of the jealousy of Lindsay.
For gif Lindsay were to hauld the possession of his paramour,

ane manifest harlot, as matter for gravest honour: then what
way could he condemn you for the murder of – of Wamphray,
is the name? Whilk murder, as I guess, bean to avenge ane
lost chastity. But ye are in dreid it has been discoverit, and
ye willna get your Royal Pardon.

GILNOCKIE. Pardon! John the Armstrang in dreid for ane
Pardon!

LADY. And for why nocht? Ye wadna hae me credit ye attach
sae mickle import to the wearen of a gilt collar and the title of
Lieutenant—

GILNOCKIE. Whist! You mak an abominable roaring with your
mou! Clap it close. Like that.

> *He closes her lips with his fingers. He lets them remain there
> longer than would seem needful, to which she does not object.
> Then he stands back a pace sharply: and unhooks his sword-
> belt.*

Here is ane brand. Aff.

> *He drops belt and sword on the stage.*

Here's a gilt collar and ane title. Aff.

> *He throws his collar down.*

Here is ane buft jacket of defence. Aff.

> *He strips off his buff coat.*

Here is my gully. Out.

> *He pulls his knife out of the top of his trunk-hose and drops it.*

I'm in my sark and my breeks wi' nae soldiers, nae horses.
As there were nae soldiers wi' David Lindsay, when he stood
before my yett. Am accoutrit convenient for ane passage of
love. Or for execution. Or for what else? Ane Pardon? Gif
the King himsel were here I wad never beg his Pardon. I wad
demand: bot defence, bot threatenens, bot alliances: I wad

demand he saw me as ane man, that he wad accord me
recognition thereas, and that he wad give me as ane man
a'thing he could conceive that it were possible I did deserve.
And what do I deserve? Ye have ane answer. Speak it.
Speak.

LADY. John, ye do deserve to be ane equal man with ony King
in Christianity.

GILNOCKIE. In Eskdale. Nae place else. I am maist moderate.
I'm nane of your presumptuous Lothian-men, ye ken. Eskdale and Liddesdale alane, that appertain towarts John
Armstrang; they are my kingdom, and I content therein my
people with the justice of my government. And my government in this small region is ane bastion for the hale of Scotland. The man that strives to pit down Armstrang is the man
that means to bring in England, whether his name be
Johnstone or Lindsay or even Stuart. They do presume to
bribe my honour with their pardons and their titles: and then
they do delay – d'ye note – in the fulfilment of their fearful
bribes. And they do justify this delay by scandalous talk of
unproven murder. They wad gain ane better service out of
Armstrang gif they were to cease to demand it as ane service:
and instead to request it – d'ye hear the word, request – to
request it in humility as ane collaborate act of good friendship and fraternal warmth!

LADY. Why, Johnny, whaur's your lockit tongue? Ye do
deliver me these maist clear words as vehement as ane mill-
wheel, Johnny. This is the first ae time ye hae been heard to
utter without ane weir of tree-trunks across your teeth. And
what has causit it, sir?

GILNOCKIE. You.

LADY. Aye, me—

When I stand in the full direction of your force
Ye need nae wife nor carl to stand
Alsweel beside ye and interpret.
There is in me ane knowledge, potent, secret,

That I can set to rin ane sure concourse
Of bodily and ghaistly strength betwixt the blood
Of me and of the starkest man alive. My speed
Hangs twin with yours: and starts ane double flood:
Will you with me initiate the deed
And saturatit consequence thereof—?
Crack aff with your great club
The barrel-hoops of love
And let it pour
Like the enchantit quern that boils red-herring broo
Until it gars upswim the goodman's table and his door
While all his house and yard and street
Swill reeken, greasy, het, oer-drownit sax-foot fou—

GILNOCKIE. Red-herring broo—

LADY. In the pot. On the fire. All the warm sliden fishes,
Johnny, out of the deep of the sea, guttit and filletit and weel-
rubbit with sharp onion and the rasp of black pepper . . .

*He leads her into the Forest. As they walk he unbuttons and
casts off her mantle, her scarf, and the tire from her head.*

SCENE TEN

[LINDSAY, MAID, MCGLASS.]

LINDSAY *appears on the roof of the Palace.*

LINDSAY. I wad never claim that I had in ony way foreseen or
contrivit this particular development. Gif I had, I wad hae
been ane pandar.

The MAID *comes out of the Castle, humming a tune.*

To the base lusts and deficiencies of humanity. The material
of my craft, in fact. Accept them, mak use of them, for
God's sake enjoy them – here is a wee maid that expresses

her enjoyment in the music of ane sang. She is betrothit to
my secretair: she has just been coverit by Armstrang's man:
and Armstrang himsel at this moment is coveren— Ach, the
deil wi' it!

MAID (*sings*).

    It was upon a day of spring
    Before the leaves were green and fair
    They led me frae my mither's house
    And bad me serve them evermair.
    Beneath the sun that in summer did shine
    And amang the rows of the harvest corn
    The young men took me in their rankit line
    Ilk ane of them of a woman born.

*She begins to pick up the various articles of dress and other
gear left on the stage by* GILNOCKIE *and the* LADY, *and
puts them in two piles.*

    Till autumn cam in grief and pain
    And the leaves fell down across the lea:
    There was naething left for me to fulfil,
    But to gather them up maist diligently
    Intil their piles like kirkyard graves –
    The snaws of December, the frost and the gloom
    Will utterly bury them after their pride,
    Deep-buried and frozen, and endit their bloom.

    MCGLASS *comes out of the Palace.*

LINDSAY. Mr McGlass, ye maun gang on your lane to
Eskdale. I canna leave the Court at this stage of the business.
MCGLASS. Will the King arrest Maxwell?

    LINDSAY *shakes his head.*

Your circuit was a yard or twae ower-large belike. A wee
King needs but a wee circuit to confine him. We wad dae
better to serve the King of England.

LINDSAY. McGlass, ye talk treason.

MCGLASS. Aye. And what am I to talk to Gilnockie?

LINDSAY. Ye are to talk of the increase of Armstrang for the
better reduction of Maxwell. And talk of it with tact. Forget
ye are ane Hielandman. Jacob, Sandy, never Esau – let
Gilnockie be your Esau. God gang with ye.

> LINDSAY *retires.* MCGLASS *comes across the stage to the*
> MAID.

SCENE ELEVEN

[MAID, MCGLASS.]

MCGLASS. *Mo ghaol, Mo ghràdh, mo thasgaidh*[1] – Sir David
sends ye his gallant salutation.

MAID. Belatit.

MCGLASS. Whaur's the lady?

MAID. It is ane question.

MCGLASS (*looking at the piles of clothes*). Aha. She wadna bide
in Jedburgh. There were nae men there sufficient large for
her capacity? Gilnockie's brand. And his coat forbye.
Whaur's his breeks?

MAID. I doubt they are nae langer on his shanks.

MCGLASS. And your shanks? Sin ye arrivit in this place I canna
believe that they've seen nae service as ane saft nakit ladder
for the ascent of some strange venturer? Ah weel, it was to
be expectit, was it no? The King did require Lindsay to win
Gilnockie's purposes – belike the lady will succeed whaur the
politician fails.

MAID. Fails?

MCGLASS. Aye. There is nae office whatever now for the
decoration of John Armstrang – this collar here will signify
him naething while Maxwell and Lindsay stand at ilk side of

---

[1] My sweet sparrow, my love, my delight.

the King's Grace, aye tuggen at his lugs, left hand and richt
hand, till the sacred Crown of Scotland is near to tumble like
a – like a ninepin. Howbeit, as I said, maybe, out of this . . .
(*He twirls the* LADY'S *head-tire in his fingers.*) . . . will we
contrive some mair sanguine conclusion. For what reason
does she lie with him? For lust, for generosity, for admira-
tion of his strength – or for ane dutiful and politic assistance
of Sir David? Gif it were the last—

MAID. Gif it were the last, she were ane true harlot, Sandy, ane
prostitute of state: and nae mair worthy of your master's
devotion than the bitter wife he had already. My lady is
awa with Armstrong because Armstrang is what he is. Gif
that be sufficient for her, ye should crave no further reason.
Ye decline to speir ower-closely intil *my* behaviour in this
castle: it was, ye said – expectit. Let Sir David accord ane
equal trust towart her, and she will wark him nae treason.
She hath her ain honour.

MCGLASS. As hath Gilnockie. Ha, here be gentlemen.

SCENE TWELVE

[STOBS, YOUNG STOBS, MCGLASS, MAID.]

The two ELIOTS *enter through the Forest. Their hands are on
their sword-hilts.*

MCGLASS. Good day to ye, sirs.

STOBS. Good day.

MCGLASS. Ye seek Gilnockie?

YOUNG STOBS. Aye.

MCGLASS. He's no here at the present.

YOUNG STOBS. We'll bide his arrival. What's your name?

MCGLASS. McGlass.

STOBS. Ye are ane Hielandman. A King's rat. I'll put my foot
upon ye, ratten. Whae's the burd? She's yours?

MAID. She's naebody's but her ain. Ye have the tongue of a
carl and ane auld carl forbye. Learn some courtesy, gif ye
can; ye are dressit like a gentleman, but your manners are
scarce concomitant.

STOBS. They are the manners of the country, lassie, and the
country's no yours. Sae adapt yoursel with speed, or else
haud your whist.

YOUNG STOBS. Will I clap her across the mou and haud it
for her, father?

STOBS. Ye will nocht. We are within Gilnockie's boundaries
and we'll leave her to him.

YOUNG STOBS. Frae what I hear, Gilnockie's dislike of
vermin in his house is no sae strang as it used to be.

STOBS. That's eneuch o' that, boy. Gilnockie is wed to my
sister. He has benefit of our good opinion until sic time as
it is proven misplacit. When does the Laird come back? I'm
talking to you!

MCGLASS. I'm no in his confidence. He will be back when he
comes.

MAID. He will be back directly, sir . . . he's here.

SCENE THIRTEEN

[GILNOCKIE, LADY, MAID, MCGLASS, STOBS, YOUNG
STOBS.]

GILNOCKIE *and the* LADY *come out of the Forest, walking
amorously, unbraced and dishevelled. When he sees the*
ELIOTS, GILNOCKIE *lets go of her. The* MAID *hands her her
clothes, etc.*

GILNOCKIE. Ah. Gilbert.

STOBS. Aye. It's Gilbert.

GILNOCKIE. Martin. (*To the women.*) Ben the house. I'll call
for ye. You, sir, gang your gate within.

MCGLASS. I will attend you, sir.

LADY (*aside to* MCGLASS). Whaur's Lindsay?

MCGLASS (*aside*). Edinburgh.

LADY. Ah . . .

Exeunt the LADY, *her* MAID, *and* MCGLASS *into the Castle.*

SCENE FOURTEEN

[GILNOCKIE, STOBS, YOUNG STOBS.]

GILNOCKIE. Gilbert—

STOBS. John.

GILNOCKIE. There is ane matter here. Is delicate.

STOBS. Aye. The day we put our blades in Wamphray he did croak ane word towarts me. He said, 'Speir at Johnny Armstrang, what betidit with his honour?' Ye are Lieutenant, are ye no? Ye are King's Warden, are ye no? And what Royal rank, then, is accordit to the Eliots? Can ye gie us the answer to that, Johnny? I wad like fine to hear ye try.

GILNOCKIE. The King of Scotland, Gibby, daurna fecht wi' me. Nor wi' you, neither. He daurna fecht wi' Eskdale: nor Liddesdale: nor Teviot. Is that agreed?

STOBS. Gif James Stuart were to levy war against us, it wad be ane sair war for the realm, and he kens that, aye, his generals ken it, and his captains: his soldiers wadna march. Our castles upon this border are impregnable, and we dwell here, and we hae dwelt, and we will dwell for ay in our ain strang integrity. Therefore, John, what's this?

He has picked up the collar.

Good brother, ye maun justify to me.

YOUNG STOBS. Aye and to me.

STOBS. Martin: I said be silent. Here is matter for the chiefs. Ye maun justify. Can ye dae it?

GILNOCKIE. We grant us then impregnable. But whilk is better: impregnable as ane outlaw – baith back to the Scots and front to the English to fecht? Or as ane friend of Scotland, be impregnable: against English alane? Gibby, we can wear the King's collar. Can tell to the King, we do serve his banner. Are nae subjects, but Officers. Ane like collar for the Eliots alsweel. And yet we fecht the English. Yet we can ride: derive our prey out of England: defend the realm: is glory, Gibby. Is greater glory than here – than hereto – heretofore.

YOUNG STOBS. Nae subjects, but Officers. I canna tell the difference. Ane officer maun obey commandment; when did ye ever hear of ane Eliot that wad obey?

STOBS. At this aye minute: or I'll split your crag, boy. Gif we are the King's Officers, we maun obey him: will he pay for that obedience?

GILNOCKIE. Is possible. Ane honourable pension—

STOBS. Aye. But he may default on it. What when we need mair kye? There's good kye across in England, we canna grip them because of the King's word. But suppose the English were to start ane war themselves? Suppose they were to brenn a goodman's house in Liddesdale? What then?

GILNOCKIE. We can then ride. Defence of the Realm. Ane just reprisal for enormity.

STOBS. Ane English provocation and ane necessair response thereto. The braw Lieutenant levies men, and fills his byres forbye. Martin, expound to the Laird what we have in our mind this day.

YOUNG STOBS. The neist full moon, Gilnockie, it's three nichts beyont the present Sabbath. We can bring ye five and twenty riders— To the south of Carlisle there is a kirk and a wee town o' the name of Salkeld.

GILNOCKIE. Salkeld. I'm no familiar. We will require ane guide.

YOUNG STOBS. We have a rogue at Stobs this minute wad

tell us the Cumberland trackways – aye and conduct us
thereacross. Does it seem to you practicable, Gilnockie?

GILNOCKIE. Practicable.

STOBS. Then ye will ride?

GILNOCKIE. Whaur's the provocation?

STOBS. Ah, d'ye hear him, Martin, the Lieutenant has his
conscience. Weel: Mickle Sim of the Mains hasna paid me
his blackmail this twelvemonth past. So neist week he wakes
at midnicht and finds his roof on fire. Wha's brent it? A
dozen hoodit riders wi' English badges on their coats: and
there's your provocation. Sufficient for ye, Johnny?

GILNOCKIE. Ach, ha: I canna tell. Is delicate. Ane sort of
cruelty belike. To brenn a Scotsman's roof, and lay the
wyte of it on the English. In time past he has, has Mickle
Sim, rade bravely at our backs. Consonant. Can we call it
consonant?

STOBS. Consonant wi' what?

GILNOCKIE. With honour, Stobs. There is in this –

He takes hold of the collar.

– ane honour. Howsoe'er we may regard it. Gey delicate. I
canna tell.

STOBS. John: we are auld companions, and Janet Eliot is your
wife. Stobs and Gilnockie thegither: aye, sin we were bairns.
What consonancy of honour was it laid ye in the arms of that
harlot of the Court before the barbican of your ain castle,
and my sister within it? I did peer with my good steel into
the red wame of Wamphray for what he did to my dochter.
It is but for ancient friendship alane I hae sparit your life
this day. And ye haver with me now upon resumption of that
friendship? Ye hae but the ae choice, Johnny: ride wi' the
Eliots, or die like a Johnstone. I will in and see my sister: I
will mak nae mention in her presence of ony ither woman:
and when ye hae decidit, inform me of your will. Ye ca' this
matter delicate. Aye, it *is* delicate – it is as delicate indeed as

the hale reputation of your name. Armstrang is ane name I
wad be richt laith to forget.

He and his son enter the Castle.

SCENE FIFTEEN

[GILNOCKIE, MCGLASS.]

GILNOCKIE *stands for a moment, toying with the collar. Then*
MCGLASS *enters on the roof of the Castle. They look at each
other.*

GILNOCKIE. Whaur's Lindsay? He said he wad come back.
That he wad bring me confirmation. I've had made me the
chain. Confirmation: hae ye brocht it?

MCGLASS. I hae brocht ye ane tidings that will emancipate your
joy: Lord Johnstone is in prison.

GILNOCKIE. For what?

MCGLASS. For prevention of feud in pursuance of the death of
Wamphray.

GILNOCKIE. What death? Wha killt him? Wamphray?
When? Obscure, ye are obscure . . . Lord Johnstone to the
black corbies: in the face of Lord Johnstone I spew. Am I
Lieutenant or no!

MCGLASS. No.

GILNOCKIE. Come down here.

MCGLASS *retires from the roof.* GILNOCKIE *puts the collar
on the end of his sword blade. When* MCGLASS *comes out of
the Castle he holds this out at him.*

Young man, will ye tak it. For me, I've nae entitlement. Tak
it: and tak the risk of what gangs with it.

He holds the sword in a threatening manner. MCGLASS *looks
at him nervously, but carefully: walks slowly towards him,*

puts the sword aside and at the same time slides the collar up the blade till it hangs round GILNOCKIE'S *wrist.*

MCGLASS. Gilnockie, it's no wise to attempt to be precipitate. There is ane reason for the refusal of the King to accord you this title.

GILNOCKIE. Wamphray?

MCGLASS. Wamphray?

GILNOCKIE. Na?

MCGLASS. Ye hae just said yersel that the matter of Wamphray was – obscure. Let us consider rather the relation betwixt ane vassal laird and his superior. Lord Maxwell is—

GILNOCKIE. Jealous! He is jealous of my merit! He has consortit with the English: there can be nae other explanation. Fornication of the Magdalene, but I will render him ane sufficient cause to feel ane jealousy of me!

MCGLASS. Ye will, sir? And what cause? For Sir David Lindsay alsweel has his merit and his honour struck at in this. Mind ye, he made you his promise—

GILNOCKIE. God, but he did! And he never meant to keep it!

MCGLASS. Sir!

GILNOCKIE. Sir, sir, sir – and whatten wass she cause offence then whateffer to the shentlemen of Rannoch Moor? Tell me for why he has no pit Maxwell intil prison!

MCGLASS. Because Maxwell had ane dangerous faction – there is Bothwell, there is Buccleuch, there is even the Cardinal—

GILNOCKIE. And what about the Hielandmen?

MCGLASS. The Hielandmen?

GILNOCKIE. They are alsweel ane faction, ane bare-leggit bloody faction. Fetch them in.

MCGLASS. I will tell you directly about the Hielandmen, Gilnockie: they combine within their character ane precellent and personal lealty with ane mislike of ignorant insult whether in their ain glens or at the Court, or – na, na, here is Jacob, never Esau, Jacob, Jacob, Jacob . . .

GILNOCKIE. I tell ye, fetch them in, mak ane balance: ane
    equal – equal—

MCGLASS. Equilibrium? The Hielandmen and Armstrang
    against the lave of all the Lawlands? Original, indeed, ane
    new and sophisticate policy: but credit me, Gilnockie, it
    wad never serve just yet. The Hielandmen are—

GILNOCKIE. Geld the bloody Hielandmen. Pluck aff their
    sporrans and geld them! I repudiate Lord Maxwell and am
    his man nae langer. The decision of my conduct, for peace or
    for war, belangs to me and to nane other!

He calls toward the Castle.

Whaur's that woman?

SCENE SIXTEEN

[GILNOCKIE, *his* WIFE, LADY, MAID, MCGLASS, STOBS,
YOUNG STOBS, ARMSTRONGS, GIRLS.]

    GILNOCKIE'S WIFE, LADY, *and* MAID *come out of the
    Castle.*

LADY. Here's three women.

GILNOCKIE. I want the splendid harlot of the Court – you!
    Ye do speak French?

LADY. I do.

GILNOCKIE. What word in Scots wad ye call Lieutenant?

LADY. Lieutenant – '*Le Lieutenant*' – the man that haulds ane
    place. As, the place of his master.

GILNOCKIE. Master: is no Maxwell. Master is ane King. And
    to haul the King's place craves ane honour of equality. Tell
    the King his Lieutenant is Armstrang. And as his Lieutenant
    I demand ane absolute latitude and discretion for my
    governance of this territory. And tell this alsweel: Johnstone

of Wamphray – I do desire reversal of that traitor's property
and lands. He did conspire against my life. I am a King's
Officer. That's treason. If the lands are no grantit me, ye can
tell the King I will grip them!

MCGLASS. But this is enormous, sir: it is inordinate: it is—

GILNOCKIE. It's what I want. Ensure I get it. Awa with ye,
the three of ye.

> MCGLASS, *the* LADY, *and her* MAID, *obedient to* GIL-
> NOCKIE'S *peremptory gesture, retire upstage among the*
> *trees. They confer together.*

GILNOCKIE'S WIFE (*brings her husband downstage*). John, ye
will never succeed.

GILNOCKIE. No?

GILNOCKIE'S WIFE. The King will never brook it, John. It is
too insolent.

GILNOCKIE. Impregnable. I canna understand why I didna
tell it to Lindsay at first. Whaur are ye, whaur are ye –
Armstrang, Stobs, whaur are ye?

> *The* ELIOTS *come out of the Castle with* ARMSTRONGS
> *and* GIRLS.
> MCGLASS *and the two women walk out into the Forest. And*
> *thence into the Palace.*

Gilbert, the neist full moon. Order your men. Gilnockie and
Stobs. Companions. Nae further word and nae need of
provocation. Gilbert, we will ride.

> *There is a general cheer.* YOUNG STOBS *kisses the two*
> GIRLS *in his excitement.* STOBS *grips both of* GILNOCKIE'S
> *hands in his own. The* FIRST ARMSTRONG *begins to sing,*
> *and the others all take it up:*

> Some speaks of Lords, some speaks of Lairds,
> And sic like men of hie degree:
> Of a gentleman I sing a sang

Sometime called Laird of Gilnockie.
He aye wad save his country dear
Frae the Englishman. Nane are sae bauld
While Johnny doth ride on the border-side
Nane of them daur come near his hauld!

Exeunt – the men into the Forest: the women into the Castle.

Act Three

SCENE ONE

[LINDSAY, MCGLASS, LADY, MAID.]

LINDSAY, *still wearing the robe he assumed in Act One, Scene two, is reclining with the* LADY, *and* MCGLASS *with the* MAID, *enjoying the pleasures of love.*[1]

MCGLASS (*improvising verse*).
> This news was brocht to Edinbugh
> Whaur Scotland's King then dwelt
> That John the Armstrang on the border
> His ain state yet upheld.

LADY (*in the same manner*).
> Riever and rebel he was before
> But now ane starker style outsprings:
> He is ane Emperour complete
> Betwixt twa petty Kings.

LINDSAY. Well, ye can baith cap verses with some truth of prosody. It is evident that companionship with the King's makar has to this extent brocht furth its fruit. But for the content of the said verses? Ane Emperour? Hardly that, I think.

LADY. In his ain een he is ane Emperour.

LINDSAY. Aye, and in his ain codpiece, I daur weel hazard. For that's whaur it began. Gif we are at wark upon the improvisation of occasional stanzas, here is ane rhyme of Lindsay's – mark:
> Lady, the love I hae maintaint
> For you nine year—

---

[1] If there is no curtain to provide a discovery here, the characters enter from the Palace.

LADY. Ten.

LINDSAY. For you ten year with nae complaint
        Should for your treason wax full faint,
        Maist shamefully expire.
        But you are ane Ashtaroth of outrage,
        Ane gowden sepulchre, ane stage
        Whaur I play out the tale of my gray age
        Aye for the increase and never the assuage
        Of venereal desire.

LADY. Jeddart is a weet and a nasty town, David. Ye left me in ane tavern there with green wood upon the fire and great gaps in the roof. And ye trippit oer the back-ankle of your ain metre in the last three lines of your – your—

LINDSAY. Doggerel? It is but doggerel. There's nae astringency left. I tell ye, I'm flatulent.

MAID. That's a puir recommendation to my lady of your venereal increase, Sir David. I think that ye should—

LINDSAY (*walking about in agitation*). I think I should postpone baith venery and poetry and set my wits to wark on policy. Lord Maxwell is richt violent angerit against us. The man's been repudiate by his vassal. Gif what he will tell the King is creditit by the King, there will be ane rope around this halse in less than two weeks.

MCGLASS. Ane noosit rope, lady. This is nae game.

MAID. Sandy, we ken that.

MCGLASS. Aye? But to her it *was* game. She did embolden John Armstrang to the extent they will impeach Lindsay!

LADY. Mr Alexander, the King will never credit Maxwell. The King hates Maxwell. He will require his Lindsay yet, the man that did divert his puberty nocht alane with the Latin Grammar, but alsweel with the bawdy satires of Petronius. My misbehaviour ye did satirize as the wark of ane Ashtaroth – ane carnal goddess, David – then accept the goddess's gift and build your policy upon it. To begin: surely Maxwell repudiate is ane benefit to the realm?

LINDSAY. Ane benefit to the Lairds on yon side of the English Border. John of Gilnockie, with nae suzerain to control him, wad be ane honest man to deal with, wad he no? For his treacheries derive frae the occult procuration of dark men that movit ahint of him: and they're gane. Sandy – what's the adage: 'The English of the North and the Border Scot'?

MCGLASS.

> The English of the North and the Border Scot
> Are ilk ane like the ither:
> Their tongue is the same and their life is the same
> Ilk man is as puir as his brither.

LINDSAY. Precise. Now: ane free confederacy of the borderers of either nation, ane alliance of mutual poverty, with their ain Parliament, gif ye will, under the leadership of – why nocht Armstrang? In the manner of the mountain cantons of the Switzers as I hae observit them on my travels. Nae hereditaire nobility, nae theft, nae feuden, and gif they lust yet for battle – ane mercenary service in the army of the Pape, or the Emperour, or the King of France. What's wrang wi' it?

MAID. England.

MCGLASS. It is ridiculous and unpractical. England wad never consent to it – why, it wad mean peace!

LINDSAY. King Henry has preoccupations. Religious, financial, amorous. I trow that he craves for peace – sincerely.

MCGLASS. He craves for the execution of Gilnockie and I think that we hae nae choice but to gie it him.

LINDSAY. What way, man? Whaur's your army, whae's your hangman – you? Wad ye mak your name ane byword for tyranny and coercion, and – and—

LADY. David, recollect yoursel – ye hae the reputation of ane man of placidity.

LINDSAY. Mak me placid, then. Love me.

She does so.

McGlass, what I hae tellt ye is practicable, and it is honourable. I hae writ indeed ane letter about it – ane treasonable
letter, to the English Ambassador.

LADY. David, that is dangerous!

LINDSAY. Agreeable danger. I did ever tak pleisure in ane
devious activity. God help me, I'm as bad as Maxwell.

SCENE TWO

[LINDSAY, MCGLASS, LADY, MAID, *the three* SECRETARIES.]

The three SECRETARIES *enter from the Palace.*

LORD MAXWELL'S SECRETARY. What do ye mean, as bad?
My master will oerwhelm you yet—

CARDINAL'S SECRETARY. Sir David Lindsay, the Blessen of
God upon you, sir; and may He in His inestimable mercy
oerlook your transgressions.

LINDSAY. What transgressions? Specify. Her, do ye mean?
Lady, will ye strip your body, stand up before them like
Phryne before the Judges of Athens, and ilk ane of them
will return ye ane similar acquittal. Though I doubt they
wad expect ye to pay for it in kind. These are gentlemen of
commerce – they buy their love and sell it: love of women
and love of country. Weel, what's the news?

LORD JOHNSTONE'S SECRETARY. What's the news, the
man demands—

LORD MAXWELL'S SECRETARY. Why, ye arrant Machiavell,
here is the news—

CARDINAL'S SECRETARY. John the Armstrang, Thomas his
brother, the Eliots of Stobs, and other of their gang, hae
ridden intil Cumberland. The town of Salkeld is brennt. The
Laird of Salkeld is slain within his ain fold-yard: and the
Lord Warden at Carlisle has ordainit ane general muster of
his levies: for revenge. That, sir, is the news. You and your

slee dalliance amang the heresies of England – ye hae brocht
war upon your native Catholic land!

LINDSAY. And are ye nocht blithe to hear it? Ye smile, the
three of ye smile! By God, I blaw my neise at ye.

He blows his nose at them.

LORD MAXWELL'S SECRETARY. The King will cut your heid
aff.

CARDINAL'S SECRETARY. The Cardinal will brenn ye.

LORD JOHNSTONE'S SECRETARY. Traitor—

CARDINAL'S SECRETARY. Satirist—

LORD MAXWELL'S SECRETARY. Englishman—

CARDINAL'S SECRETARY. There is nae more to say.

The SECRETARIES *go off into the Palace.*

SCENE THREE

[LINDSAY, MCGLASS, LADY, MAID, ENGLISH CLERK.]

LINDSAY. There is a great deal mair forbye. But we maun wait
for it – out of England. Placidity, and patience . . .
Retournons-nous à nos fesses.

LADY. *Mais c'est une situation très grave, mon chéri: il nous
faut penser à notre propre sécurité: pas de fesses et pas de
tétins aujourd'hui – par dieu, c'est terrible!*

LINDSAY. *Non, ce n'est que ridicule – une connerie inévitable,
et c'est une connerie de ton con – tu as tourné le monde entier
tout à fait de haut en bas . . Tais-toi, et baise-moi . . .*
Aha, here he is: I thocht he wad come soon.

Enter the ENGLISH CLERK, *with a letter.*

ENGLISH CLERK. Sir David, we can prevent open war, and
we must prevent it – now. The English Ambassador has sent
me to tell you—

LINDSAY. Did he read my letter yet?

ENGLISH CLERK. He did: I have it here. A very cunning letter, Sir David; you have not even signed it. But nobody could doubt that it came from your hand.

LINDSAY. Absence of doubt is nae presence of proof.

ENGLISH CLERK (*laughs a little*). Your curious proposals, for the establishment of what amounts to an independent sanctuary for outlaws and masterless men between England and Scotland, have been examined with a more sympathetic attention than perhaps you will give credit for. . . . Why not go back to Eskdale and put your ideas to Armstrong? We can do the same to our own rude gentlemen in Cumberland and Northumberland. But we must have assurances that they will remain content within their own boundaries. Your Maxwells and your Douglases will certainly endeavour to stir up disharmony. Will they be controlled, Sir David? This is absolutely cardinal.

LINDSAY. Ach, I canna tell ye: but I'll dae the best I can: creep in and creep out and tangle them whaure'er it's possible. I doubt I'm a wee bit discreditit at the Court here at present.

ENGLISH CLERK. Yes, we have heard so . . .

He goes out.

LINDSAY (*calling after him*). Hey – hey – brenn that letter!

SCENE FOUR

[LINDSAY, MCGLASS, LADY, MAID, PORTER.]

LINDSAY. Aha, they've heard it, have they? Mr McGlass, we maun put it tae the proof. Blaw your horn, we're gangen in.

MCGLASS. Ye'll no be permittit.

LINDSAY. Blaw it.

MCGLASS *blows the bugle. The* PORTER *appears on the Palace roof.*

PORTER. The King's Grace regrets that he is unable this day to find occasion to speak with Lord Lyon.

The PORTER *retires.*

SCENE FIVE

[LINDSAY, MCGLASS, LADY, MAID.]

MCGLASS. Sure it was inevitable that he wad become ane adult.

LINDSAY. God, McGlass, he's nae adult yet. He has acquirit ane different dominie, but he's still *in statu pupillari*. And it is for you and me to pull him out of it this minute. We will accept the advice of our consequential English friend, and gang directly to Eskdale. I intend to bring Gilnockie to a *de facto* truce and handfast with the lairds beyond the border. That includes the Salkeld men: ane strang immediate torniquet before the wound bleeds further. I ken very weel what is in John Armstrang's mind—

MCGLASS. There is naething in his mind but the enjoyment of manslauchter.

LINDSAY. Na, na, the man desires – he yearns in his mirk bowels, Sandy, for ane practicable rational alternative: and I trow we can provide it him. He is ane potential magnificent ruler of his people – he did steer *you* to your muckle pleisure; you tell us what ye think of him!

LADY. Potential, true indeed: but unpredictable, David. Whiles he is generous and intelligent, ane lion, gif ye will – but when he turns intil ane wolf . . . Besides, ye will be rebel; ye will be against your ain King for this.

LINDSAY. Rebel? I am already traitor, it wad seem. Certain it is ane risk. I am about to set ane absolute trust upon King James. This is ane test for him, ane precise temptation: he kens my value, gif he will bethink him: let him see my purposes, and let him see the purposes of Lord Maxwell and the lave: and mak ane clear choice betwixt them. There was a time when his father was your lover. Explain to the son then, what it is I intend.

LADY. I will do what I can, David.

LINDSAY. Gif he be at last ane man, he will discern what David Lindsay means, and then there will be nae mair talk of rebel or of traitor. But gif he prefer to remain for ever the schoolboy that he has been, he will put himself for ever outwith all hope of stringent kingly government. It is ane act of faith to trust him: Sandy, will ye come?

MCGLASS. *Amadain, Tha thu clis is cearr ach tha mise leat agus thig mi.*[1] I will come.

LINDSAY. Ladies, this wark is yours. Begun within the wames of women: now it maun be carryit through, at the hands and brains of men, tormentible, destructible men. Accord us your bitter blessen and get within your doors.

LADY. There are ower-mony brands and lang guns in the forests of Eskdale. Gif ye shouldna return hame—

LINDSAY. Ye may get intil the King's bed. He is of ane age for it, I think.

MCGLASS (*to* MAID). I shall return: in whatever shape they bring me, ye wad never withauld me welcome?

MAID. *Tha thu ro óg airson a'bhàis.*[2]

MCGLASS. *Na creid facal dheth.*[3] Lindsay, are ye ready? Then let's gang: and the de'il gang wi' us, for I doubt that naebody else will.

The women kiss them and go into the Palace.

[1]'Stupid, impulsive, a miscalculation, but I am your man and I must come.'

[2] 'You are too beautiful to die.'

[3] 'Never believe it.'

SCENE SIX

[LINDSAY, MCGLASS, GILNOCKIE, *his* WIFE, ARMSTRONGS, MEN, GIRLS, EVANGELIST.]

LINDSAY *takes off his robe and puts on a buff coat. He and* MCGLASS *walk across the stage, and call out at the Castle gate.*

LINDSAY. Now then, for Eskdale . . . Gilnockie, are ye there?

MCGLASS. Mr Armstrang!

LINDSAY. Johnny!

GILNOCKIE *comes out of the Forest.*

GILNOCKIE. Here.

LINDSAY. Ah, out of the wynds of the forest, as befits a rank reiver that recks little of King or Baron but uphaulds for a' time the standard of his ain strength. Sir, I do salute you: you are lord entire within your boundaries.

GILNOCKIE. And what are you?

LINDSAY. The salamander of sanity, belike, betwixt the gleeds of your het fire.

The EVANGELIST *and all* GILNOCKIE'S *household come out of the Forest behind him.*

EVANGELIST. Sanity or sanctity, Sir David?

LINDSAY. Ah? Gilnockie, the English are preparen war. I have come to preserve your manhood and your liberty in the face of either nation.

EVANGELIST. You do interrupt with your feckless brawlen the service of the Lord God. The Laird of Gilnockie has declarit himself at last amang the congregation of the Elect. We were about to sing ane haly sang of praise.

He leads them all in a hymn, speaking each line, which is then sung by the congregation:

ALL.   Lord God of Wrath, our arms mak strang
            To deal the right and hale down wrang

            Thy people are but few and faint
            And Thou wilt hear their just complaint.

            Our native land, O Lord doth bleed:
            Assist us to fulfil her need.

            We praise Thee and adore Thy rage:
            Thy words are writ upon our page.

            We praise Thee and adore Thy love:
            O cause, O cause our hearts to move.

EVANGELIST. Again, again, brethren, assail the ears of God!

ALL. O cause, O cause our hearts to move!

> *The* EVANGELIST *launches into an ecstatic homily, while the congregation, moved to excess, interject cries of religious passion.*

EVANGELIST. Let them move indeed, let them pursue Thy impeccable purpose notwithstanding fear and feebleness of spirit—

ALL. We are but few and faint—

EVANGELIST. —until that we can at the last within this barren land of Anti-Christ and corruption declare to the uttermaist—

ALL. Lord, Lord, declare it—

EVANGELIST. —and out of ane hale and sanctifyit mind give furth with pregnant voice the fervent utterance of Thy glory—

ALL. Glory, glory, glory—

EVANGELIST. —and thereupon erect Thy temple—

ALL. Lord, Lord, Thy true resplendent temple—

EVANGELIST. —upon the banks and braes of Eskdale!

ALL (*including* EVANGELIST). Glory, glory, glory, Lord, Lord, whaur is Thy temple?

MCGLASS. And is this what ye want the Lady to tell the King was your intention – to set up ane temple?

LINDSAY. Never.

MCGLASS. It wad hae been better to hae deliverit up this Evangelist to the fires of the Cardinal, as prescribit in the law, and never mind in what tongue is writ the orthodox Gospel.

LINDSAY. Na, na, Alexander – never that neither! God, I am at my wits' end. I had come to maintain Gilnockie by ane argument to his ain self-interest – but this is nae self-interest: this is ane coercive zeal for martyrdom and fanatic excess that I am scarce able to credit.

MCGLASS. Ye trow that our Johnny isna sincere?

LINDSAY. I trow that he isna godly. The man is exceeden politic: mair politic than me. I will ask him ane question.

During the above dialogue the drone of devotion has been continuing, but more subdued. Now the EVANGELIST *cries again in full strength.*

EVANGELIST. For the sins and the errors of our past life, we maun shew furth our sober penitence. John, are ye indeed washit white in the Blood of the Lamb?

GILNOCKIE. White, washit, clean, pure. Glory to God for that I did sin with ane carnal and abominable sin, but glory, glory, glory—

ALL. Glory, glory, glory—

GILNOCKIE. But all is turnit now towart election and salvation—

EVANGELIST. This brand that ye do bear—

GILNOCKIE (*draws sword*). Is the Lord's brand and consecrate—

ALL. Glory, glory, glory—

GILNOCKIE. For the execution of God's enemies and the renovation of His Kingdom!

ALL. Glory, glory, glory. Hallelujah upon Mount Sion . . . *etcetera.*

The religious orgasm fades away: GILNOCKIE *comes down to* LINDSAY.

GILNOCKIE. Delamont, ye are ane vanity. Ye are ane warldly infection with your collars and vile titles. I am naebody's man but God's.

LINDSAY (*takes him aside*). There is nae credibility in this, Johnny, and I think nae practicality—

GILNOCKIE. Ah. Practicality. Hear ye this, Lindsay – your wee man Evangelist there – ye canna ca' him unpractical. We intend to extend the Kingdom of Christ—

LINDSAY. Northwarts, or south?

GILNOCKIE. Whilkever direction can ensure me the best wealth and food for my people. There are monasteries in the Scots Lawlands. They tell that in Germany Martin Luther has made free the nuns and monks. And why nocht alsweel in Scotland? And Johnny will prove ane gey furious fechter, new-washit as ye see him, white in the Blood of the Lamb!

SCENE SEVEN

[LINDSAY, MCGLASS, EVANGELIST, GILNOCKIE, *his* WIFE, ARMSTRONGS, MEG.]

MEG *comes out of the Forest.*

MEG. Lamb's blood or man's blood, it was never white, but mirk, thick, blue-red, and it dries upon the bleachit linen stiff as ane parchment.

EVANGELIST. Be silent.

MEG. I wad speak like yoursel the day, master, I wad speak the prophetic tongue. I was possessit twa year by the fury of

Lucifer: he drave me like a packmare intil the moss and mire of iniquity: in the fleshly beds I did roll and I did wallow.

GILNOCKIE'S WIFE. Haud fast your gapen slot, cousin, ye incontinent wee carline – did ye no hear the good preacher—

MEG. —but there is mair shame than mine craves absolution here. Aye and chastisement forbye. For ane secret murder done on the riggs of the moor – what chastisement for that, master – punition, revenge, ane heavenly correction – I cry, I cry, I cry: Glory, glory, glory, Lord God amend all, strike down the men of blood, strike down Armstrang, strike down Eliot. Glory, glory, Lord—

GILNOCKIE. She's runnen mad—

GILNOCKIE'S WIFE. Ye will no hear her further; she brings scandal upon the conventicle—

GILNOCKIE. It is the fiend speaks within her. Or witchcraft—

GILNOCKIE'S WIFE. Aye, witchcraft—

EVANGELIST. I did trow she wad be penitent . . .

GILNOCKIE. Penitent. *I'm* your penitent here. Wamphray was slain for ane lustful confederacy against me and against the Eliots, and *she* was part of it! Gif she in truth be penitent, God's throat, she should be *glad*! Ben the house, cast her awa, she is ane withcraft adversary – ben!

He leads his WIFE *and people into the Castle.*

SCENE EIGHT

[LINDSAY, MCGLASS, EVANGELIST, MEG.]

MEG (*sings*).

> Fall, Sword of God, upon his heid
> And bite intil his brain
> For he slew the lovely lover of me
> That will ne'er love me again.

EVANGELIST. I did trow that she was penitent.

MCGLASS. Ha, but she is, master. She is your child and your disciple – a wee bit difficult to control, whatever, but yours – observe her, sir, she hath ane strange passion for you. Is it no reciprocate in your ain body? It is indeed, consider: maist certain ye do feel ane risen lust within you! She hath hauld upon your garment – look!

EVANGELIST (*withdrawing his skirts from the kneeling woman*). This is filthy and incomprehensible.

MCGLASS. Then attempt to comprehend it! The cause of her distraction is John Armstrang, that did kill her man. And ye hae sanctifyit that murderer in all verity with the words of the Gospel? Whilk of these twa penitents of yours will ye accept or reject? Ye canna credit the baith of them? They canna be baith guests at the same Christian marriage table.

LINDSAY. McGlass, that's sufficient.

MCGLASS. Na, na—

LINDSAY. It is! Ye will confound all my policy with this fool's talk of marriage tables. McGlass, ye maun tak tent—

MCGLASS. Aye, aye, and gang ane circuit! You put temptation upon the King, very weel – I put it in this minute upon this Evangelist: whaur is conscience and humanity, master – with this tormentit lassie, or with Gilnockie and his brand? Whaur is your conscience – whaur is Christ, this minute!

EVANGELIST. Here, Satan, here—

He snatches the knife out of MCGLASS's *belt and stabs him with it.*

The flesh prevails ever. The Lord hath hid his face. Within three days I could hae biggit the temple in Eskdale. Oh, ye mountains of Gilboa: cover me, cover me frae the abundant wrath of God—

He runs out into the Forest.

MEG. Never forsake me now, master, I will despair; never forsake me, master—

She follows him, crying.

SCENE NINE

[LINDSAY, MCGLASS.]

MCGLASS *has sunk down at the edge of the stage, so that he is half-seated, half-propped against the wall. The knife is still in the wound. He laughs.*

LINDSAY. Sandy, did he wound you? What's sae damn droll, man? Here is nocht but bloody frenzy. Maintain your manly dignity, stand upon your feet – Sandy, do ye hear me?

MCGLASS. Sir David, there is ane gully-knife sticks out at my side. Look. Whaurever we gang now there is ever ane gully-knife, or ane brand, or ane lang rope, Sir David. Nae circuit nae langer: finish it, sir, finish it.

LINDSAY. I will bring ye intil the castle—

MCGLASS. Na, na: finish it. Edinburgh. Finish it.

LINDSAY (*helping him up*). Finish it? Finish it what way?

MCGLASS. The way of the Cyclops, or Gogmagog or whatever. He has deliverit himself, has Johnny, intil the hands of Evangelists: and in the hands of Evangelists there are red reeken gullies. Ye did tak pride in your recognition of the fallibility of man. Recognize your ain, then, Lindsay: ye have ane certain weakness, ye can never accept the gravity of ane other man's violence. For you yourself hae never been grave in the hale of your life!

LINDSAY. That is entirely untrue—

MCGLASS. Na, na, it is utter verity. But John Armstrang is ane gey serious boy: and gif he claims to be ane Luther – he may

nocht be sincere in it – but I tell ye, I tell ye, he will be as
dangerous – and as lunatic – as the maist promiscuous
Evangelist that ever held a book. Now get me intil Edinburgh.

LINDSAY. Ye canna mak the journey in that condition,
Sandy—

MCGLASS. I can. Observe me, sir: I'm maken it. Observe, I'm
upon the road.

> *He staggers round the stage, supported by* LINDSAY. *As he
> goes, he sings:*

> O lang was the way and dreary was the way
> And they wept every mile they trod
> And ever he did bear his afflictit comrade dear.
> A heavy and a needless load.
> A heavy and a needless load.

Ye should hae heard me at the first – your rationality and
practicality has broke itself to pieces, because ye wad never
muster the needful gravity, to gar it stand as strang, as
Gilnockie's fury . . . There is naething for you now but to
match that same fury, and with reason and intelligence, sae
that this time you will win.

LINDSAY. Will win and win damnation.

MCGLASS. Aye, man, ye'll win and be damned . . . Do ye
mind what ye said to Gilnockie the first time ye met him?
'There is ever ain sair question when a man sees his ancient
life upon the brink of complete reversal!' For my sake, Sir
David, will you reverse your life for me? Show to the King
the gully in my side: and tell him to act: and first he maun
put intil prison: Johnstone – he's there already: Maxwell:
Bothwell: Buccleuch: ony man else? I canna mind . . . But
let them all be lockit up, upon the same hour, of the same
day, and let the King, alane, ken in what prison, they are
keepit. Then let him come to the conclusion of Gilnockie . . .
        A heavy and a needless load . . .

SCENE TEN

[MCGLASS, LINDSAY, MAID, LADY, PORTER.]

They have come to the entrance of the Palace. The LADY *and the* MAID *look over the walls and see them: the* MAID *gives a cry: and they come down and receive them at the doorway.*

LADY. David, what's to happen now? Ye wad never kill Gilnockie – David, he was my lover, David—

MAID. Can ye find ane policy to gang ane circuit around this?

LADY. Hauld your tongue, burd: Sir David makes his ain decision here.

LINDSAY. McGlass, ye do disgrace your master. Ye bring the gully in your side for ane nakit witness against me.

MAID. How lang is there left of him of life?

MCGLASS. Burd: I'm a deid man before my dinner. Will ye show it to the King! *Greas ort, greas ort, iarr air an righ Gilnockie a mharbhadh. O mo gheol ghadl bhithinn sona gu bràth na d'aclais.*[1]

LINDSAY. The King will hear me: I will nocht brook prevention. Whaur's his Porter? Whaur?

The PORTER *appears on the Palace roof.*

The King shall hear me: the King shall see this: the King shall! Let me in!

PORTER. Lord Lyon, please to wait in patience, sir. I will inquire.

He retires from the roof. MEG *is keening.*

LADY. David, you are ane new man. I am unable to recognize you, David.

LINDSAY (*indicates* MCGLASS). Can ye recognize him?

LADY. I am talken about you. I tellt ye, I am unable.

[1] 'Quick, quick, and tell the King to kill Gilnockie. O my lovely girl, I would have lived within your arms for ever.'

The PORTER *beckons them into the Palace.*

Belike the King will fare better. Ye may divert wi' this his manhood as ance ye did his puberty. Indeed, it is provocative of comedy and mirth.

They carry in MCGLASS'S *unconscious body to the Palace.*

SCENE ELEVEN

[GILNOCKIE, *his* WIFE, ARMSTRONGS.]

GILNOCKIE *appears on the roof of the Castle.*

GILNOCKIE. Whaur's he gane? Whaur's the Evangelist? He's no within the Castle – gang out and find him. Whaur did ye leave him?

The ARMSTRONGS *come out of the Castle gate.*

I tell ye, that man, he is the word of Jehovah God, he is the good fortune of Gilnockie, he is the luck of Johnny's house.

GILNOCKIE'S WIFE (*appearing also on the roof*). Be patient, Gilnockie; he will return in his ain good time. Belike he has stayit to pray.

GILNOCKIE. Pray, woman? What? What's it, pray? Find him, bring him in—

The men run into the Forest.

SCENE TWELVE

[LINDSAY, GILNOCKIE, *his* WIFE.]

LINDSAY *comes out of the Palace. He is wearing his herald's tabard, and carries a scroll.*

LINDSAY (*to audience*).

> I did swear a great aith
> I wad wear this coat nae further
> Till Armstrang be brocht
> Intil the King's peace and order.
> To gang against his house
> As ane man against ane man,
> Through craft and through humanity –
> Alas, and mortal vanity,
> We are but back whaur we began.
> A like coat had on the Greekish Emperour
> When he rase up his brand like a butcher's cleaver:
> There was the knot and he did cut it.
> Ane deed of gravity. Wha daur dispute it?

He walks across the stage to the Castle.

John, I have ane letter. It is ane letter of love frae the hand of the King. Will ye come down and read it? Or will ye let your lady read it? Or will *I* read it, John? I wear my Herald's coat the day: it is ane surety of Royal honour that there will be nae deception.

GILNOCKIE. Read.

LINDSAY (*reading*). 'We, James, by the Grace of God,' and so furth and so furth, 'to our weel-belovit—'

GILNOCKIE. Our weel-belovit subject?

LINDSAY. Subject? Na, na, I canna see it writ here . . . 'To our weel belovit John of Gilnockie,' that's what he says, 'Our weel-belovit John of Gilnockie, Warden and Lieutenant . . . we do hereby send our Royal greeten. We intend to mak ane sportive progress for the improvement of our health and for the pursuit of the wild deer, throughout the lands of the Border. Gif John of Gilnockie, and sae mony of his people as do desire to come with him, will attend our person and household at the place callit Carlanrigg: he may there be assurit of ane richt cordial and fraternal welcome.'

GILNOCKIE. Fraternal?

LINDSAY. Fraternal.

GILNOCKIE. That means he calls me his brither. He wad call King Henry brither?

LINDSAY. Listen to the lave of it. 'This letter will serve the recipient baith as ane Free Pardon and as ane Safe Conduct upon his arrival at Carlanrigg.' The signature 'Jacobus Rex', and the seal appendit. Ye will recognize the seal.

GILNOCKIE'S WIFE. And we are to trust to this letter?

LINDSAY. Safe Conduct, Free Pardon, the King's seal, the Herald's coat upon me? Remember the words of Virgil Mantuan, madam: '*Timeo Danaos et dona ferentes !*' – 'The gifts of your enemies are e'en sweeter to the taste than those of your friends!' The King hath said 'fraternal'. Do ye mean to reject him?

GILNOCKIE. Lord Maxwell?

LINDSAY. He is in prison.

GILNOCKIE. Bothwell?

LINDSAY. In prison.

GILNOCKIE. Buccleuch?

LINDSAY. Prison.

GILNOCKIE. The hale gang of them. I'll no believe it.

LINDSAY. John, ye had best. The King has become ane adult man this day. Ride out, sir, and bid him welcome to your lands. At last, at last, Gilnockie, he has listent to my advice!

GILNOCKIE. It is necessair, this matter should, with earnest deliberation, be embracit.

He and his WIFE *descend from the roof. They come out of the Castle.*

It is necessair, ane good preclair appearance: as in dress, and plumage. Whaur's the men?

GILNOCKIE'S WIFE. Ye sent them to the wood, for the Evangelist.

GILNOCKIE. Evangelist? What's an Evangelist? Call 'em back! Whaur's the women? Armstrang! Armstrang!

SCENE THIRTEEN

[LINDSAY, GILNOCKIE, *his* WIFE, ARMSTRONGS, GIRLS.]

His MEN *reappear from the Forest, and the* GIRLS *come out of the castle.*

GILNOCKIE. The King has callit me brither! My gaudiest garments, ilk ane of them, a' the claiths of gowd and siller, silk apparel, satin, ilk ane I hae grippit in time past out of England. Fetch 'em here.

The GIRLS *bring out a chest which they open and take out rich clothes.*

Lindsay Delamont: tak tent: ye see Gilnockie's putten on his raiment. It is the ceremony: John the Armstrang's pride and state.

He looks at the garments presented him, and strips off his buff coat, and under-tunic.

Here, this yin, that yin – no that, carl's claithing – rags and tatters – that: ane coat of glory for ane glorious King to hauld the hand of his brither! The King has callit me brither!

GILNOCKIE'S WIFE. He did call ye Lieutenant alsweel.

GILNOCKIE. Lieutenant? What's Lieutenant? Forgotten: subordinate, nocht . . . (*He is now dressed in a fine cloth-of-gold tunic and accessories.*) Aha: and now a bonnet.

FIRST ARMSTRONG. The Laird wants his bonnets.

A GIRL *fetches a number of hats.*

GILNOCKIE (*looking through them*). Na, na, for ane cattle-drover, that . . . ane Carlisle bloody burgess, that . . .

belike, but whaur's the feathers? . . . Aha, ye've brocht it.
This did belang to the Lord Warden of the English side; I
dang it aff his heid wi' my fist at the conclusion of ane parley.
Mair of these targets; pin 'em in. (*As an afterthought he puts
on the Lieutenant's collar.*)

FIRST ARMSTRONG. Mair targets, pin 'em in.

*The hat he has selected has a wide brim turned up over the
forehead, with one or two jewelled badges pinned on the
underside. The* GIRLS *now fetch out a box with more badges
in it, and they set to work to add these to the hat.*

GILNOCKIE. On the road to Carlanrigg, Johnny Armstrang
requires his music. Whaur's the piper?

FIRST ARMSTRONG. Whaur's the piper?

THIRD ARMSTRONG (*fetching the pipes*). Whatten air d'ye
want me to play, Gilnockie?

GILNOCKIE. Ane new-made air: I made it mysel': ye havena
blawn it before. It rins in my heid these twa-three days – nae
words to it yet, but they'll come – wait, I'll gie you the line
of the melody.

He hums a tune, carefully.

Can ye follow it?

The PIPER *tries it out.*

THIRD ARMSTRONG. Aye, belike.

GILNOCKIE. Play . . . Set onwards then, we march.

The PIPER *plays the tune, and they start to march about the
stage. They form a little procession, first the* PIPER, *then*
GILNOCKIE, *then the other* ARMSTRONGS, *and* LINDSAY
bringing up the rear. GILNOCKIE *carries his sword drawn,
and holds the scroll, which* LINDSAY *has given him, in his
other hand. His two men carry hunting spears.* GILNOCKIE'S
WIFE *has gone up to the roof of the Castle, and the* GIRLS
have gone inside.

GILNOCKIE'S WIFE (*calling from the roof as they march*). John – John – God send ye safe, John: remember the King is—

GILNOCKIE (*stops briefly to reply*). The King is what? The King's fraternal!

GILNOCKIE'S WIFE. God send ye safe.

She retires from the roof.

SCENE FOURTEEN

[GILNOCKIE, LINDSAY, ARMSTRONGS, HIGHLAND SOLDIERS, *the* KING.]

A HIGHLAND CAPTAIN *comes out from the Forest. He intercepts the procession, with his drawn claymore.*

HIGHLAND CAPTAIN. Stand whaur ye are. Declare your name and business, sir, gif ye please.

GILNOCKIE. Wha's this?

LINDSAY. It is the Captain of the King's Guard. Show him your paper.

GILNOCKIE. Ane draff-black bare-arse Hielandman, the Captain of his Guard – when he rides intil the Lawlands! Hechna hochna hochna hoo – it is a'thegither inconsiderable. Gang past him: blaw your pipe!

More HIGHLAND SOLDIERS *have entered and taken up positions behind the* CAPTAIN.

HIGHLAND CAPTAIN. Sir, I said stand. Gif you be indeed ane gentleman that hath business with the King's Grace, you will have papers thereto anent: and it is to myself that you maun shew them, gif you please.

The KING *is standing among the* SOLDIERS, *but he is inconspicuous in a plain Highland dress.*

GILNOCKIE (*jeering at the* CAPTAIN). Loòk at the legs of him, the puir ignorant cateran – I ken a whin bush in Eskdale that'd wark some damage there, gin ye daur to trample through it!

LINDSAY (*to the* CAPTAIN). Captain MacFadyan, this is Mister John Armstrang of Gilnockie, and here is his Safe Conduct.

> *He takes the scroll from* GILNOCKIE *and gives it to the* CAPTAIN.

KING. *Am bheil fios aige gum feum iad an armachd fhagail an seo? Thu fhein a dh'iarr sin a dheanamh, nach tu, Shir Daibhidh?*[1]

LINDSAY. *Innsidh mise sin dha.*[2]

HIGHLAND CAPTAIN. *Faodaidh tu innse dha cuideachd e nas lugha mhimhodh a nochdadh do Ghaidheil an righ.*[3]

LINDSAY. *O tuigidh e sin an uine gun bhi fada.*[4] It is the King's desire, Gilnockie, that baith you and your men remove your weapons and leave them here.

GILNOCKIE. What? Na—

LINDSAY. Peace, good fellowship, fraternity. Wad ye spite the King's intention?

GILNOCKIE (*to his men*). Aye. Did ye hear him? Spears down, gullies out.

FIRST ARMSTRONG. Dangerous.

GILNOCKIE. Peaceable. Obey it. We are here upon ane trust.

> *The weapons are piled, and one of the* SOLDIERS *carries them away.*

Now then, whaur's the King?

[1] 'Does he know that they must remove their weapons and lay them down here? Your own instructions, Sir David, were they not?'

[2] 'I will tell him, sire.'

[3] 'Perhaps, sir, you would also tell him to restrain himself from insults to the King's Gaelic subjects.'

[4] 'He will understand in good time.'

KING. Sir, I will conduct you to His Grace.

He leads GILNOCKIE *downstage.*

GILNOCKIE. And what are you?
LINDSAY. Ane Officer of his Household, Gilnockie.
KING. Will ye please to come this way.

As they walk across the front of the stage, GILNOCKIE'S
men behind them are silently taken away by the SOLDIERS.

GILNOCKIE. They tell't me it was ane progress of sport,
against the wild deer of the forest. Wherefore soldiers?
Wherefore bloody Ersemen, here?
KING. As it were, ane time of solace and recreation for the
King's dependents: the Border lands are weel notit for the
joy of the chase. Ye wad never wish to withhauld your
hospitality frae men of sic gallantry? Will ye tak a wee dram
with me, Gilnockie, before we see His Grace?

He offers a flask.

GILNOCKIE. Aha, boy, I will that. (*He drinks.*) Ersemen or
Norsemen, Spaniards or heathen English, they're free and
welcome here, every man, every bonny fechter! Gilnockie
bids ye welcome. It's Gilnockie's land: it's no the King's,
mind that. Gilnockie's land and God's. We are reformit,
here, sir: we have ane true religion here; aye, aye, the verity
of the Gospels . . . Whaur's the King?
KING. Aye. Whaur is he?
GILNOCKIE. Hey – what?
KING. There is ane richt curious circumstance, Gilnockie, doth
attend the King of Scotland. When he stands within ane
company, he will be the anely man present wi' a hat on his
heid.
GILNOCKIE. Aye? (*He looks round and realizes that he and the*
KING *alone wear hats. He laughs – a little uncertainly.*) Aye:
nae doubt he will: then it's either you or me, boy.

KING. It's no you, I'll tell ye that! Ye are ane strang traitor. The hale of your life ye have set at nocht the laws and commandments of the kingdom: ye have made mock of our person and the Crown and the Throne of Scotland: ye have embroilit and embranglit us with England the common enemy: and by dint of malignant faction ye have a' but split the realm! What in the Name of God gars ye believe I wad pardon ye now? Gilnockie, ye maun be hangit: furthwith, direct, nae process of law: our word in this place is sufficient. Hang him up.

The KING *turns his back abruptly. The* SOLDIERS *close in upon* GILNOCKIE.

GILNOCKIE. Hang? Hang me up? But ye sent me ane letter – ane letter of Safe Conduct—

KING (*without turning round*). Whaur is it then?

GILNOCKIE. Lindsay, I gave it to—

LINDSAY (*deadpan*). What?

GILNOCKIE. Whaur hae ye taken my men? Ane letter. Delamont. The King's letter. The King's honour, the Royal seal – but nae man can say a word against *my* honour: the elect, the godly, me: washit white in the Blood of the Lamb! Whaur are my men, my leal people? Delamont, they are my kinsmen. Delamont, d'ye hear me? What hae they done with my piper?

LINDSAY. What good's your piper now?

GILNOCKIE. For music, what else? Johnny wants his music. He has fand him words to his new air. Nae piper: nae music: Johnny maun sing on his lane.

(*Sings.*)

> To seek het water beneath cauld ice
> Surely it is ane great follie
> I hae socht grace at a graceless face
> And there is nane for my men and me.

KING (*stamping his foot*). I said to you to hang him up. For what do you wait?

> *The* SOLDIERS *lay hold of* GILNOCKIE *with considerable violence: he struggles: they rip the fine clothes off his back, and wrap ropes around him: they force him on to his knees and drag him with the ropes upstage to the big tree. Throughout this he tries to complete his song.*

GILNOCKIE (*singing*).

> But had I wist ere I cam frae hame
> How thou unkind wadst be to me
> I wad hae keepit the border side
> In spite of all thy men and thee—

> *The words of the song are all broken up in the struggle. They stand him under the tree, throw a rope over the bough, place the noosed end round his neck.*

For God's sake let me finish my sang! I am ane gentleman of land and lineage – and ane Armstrang for ever was the protection of this realm—

> *They hang him.*

SCENE FIFTEEN

[LINDSAY, KING, HIGHLAND CAPTAIN, *and* SOLDIERS.]

> *The* KING *picks up* GILNOCKIE'S *coat and hat and other articles of his adornment.*

KING. Will ye look at what the man was wearen? Gif we were to set ane crown upon the carl, he wad be nae less splendid than ourself. The noblemen that we hae wardit intil prison may be releasit upon surety of good behaviour. The good behaviour of Lord Maxwell in particular will carry with it

ane grant of the lands heretofore held by the late Armstrong
of Gilnockie – thereby we may hope to secure his further
lealty to our person. Ane message direct to the English
Ambassador – ye will attend to it, Sir David – recount to
him briefly the course of our Royal justice here at Carlanrigg:
and express our trust in the eternal friendship of King Henry
his master. What mair – can ye think?

LINDSAY. Naething mair, sire. The man is deid, there will be
nae war with England: this year. There will be but small
turbulence upon the Border: this year. And what we hae
done is no likely to be forgotten: this year, the neist year,
and mony year after that. Sire, you are King of Scotland.

KING. We do think we are indeed. Henceforwart, we require
nae tutor, Sir David. But we have ever ane lust for good
makars and faithful heralds. Continue to serve us in either
capacity. Our gratitude is as mickle as our state can contain.
Gentlemen: we will ride to kill the deer.

A horn blows. Exeunt all, save LINDSAY, *into the Forest.*

SCENE SIXTEEN

[LINDSAY, GILNOCKIE'S WIFE, *the* ARMSTRONG GIRLS,
LADY, MAID.]

The LADY *and her* MAID *appear on the roof of the Palace.*
GILNOCKIE'S WIFE *and the* GIRLS *appear on the roof of the
Castle.*

LINDSAY. There was ane trustless tale grew out of this conclusion—

GILNOCKIE'S WIFE. That the tree upon whilk he was hangit
spread neither leaf nor blossom—

LADY. Nor bloom of fruit nor sap within its branches—

LINDSAY. Frae this time furth and for evermair. It did fail and it did wither upon the hill of Carlanrigg, as ane dry exemplar to the warld: here may ye read the varieties of dishonour, and determine in your mind how best ye can avoid whilk ane of them, and when. Remember: King James the Fift, though but seventeen years of age, did become ane adult man, and learnt to rule his kingdom. He had been weel instructit in the necessities of state by that poet that was his tutor.

If there is a curtain it falls upon this tableau.
If not, LINDSAY *concludes his speech with a bow to the audience, and turns away. Other members of the cast immediately re-enter and* GILNOCKIE'S *body is lowered and released before they all make their bows and then exeunt.*

Glossary of old Scots terms

Certain regular usages should be noted:

gh becomes ch: as	'brocht' for 'brought'.
o becomes a: as	'haly' for 'holy'.
ea becomes ei: as	'heid' for 'head'.

also read:

'money' for 'many'.	'no' or 'nocht' for 'not'.
'hae' for 'have'.	awa' for 'away'.
'nae' for 'no'.	'deil' for 'devil', etc.
o (long) becomes ai: as	'baith' for 'both'.

The past tense ends 'it' instead of 'ed' thus: 'defendit' for 'defended'.

'ing' becomes 'en' or 'an' as: 'riden', 'sleepen', etc.

Aboon	Above
Alsweel	As well
Ane	A, An, One
Anent	Concerning
Ben	In
Brand	Sword
Brenn	Burn
Bot	Without
Broo	Soup
Buft	Untanned leather
Burd	Girl
Carl	Person of the lower classes
Complot	Plot
Corbie	Crow (a bird)
Chaumer	Chamber
Crag	Neck
Creish	Fat
Dang	Knocked (past tense)
Daur	Dare
Dominie	Schoolmaster
Draff	Rubbish (a technical term from brewing, I think)
Dram	Drink
Eneuch	Enough
Erse	Gaelic
Fecht	Fight
Flair	Floor
Forbye	Moreover
Fou	Drunk (literally, Full)
Gate	Way
Gat-leggit	With legs outspread
Gey	Very
Gif	If
Gleed	Hot coal
Gin	If
Gully	Dagger
Graith	Girth
Greet	Weep

Halse	Neck
Hinnie	Darling (literally, Honey)
Howkit	Hooked
Jeddart	Jedburgh (a town)
Kirkfast	(of a wedding) made in church
Lave	Remainder
Laverock	Skylark
Lealty	Loyalty
Makar	Poet
Mickle	Big
Muckle	Much
Mou	Mouth
Mushrump	Mushroom
Neise	Nose
Nicker	Neigh (like a horse)
Nolt	Cattle
Paddock	Toad
Quern	Hand-mill
Ratten	Rat
Reeken	Smoking
Riever	Thief
Rigg	Ridge
Sackless	Helpless
Sark	Shirt
Slee	Sly
Speir	Ask
Steer	Have sexual intercourse with
Strae	Straw
Swyve	Have sexual intercourse with
Tawse	Strap (used to whip schoolboys)
Target	Jewelled badge in a cap
Thrawn	Twisted
Toom	Empty
Umwhile	Sometime
Usquebaugh	Whisky
Wame	Stomach or Womb
Wean	Child
Weird	Destiny
Wha	Who
Whae ?	Who ?
Wheen	Few
Whilk	Which
Weet	Wet
Whoor	Whore
Wynd	Path or passage
Yett	Gate